C0-AMO-611

Managing and Controlling Small Computer Systems Including LANs

all Computer Systems Including LANs

Gaston, FCA

CA The Canadian Institute
of Chartered Accountants

Canadian Cataloguing in Publication Data

Gaston, S. J. (Stephen James), 1943–
    Managing and controlling small computer systems including
LANs

ISBN 0-88800-278-5

1. Small business — Data processing.   2. Electronic data
processing — Management.   3. Local area networks
(Computer networks).   4. Microcomputers.   5. Small
business — Management.   I. Canadian Institute of Chartered
Accountants.   II. Title.

HF5548.2.G37 1992   658'.05   C92-094568-6

Copyright © 1992
The Canadian Institute of Chartered Accountants
Printed and bound in Canada
Disponible en français

ISBN 0-88800-278-5

Table of Contents

Table of Contents

Preface to the Second Edition

Since the first edition of this book was published in 1986, rapid advancements have occurred in information technology. Microcomputers have truly come into their own and through local area networks (LANs), can now be tied together into powerful structures to support the information systems and office automation needs of many organizations. Software suppliers have responded by creating a variety of powerful, flexible, and relatively inexpensive microcomputer and LAN based software to meet the accounting, office automation, and personal computing requirements for a wide variety of organizations.

With the advent of these powerful microcomputers and LANs and new application software, powerful and flexible information systems are within the reach of virtually every organization.

The microcomputer has truly become the window on the world of information technology. It can be used alone for personal computing and can also serve as a work station on a LAN, providing access to the organization's accounting and office automation systems. Through modems and telecommunications, microcomputers and LANs can be tied into vast and complex information networks spanning cities, countries, and now even continents.

These expanded, flexible microcomputer capabilities have given birth to the phenomenon of end user computing. In even the largest organizations, departments are acquiring, implementing, and managing their own powerful systems running on local area networks. Departments in these large organizations are seeking ways to gain the benefits from directly managing their own systems while respecting the need for overall information technology strategies and the requirement to ensure reliable systems and data.

In both large and small organizations, users now look to their microcomputer hardware and software as a daily business resource to prepare financial models and spreadsheets, create documents and reports, communicate with others through electronic mail and complete other activities.

To respond to these changes, this second edition contains additional chapters focusing on local area networks, end user computing, and office automation.

Unfortunately, all developments since 1986 have not been good news. In the last few years, computer viruses have started to plague microcomputer and LAN users. The purpose of these viruses is to destroy the capability to use the microcomputer or its programs and files. Viruses have become prevalent and the majority of organizations will probably suffer from a computer virus at least once over the next few years. As our dependency on our microcomputers grows, the pain caused by a computer virus increases accordingly.

To assist in addressing this serious problem, a special chapter has been added to help users decrease the likelihood of "catching" a virus in the first place. Of equal importance, it outlines the steps which should be put in place today so that recovery from a virus infection can be well managed and quickly carried out.

This second edition draws considerably on the first book. Thus, it is appropriate to repeat my thanks to my many colleagues including Bob Semple and Pat Allin, who together with Ron Salole of the staff of the Canadian Institute of Chartered Accountants, made the first edition possible. In creating the second edition, I would like to add special thanks to my many colleagues at the Price Waterhouse World Firm Technology Centre in Palo Alto, California. Their world class expertise and knowledge have been invaluable in writing the second edition. I would also like to thank my colleagues at Price Waterhouse here in Toronto including Mike Hetherington and Tom Whelan, who with good humour and vast knowledge have contributed much to this book.

Introduction

In today's highly competitive economy, accurate and timely information obtained at a reasonable price is essential for business success. Besides its importance to the management decision process, good information is part and parcel of the goods and services which any organization provides. For example, customers want to know when the goods and services will be available and at what price, and they want to acquire them promptly and on schedule. None of this can be accomplished without a good, reliable, and well controlled information system.

In addition, a host of office automation software is available which can help employees be more effective in supporting each other and in serving customers. Electronic mail, word processing, spreadsheets, and desktop publishing are only a few examples of tools which are now in widespread use.

Any business organization requires a well developed and coordinated overall plan to evaluate, acquire, and then successfully use and implement information systems. In short, good strategic planning for information systems is a must as are controls to ensure systems are properly operated and maintained. This book has been written to assist management in these areas, as well as Chartered Accountants and other external advisors who may provide advice and assistance on these matters.

What Is a Small Computer System?

The smallness of a computer system is not defined by its power or importance but rather by the size of the full time professional EDP staff that support and run it. Thus, a computer system that is only supported by a few full time EDP professionals is a small computer system, whereas one supported by a cadre of information systems specialists is large.

Small computer systems often have the processing power of yesterday's mainframe. The software can be complex and provide all the functions an organization may require. Small computer systems, far from being of marginal importance, are often backbone systems supporting the basic daily needs of the organization.

Small computer systems are found in all organizations. By definition, smaller companies or organizations have small computer systems as they cannot afford, nor do they necessarily need, large numbers of EDP professionals.

But with the advent of local area networks and end user computing, small computer systems are found in at least some departments or branches of virtually every large organization. These information systems are "small computer systems" when they are acquired, implemented, or managed by only a few departmental employees rather than being under the direct control and daily supervision of the organization's central information systems department.

As small computer systems are used in many ways by many organizations, so can this book be useful to many readers as follows:

- owner managers or those responsible for information technology in small businesses or organizations;
- those concerned with departmental systems in larger organizations, including local area networks;
- Chartered Accountants and other external advisors to management on small computer systems; and
- internal and external auditors confronted by such systems.

Below is an outline of how the book is organized and its contents. Following this, some comments are made as to how each reader might make the best use of the book.

An Overview of the Book and Its Contents

The book is designed to provide guidance on the acquisition, implementation, and then successful ongoing use of information systems for accounting and financial purposes, as well as office automation and personal computing needs. It does not address additional special considerations that are usually required to support just-in-time inventory systems or systems used for production or production control.

This book places special emphasis on internal controls which are series of policies and procedures designed to ensure that all and only authorized data is completely and accurately processed and that systems and data will remain available to serve the needs of the organization. Because internal control is most challenging in accounting systems where the need for completeness and accuracy is highest, the core of the book is written from this viewpoint. In later chapters, internal control considerations arising directly from local area networks, end user personal computing and office automation products are visited against the rich framework of controls for computerized accounting systems already established. An additional chapter has been written to directly address the threat of computer viruses which are unfortunately becoming an increasing problem for users of microcomputers and LANs.

The book is also written on the premise that any organization needs to have an overall strategic information systems plan. Every organization, regardless of size, needs such a plan which can range from simple to elaborate depending on the size and complexity of the organization. Departments in large companies considering their own departmental systems and local area networks not only need to understand and adhere to overall corporate plans and policies, but need to make sure there is a coordinated and logical plan for their own additional and unique information systems activities.

In all circumstances, it is vital to consider the total needs for information processing of an organization and then develop a strategic plan to address them. If accounting systems, office automation, and personal computing needs are considered in a vacuum, the almost certain result will be confusion.

Accordingly, all readers are strongly urged to read Chapter 1 on Acquisition Decisions in conjunction with Chapters 8 through 10 which address local area networks, end user and personal computing, and office automation. By considering these chapters together, the reader can focus on overall information needs, or consider individual systems of any type in an overall context. Furthermore, local area networks are no longer limited to personal computing or office automation but are a viable alternative for financial and accounting systems. Acquisition decisions should not be made without considering local area networks and the many uses to which microcomputers and LANs can be put.

Chapters 2 through 7 address internal controls which help safeguard assets or help ensure that all and only authorized data is completely and accurately processed and that computer systems and related data remain available to support the activities of the organization. These chapters focus on financial and accounting systems where the need for control is greatest and most difficult to achieve.

Chapters 8 through 10 revisit acquisition and control decisions from the viewpoint of local area networks, end users or personal computing and office automation respectively. They also provide guidance on how the internal control policies and procedures in Chapters 2 through 7 may be adapted to these different environments.

Three appendices are provided. Appendix A is a condensed summary of control considerations from a management perspective. In effect, it constitutes a brief summary of the entire book for members of senior management seeking an overview.

Appendix B provides a list of control considerations designed to help the reader review whether or not all areas of control are being properly addressed in acquiring, implementing, or managing a small computer system. It is especially useful in ensuring important areas are not overlooked.

Appendix C is a glossary of terms.

How This Book will Benefit Various Readers

Those Working for Small Organizations

This book will be especially useful to those members of management with overall responsibility for acquiring, implementing, and ensuring the successful use of computer systems from a management perspective. Often, key decisions will be made by the person owning the business, that is the "owner/manager". There may be a chief operating or financial officer who manages the business on a day to day basis on behalf of the owner/manager. Or indeed, the organization may be a smaller public company or not-for-profit organization run by professional management.

Throughout this book, the term owner/manager has been used to mean the owner, the president, chief operating officer, chief financial officer, etc. or any member of senior management who carries executive responsibility for information systems.

Such executives will need technical advice and support in making certain decisions or in controlling certain activities. References are made throughout the book whenever such may be required.

The author hopes that owner/managers (as defined above) will take the time and trouble to read the entire book. Indeed, this would be highly desirable for the one member of the management team who has overall responsibility for EDP systems. In order to provide some background reference and understanding for other members of the management team, a brief "executive summary" of the book has been provided in Appendix A.

In addition, management will find the checklist of control considerations in Appendix B useful as an aid in assuring that all areas of control have been appropriately addressed. This appendix also indicates those areas where management is most likely to require help from outside consultants or EDP specialists.

Those Working for Large Organizations

As stated earlier, departments which acquire, implement, or maintain their own departmental computer systems are indeed using "small computer systems". There is a very close analogy between the owner/manager of the small organization and the department head and his management team for the department in the large company. In addition, that department would look to the company's centralized information systems department as an external advisor or consultant when help with specific technical problems is needed.

The use of end user or departmental systems in large companies has expanded very rapidly. This growth has been driven by the desire of departments in many large organizations to have an information systems structure that is more responsive and agile in meeting the department's needs. The increasing power of LANs and microcomputer hardware combined with the availability of powerful microcomputer software have made these goals possible.

Senior management of large organizations usually want to provide departments with the opportunity to benefit from departmental systems and end user computing. They also want employees to have individual or personal computing resources to enhance productivity. On the other hand, senior management should ensure that such systems and data they contain will be accurate and reliable, will be properly backed up to ensure the continuity of processing and will have proper security and internal controls. They may also want to ensure that data can be exchanged in electronic form. Thus, most large organizations set down policies to be followed by all departments. Those responsible for creating or approving such policies may find Chapters 8 through 11 to be useful background material when developing them.

With the additional requirement to always work within the framework of overall corporate policy, departmental managers in large organizations find themselves very much in the same position as the owner manager of a small business. Thus, those responsible for the acquisition or ongoing management of departmental systems or end user computing will find the entire book useful and can use it in the same manner as described above for the owner/manager of a small business.

Chartered Accountants and Others Acting as External Advisors

Chartered accountants are often called upon to advise management in acquiring, implementing, controlling, or using small computer systems. The detail guidance and commentary given in this book should be of assistance to Chartered Accountants in discharging these responsibilities.

In providing such advice, the Chartered Accountant often has to review with the client the overall nature of small computer systems and to explain to the client the role and responsibilities of senior management regarding them. In these activities, Appendices A and B can be a useful vehicle to assist the Chartered Accountant in communicating these concepts to his or her client, and in pointing out where the CA's services may be most useful.

Chartered Accountants are also owner/managers of their own firms and require their own accounting and office automation systems. Thus, Chartered Accountants will find this book useful in the same way as other owner/managers.

It is beyond the scope of this book to discuss how information technology can be used to support the planning or conduct of an audit examination or assist in the performance of other professional engagements. However, the companion volume to this book, "**Auditing Small Computer Systems Including LANs**" addresses these subjects.

Internal and External Auditors

Increasingly in large organizations, internal auditors are faced with the challenge of evaluating overall corporate policies and procedures for departmental systems and end user computing. The information provided in this book should be useful to internal auditors when evaluating such corporate wide policies and procedures.

As previously pointed out, any departmental system (including LANs) in a large organization probably is a "small computer system" as described in this book. Accordingly, internal auditors may find this entire book useful reference material when creating audit guides and programs for the examination of departmental systems, including local area networks.

Under generally accepted auditing standards (GAAS), external auditors engaged to express an opinion on the fairness of general purpose financial statements need to properly plan and then conduct their audit examination. GAAS requires that the auditor consider "accounting policies and degree of complexity of the accounting systems" and also requires that judgements be made concerning intended reliance on internal controls.

This book should help the Chartered Accountant gain an overall understanding of the nature of small computer systems. This in turn will result in a better understanding of the overall accounting process. At both an overall and component level, the Chartered Accountant will be better able to judge whether the planned audit examination should contemplate reliance on internal controls.

There is a widespread belief that, when confronted with a small computer system, auditors have no choice but to conduct examinations on a fundamentally substantive basis. The presumption is that internal controls are not sufficiently strong to be a cost effective source of audit satisfaction. These basic presumptions may be false for many of today's small computer systems. Local area networks can provide a significant degree of logical access controls if user identification and password capabilities for these systems are properly used. When packages are purchased from outside suppliers or off the shelf, there is generally good control (or indeed inability) to make fundamental changes to the computer programs and to the calculations of accounting significance which they perform. Both these factors set the scene for a very strong control environment. As pointed out in Chapter 2 on Non-Processing Controls, often an acceptable division of duties over computer operations to segregate these functions from the recording of transactions can be achieved with only three or four employees. All these factors when combined with asset protection and comparison controls (discussed in Chapter 7) can create a control framework which is comparable in quality and reliability to that found in many large organizations.

Of course, the decision as to whether internal controls should be tested as a source of audit satisfaction is a matter of professional judgement in each individual audit examination. The decision is both a question of audit efficiency (conducting the audit as the lowest possible cost) as well as client service (meeting client expectations). Given the importance of information technology for most organizations and the fact that small organizations can and often do have very strong overall systems of internal control, auditors should approach each assignment with an open mind as to whether reliance on internal controls is a valid audit strategy.

It is beyond the scope of this book to specifically address the external audit of small computer systems. These subjects are addressed in a companion volume called **Auditing Small Computer Systems Including LANs**.

However, this volume can be of considerable help in obtaining or deepening an understanding of internal controls for small computer systems, or in developing audit guides or programs to evaluate inherent and control risks for general and environmental controls as well as for individual applications.

This volume may also be a useful reference source when drafting internal control recommendations or discussing them with the client.

CHAPTER 1

Acquisition Decisions

INTRODUCTION

The purpose of this chapter is to discuss key factors to be considered when acquiring computer hardware, operating systems, or application software. Its primary focus is on financial systems. However, information processing decisions need to be made on an overall basis to meet the total needs of the organization. Thus this chapter should be read in conjunction with chapters 8 through 10 which review other information processing requirements as well as providing a detailed discussion on local area networks or LANs.

Information technology now affects virtually every service provided by an organization as well as most of its internal activities. Thus, every organization needs a strategic information systems plan or SISP. The basic purpose of a SISP is to determine that the required information technology will be available to support the strategic goals of the enterprise and that more detailed decisions on particular pieces of hardware and software will be made in a consistent manner as part of an overall, coordinated strategy.

A SISP cannot be properly prepared unless the organization has a strategic plan. Conversely, the development of a SISP may affect or cause revisions to be made to the overall strategic plan. During SISP activities, the company may find new ways of using technology which could affect the nature of goods and services being sold or the manner in which they are delivered.

A good SISP will address all the information technology needs of the organization including:

- financial systems;
- operational systems such as order entry, purchasing, inventory control and production scheduling, etc.;
- office automation requirements such as word processing, financial modelling, desktop publishing, electronic mail, etc.;
- personal computing requirements of individual employees;

1

- requirements to interface with customers, suppliers, and bankers through such means as electronic mail, electronic document interchange (EDI), or electronic transfer of funds and,
- the ways in which these requirements may change in nature or scope over the next few years.

All of these needs can then be blended into an integrated and overall plan for the organization to acquire or replace existing systems and hardware over a period of time and to prioritize the order in which new technology capabilities will be obtained. The SISP would also address the organization's needs for skilled resources to select, install, and maintain computerized systems and to determine which functions will be performed by employees or contracted for with outside suppliers.

The importance of a SISP to ensure that hardware and software decisions are made in a controlled and consistent manner cannot be overemphasized. In the absence of a SISP, the following are only some of the problems that may arise:

- systems may be acquired that do not support the critical needs of the organization.
- the organization can end up with a variety of hardware and software that cannot easily exchange programs or data. Expensive or time-consuming efforts may be required to overcome these problems or the business may be unable to implement its plans for office automation and other sharing of information. For example, financial systems could be running on a minicomputer and office automation on a local area network (LAN). Possibly all these requirements could have been fulfilled on either the minicomputer or the LAN.
- the organization has a proliferation of microcomputers of different models and makes. This is frustrating and prevents their use as part of a LAN that the organization now wishes to install, as well as increasing maintenance and support costs.

When considering overall strategies, the multiple purposes which microcomputers can serve should be considered. For example, they can support:

- office automation;
- access to data or programs stored on a LAN;
- input terminal activities to record financial transactions (connected either to a LAN or to a minicomputer), and
- additional personal computing requirements of individual employees.

Failure to develop an overall SISP can result in unnecessary layers of hardware and software, frustrations in moving data from one system to another, under utilized equipment, and extra layers of complexity in supporting many platforms and technologies.

In the past, small business (or individual departments in large companies in respect of their departmental systems) generally looked only to minicomputers as the overall solution to their information processing needs. LANs are now a viable alternative for these needs, including financial systems.

For all the above reasons, the reader who is making or contemplating acquisition decisions is strongly urged to read the following chapters of the book in conjunction with this chapter:

- chapter 8 on local area networks
- chapter 9 on end user and personal computing, and
- chapter 10 on office automation.

The rest of this chapter is written to address those acquisition decisions that are appropriate regardless of whether LANs or minicomputers are being used or considered by an organization. It focuses on financial information systems which are the main theme of this book and is written in the spirit that decisions on financial systems will be made in the context of an overall SISP.

The owner/manager of a small business usually starts to consider a particular new computer system when the current system has begun to suffer from one or more of the following symptoms:

- Information is costly to obtain.
- Information needed by management is not produced by the current system.
- Information is not available or difficult to obtain.
- Information is inaccurate or incomplete.
- Information is not available on a timely basis.

Although causes of such problems vary from business to business, some of the more common include:

- Changing needs. The business may have changed and thus the system may no longer meet business requirements.
- Rate of growth. Increased business volumes can often overload the best of manual or computer systems. This can result in an increased number of errors, and delays in routine business operations (for example, customer statements, overtime payroll costs, customer complaints, etc.).
- Staff turnover/retirements. Retirement of long-term employees often reduces the effectiveness of existing systems. Staff turnover has a similar effect.

- Need for more detailed management information. Additional or more timely information about inventory control, production scheduling, accounts receivable, etc. may be appropriate.
- Competitive disadvantage caused by the competition modernizing.
- Existing, record-keeping procedures becoming too complex to be dealt with at current or anticipated volumes.
- Clerical costs may be increasing at an unacceptable rate.

This chapter addresses the controls and procedures that should he applied whenever a company is contemplating the acquisition of computer software and hardware. The procedures to be carried out by the owner/manager of a small business are similar to, and just as important as, those which would be applied by a larger business. Due to the technical knowledge and skill levels required and the time commitments necessary, an owner/manager of a small business will find it more difficult to perform this work. Nevertheless, acquisition decisions have a major effect on the success of the computerization project. Without enough time and careful consideration, the anticipated future benefits to be derived from using EDP (electronic data processing) or acquiring a new EDP system may not be realized.

It should be noted that this publication assumes that the small business owner/manager has determined, at each phase of the computerization project, whether or not the company personnel involved have the experience and technical skills necessary to perform the work. At specific points in the process, the services of an external advisor (EDP consultant) may be required to provide experience and guidance.

Interrelationship of Acquisition Decisions

The acquisition of application software, computer hardware, and operating software is a highly interdependent process. Acquisition decisions in any one area (e.g., computer hardware) will automatically impose limitations on the choices available in the other areas (i.e., compatible operating software and application software). In addition, the initial selection of hardware and software may have a significant effect on the level of control that can be achieved once the system is implemented. For example, if it is determined that password controls will be necessary to protect data files and programs, the need for this control feature in the software must be taken into account from the outset.

Because each acquisition decision will impose a certain degree of inflexibility on subsequent options, it is important that the decisions be made in the appropriate sequence so that overall systems requirements will be achieved.

Computer Software

Until recently. the primary emphasis during the selection process was on hardware or machine capabilities. Less emphasis was placed on the software to be used on the selected equipment. The main reason was the relatively high cost of the central processor and/or peripherals (particularly memory, on-line disk capacity, and high speed printers) in relation to the cost of the software programs. It was not uncommon to encounter a typical configuration where the hardware costs exceeded software costs in a ratio of five to one.

In the past several years, however, computer technology advances have removed many of the machine performance limitations, and the manufacturers can now supply more powerful equipment with increased capacity at a much lower cost. As a result, the actual processing capabilities have become a less important selection criteria. As the relative cost of hardware continues to decline, more emphasis is being placed on computer software capabilities and requirements.

As explained later, it is usually much more economical for a company to purchase packages rather than creating original programs. The owner/manager usually has the choice of several software packages for each piece of equipment, including minicomputers and LANs. The selection process involves determining which package best meets the requirements of the particular small business.

Computer software can be classified into the following major components:

1. Application software.
2. Operating software which consists of:
   a) Operating system software, and
   b) Application support software.

Application software is software written to perform a specific function or task, such as to maintain payroll or accounts receivable records. Application software runs "under" an operating system which provides certain basic capabilities required by all applications.

Operating system software is a set of programmed routines, often supplied by the equipment manufacturer, to control all operations of the computer hardware. For example, each time an application program requires an input/output to be done or processing operation (e.g. mathematical) to be carried out, the operating system performs the function and delivers the results back to the application software for further use. Thus, it is not the function of the operating system software to perform any specific business task. Rather, it ties the various parts of computer hardware together in a way that makes them useable by the application systems.

Application support software is a term used to describe a variety of programmed routines (normally supplied by the equipment manufacturer but also available from independent software suppliers) to perform standard recurring functions, thus enhancing the capabilities of the operating system software. Examples of application support software include language compilers (such as BASIC, C, etc.), general utility programs (for example to sort files of data in various orders), on-line support software to allow for the use of on-line terminals, and file organization support software (such as database management capabilities). Application support software makes it unnecessary for those writing application programs to continually code instructions to perform routine tasks. Instead, the application system can call on the application support software to perform the work.

The development and implementation of application software and operating software is discussed later in this chapter.

Computer Hardware

As previously mentioned, hardware decisions should always be made in accordance with an overall strategic information systems plan. Otherwise, the organization may end up with a variety of computer hardware and software that can be difficult and expensive to interconnect and have work together as an integrated whole.

Technological advances have dramatically increased the speed and accuracy of data processing. Perhaps of greater significance, the costs of computing resources have been dropping at a rate unparalleled in most industries. As a result, electronic data processing resources previously affordable by only larger companies are now within the reach of the small to medium-sized business.

Prior to the many enhancements to internal processing speeds and storage capacities permitted by improved technology, the adequacy of the hardware used in small computer systems was a major concern. Better prices for equipment (including the computer, disk storage devices, and printers) and significantly increased capabilities have alleviated the problem to a large degree. As long as the system requirements and business transaction volumes have been adequately defined, the prospective buyer now has a broad range of vendors to choose from, each one having a range of equipment capable of handling the customer's current and future requirements.

The major hardware decision centres around choosing between a local area network or LAN or a minicomputer. Both are indeed viable options for a smaller organization or departmental systems within a large company. However, there are important differences and impacts on the organization.

Chapter 8 includes a detailed discussion on the differences between minicomputers and LANs and the impact these two alternatives can have, especially in the areas of outside support and the need for in house expertise. Thus chapter 8 should be read in conjunction with this discussion.

Once a decision has been made on the overall approach, then a supplier needs to be chosen as well as the model or capacity of the central processing unit, disk drives, printers, etc. that are required. These decisions should be made in accordance with the SISP and provide not only for today's needs but for the growth in business volumes that can be reasonably anticipated for the next few years. These kinds of decisions are quite technical in nature and usually require the help of an EDP consultant.

Deciding on Application Software First

In the absence of unusual circumstances, it is best to choose application software first and then proceed to other decisions. Application software decisions have an impact on the availability of alternatives for computer hardware and operating software. In addition, the ability to incorporate control features or take advantage of existing control features will be affected.

Effect on Computer Hardware

Deciding on the application software will affect the choice of hardware in three specific areas:

1. *Equipment manufacturers.* Deciding on specific software applications will limit the number of available suppliers because only certain manufacturers have equipment capable to support the application systems chosen.
2. *Programmers.* It may or may not be difficult to find programmers with the necessary experience in the given application area on a specific manufacturer's equipment.
3. *Industry packages.* Specialized software packages intended for particular industries may have been developed on one manufacturer's equipment. Use of this application software may therefore preclude consideration of other computer hardware.

Effect on Operating Software

Choice of operating software will also be affected in three areas:

1. *Utility programs.* The use of specific application systems may require that the operating software contain certain utility programs to support normal processing (e.g., sorts).
2. *Compilers, interpreters.* The selection of certain application packages may require the availability of a specific compiler or interpreter to support certain computer languages.
3. *Industry packages.* Specialized software packages written for particular industries may require specific operating software as well as a particular equipment configuration.
4. *Where a local area network or LAN is considered*, a network operating system must be selected. Certain application packages may only be compatible with certain network operating systems.

General purpose utility software routines are available with most operating software packages and should not seriously restrict the alternatives of equipment and operating software.

Control Features

Two areas are affected here:

1. *Mix of controls.* Acquisition decisions about application software will have a significant impact on the control features that should be incorporated in the applications themselves and those that are accomplished through the operating software or through manual control procedures, as discussed in Chapters 2 to 7.
2. *Built-in controls.* Application software packages should have useful controls built into them which should be incorporated in the company's overall control structure. If the application package does not contain adequate control features, additional compensating manual control features may be required or the packages may require modification. Application systems designed and developed in-house should have adequate controls built into them. This would require control features to be defined prior to the actual development of the system. One important built-in control feature is password security.

The owner/manager may require assistance from knowledgeable personnel outside the organization to assess the adequacy of EDP controls in application systems.

Deciding on Computer Hardware First

As previously mentioned, it is usually best to consider application systems first. However, in some circumstances, hardware decisions will have already been made and decisions on operating systems and remaining applications need to be made accordingly.

For example, hardware decisions may already have been made to support the applications that are of greatest importance to the business. Thus for the remaining applications, a hardware decision has already been made and the task is to choose the best available software that will run on the selected hardware. Or, the organization may be considering replacing only one application system and for economic reasons it is not justifiable to change the hardware for this one application alone.

If the computer hardware is chosen first, options that can be exercised exist in the areas of application software, operating software, and control features are:

Effect on Application Software

1. *Software suppliers.* Choosing computer equipment first may restrict the number of potential suppliers of application software. Certain small computer system manufacturers do not supply application software with their equipment. As a result, customers are obliged to obtain software development and support services from software suppliers or through the purchase of packages.
2. *Software packages.* Choosing a specific type of computer hardware may affect the availability of application software packages.
3. *Industry packages.* Selecting computer hardware first may preclude the use of a specialized application package intended for a particular industry if it has been developed to run on different equipment.
4. *Programmers.* Computer programmers usually restrict their work to specific equipment manufacturers. Choosing computer equipment first may restrict the availability of application programmers.

Effect on Operating Software

1. *Manufacturer's software.* There is a close interdependence between computer hardware and the operating software designed to run on it. Given a specific piece of equipment, there is usually only one (or possibly two) operating software packages to support that hardware.
2. *Compilers, utilities.* Selecting specific computer hardware may restrict operating software to a product that does not offer necessary and/or desired language compilers, interpreters, or utility programs.

Choosing computer hardware first will severely restrict operating software availability. Hardware acquisition decisions should only be made in conjunction with operating software considerations.

Control Features

1. *Backup, recovery.* Equipment selected may not provide adequate backup and recovery procedures.

Choosing Operating Software First

Only rarely would operating systems be chosen first. If this is the case, operating software decisions will have the following impact on application software, computer hardware and control features:

Effect on Application Software

1. *Industry packages.* It will preclude the use of some specialized industry application packages which run under other operating systems.
2. *Programming languages.* The availability of specific language compilers or interpreters will restrict the programming language(s) supported.
3. *Utility programs.* The general utility programs included in the chosen operating software package will affect the use of application software packages or the programming effort required for in-house developed software.
4. *File organization.* File organization structures supported by the operating software will have an impact on the application software that can supported.

Operating software acquisition decisions will impose significant restrictions on the application software that can be purchased on a package basis and on the application software that can be custom developed for the system.

Effect on Computer Hardware

1. *Manufacturer's equipment.* The operating software package chosen will impose significant restrictions on the computer hardware to be used because specific operating software packages are designed to be used with specific equipment configurations.

The selection of an operating software package and the computer hardware on which it will be used is so interdependent that the buyer should not decide on one without thoroughly considering the other.

Control Features

Although the following features can be built into individual application systems, it is often more efficient to implement and maintain them via the operating system.

1. *Terminal security.* The chosen operating software package or network operating system may not support adequate terminal security features.
2. *Password protection.* The operating software may not support an adequate system for password protection of programs and data files. Compensating controls within the application software may be required.
3. *Operator or machine malfunction.* Operating software may not incorporate adequate control features to detect operator or machine malfunction.

The absence of specific control features in the chosen operating software package may adversely affect the overall level of control that can be achieved. Minimum control standards for operating software should be established and incorporated into the selection criteria.

Control Features

As indicated above, certain key control features pertaining to application software, computer hardware, and operating software should be included when establishing selection criteria. The absence of such control features does not imply that it is impossible to achieve an appropriate level of control with compensating control procedures. It will, however, be easier to do so if the following control features are present:

KEY CONTROL FEATURES	
Application software	Programmed edits Transaction lists or other control reports Master file change reports
Computer hardware or Application software	Hardware failure checks Backup (files) Backup (equipment)
Operating software	Terminal security Passwords Sorts

THE ACQUISITION PROCESS

Having decided to computerize their accounting systems, owner/managers should make decisions regarding the overall approach to using EDP within the company. Once those decisions have been made, the system requirements can be formulated. Information should be gathered to assess which software and hardware products best suit the company's needs.

The ideas presented are relevant regardless of the nature of the system being replaced or the new one being contemplated. The acquisition decisions should all be made carefully as good systems are important for business success and the decisions made may have to be lived with for quite a long time.

Organization of the Data Processing Activity

Owner/managers must first decide who will develop the system initially and who will be responsible for maintaining it on an ongoing basis.

In the majority of cases, first-time EDP users will choose the strategy of implementing purchased application packages, and will rely on outside software organizations or EDP consultants to help implement and maintain the systems. That means relying on the outside software company to provide personnel with the expertise required to implement the computer system, rather than having to hire full-time EDP staff. Once the system is installed and accepted by the business, the software organization normally provides ongoing maintenance support. It will also make, test and implement any necessary program modifications.

In the microcomputer and LAN environment, application packages are purchased off the shelf in a retail store or through the mail. In this environment, owner/managers or their staff usually select from various options available within each package those they want to use when installing the programs on the computer hard disk. Updates or amendments are received through the mail from the supplier. As discussed in chapter 8, at least one employee needs to be trained as a network administrator to operate and support the LAN.

On the other hand, as a strategy some owner/managers may choose to employ full-time staff with EDP training and expertise. There are also situations where first-time EDP users immediately hire EDP staff, but caution should be exercised in proceeding this way.

There are advantages and disadvantages in relying on outside advisors or in establishing an in-house EDP function. The decision does not rest solely on whether or not custom programming will be done, but also should take into account the magnitude and complexity of all intended computer applications. As a result, the owner/manager's first priority is to decide how the data processing activity is to be organized.

Acquiring Application Software

The next step is to decide which specific accounting and financial applications are to be computerized, or replaced, with newer applications to meet current and future business needs. In effect, the entire acquisition process depends on that decision. Once the application requirements have been defined and the application software chosen, the appropriate computer hardware and operating software alternatives can be evaluated.

Application systems include not only the program code used by the computer to perform various tasks, but also the following elements:

- Manual procedures for capturing information to be used as input to the computer system.
- Data entry procedures.
- Procedures used to operate programs.
- Procedures to produce reports and copy (backup) files.
- Manual procedures to review, balance and utilize data output by the system.
- Alternative procedures to be employed when the computer system is inoperative.

Application software can be acquired or developed in several different ways. Whether the owner/manager has decided to organize the EDP activity by purchasing packages and relying on third parties to help implement them or to put it in the hands of in-house EDP staff, he or she can choose to use standard application packages, specialized industry systems, or custom-developed application software — or even a combination of all three to meet the company's established requirements.

Standard Application Packages

A variety of generalized application software packages is available for the processing of standard accounting functions (e.g., general ledger, payroll, accounts payable). Such packages usually require the use of standardized input forms and procedures that may well differ from the company's current procedures. The package will provide most of the standard management information and transaction reports common to the specific business applications. Most packages offer alternatives at the installation stage of a new system. For example, it may be possible to choose between a "balance forward"

13

or an "open item" accounts receivable system. Some packages can be modified to produce additional information beyond that initially provided but this requires extra programming and such modifications are usually very expensive.

Prices of packages can vary from a few hundred dollars for simple microcomputer or LAN based software to many thousands of dollars for complex software that is integrated and runs on minicomputers.

Specialized Industry Systems

Application software packages have been developed for many industries (e.g., insurance agencies, law practices, doctors' offices, travel agents) based on the common information needs and business practices of businesses in those industries. Most of these packages include application modules for the major accounting functions particularly unique to the industry. In addition, nonspecialized applications (e.g., payroll, general ledger) are normally supplied. By using an industry-based package, a business can often meet its special information and processing requirements without incurring the costs associated with custom-developed application software. Specialized industry systems are normally intended to be used as originally designed without programming modifications.

Custom-Developed Application Software

In situations where standard application packages and/or specialized industry systems are not available or would require significant modification to be effective, custom-designed application software may be the answer. Such application software is designed and developed to meet detailed system specifications established by the business. In these circumstances, it may be best to consider database packages which can be readily programmed. These packages supply a means of writing high level code to create applications. They often provide English-like programming commands that accomplish with one statement what would usually require 10 or even 100 COBOL or BASIC commands.

With the widespread availability of good accounting and specialized industry packages, owner/managers should be wary of incurring the comparatively much higher costs of custom-developed software. Usually, there is a package available that will meet 90% of software needs at a fraction of the cost incurred to develop custom application software.

Defining Requirements for a Specific Application

Experience has indicated that the most common factor in the majority of computer system failures is an inadequate statement of system requirements at the outset. Although this may not result in complete failure, the system may:

- Not perform all of the desired functions.
- Not achieve an adequate level of control.
- Not realize all of the benefits initially hoped for.
- Be more expensive than originally forecast.
- Require major modifications shortly after implementation.

These problems can be avoided with a properly planned and organized approach to the acquisition of computer software. Paying sufficient time and attention to the necessary details will pay off with well-controlled, technically sound computerized accounting systems.

The amount of time and effort required for this initial information gathering and documentation stage will vary significantly, depending on the complexity of the business operations and the number of applications to be converted to computer processing. The intended organizational structure of the EDP activity (reliance on third parties vs. in-house EDP staff) and the type of application software to be used (packages or custom software) will also influence the time requirements for this process. The owner/manager of the business should be directly involved in the process but may require assistance from external personnel as noted.

This initial information gathering process should be followed even when the perceived solution is the purchase of relatively inexpensive microcomputer software and hardware. Although the costs of purchasing the system may be low, buying the right one for the business is the key to the system successfully producing relevant, accurate, and timely information.

Preliminary Survey/Request for Proposal

The purpose of the preliminary survey is to gather and organize pertinent information about the business, its activities, and its information system, and to identify future business and information requirements. If appropriate, the information is then supplied to potential suppliers who, in turn, will use it for hardware and/or software proposals and price quotations.

It is necessary to review general corporate objectives and future plans to ensure that this proposed system takes into account any foreseen changes in company strategy or activity. For example, if future plans include expansion and operation of multiple physical locations, that should be reflected in the statement of system requirements. Contemplated changes in product lines or marketing methods will also affect information requirements.

Current information systems should be documented in detail. The purpose here is to:

- Identify current procedures and determine the need for a revised system.
- Identify problems or weaknesses in the current system.
- Identify additional information requirements, now and in the future.
- Provide a documented description of current procedures which can be used as key information in designing the new system.

The final product of a preliminary survey often includes the following information:

- *General business information.* This addresses such matters as the overall business objectives, the organizational structure of the business, formal/ informal reporting relationships, and the growth potential of business.
- *Documentation of current system.* This information might describe, in detail, current systems and procedures, including flowcharts outlining the flow of documents and information throughout the business, copies of all documents used and reports produced, and volumes of all types of transactions handled (both average and peak workload). In addition, there should be descriptions of all formal and informal files maintained and detailed descriptions of procedures for all types of transactions.
- *New system requirements.* To ensure that the system will provide the required management information, detailed definitions of outputs (management and exception reports, displays, documents, audit trail, and management reports) should be defined in detail. A description of inputs to the proposed system should also be provided, including any new transactions or files not in the current system.

If it appears that the requirements identified can be satisfied by a standard software package, those requirements would be compared to the capabilities of the package.

The next step is to collect the costs and benefits of the proposed new system. As a start, the cost (actual or estimated) to operate current systems and the estimated costs of operating a new system (to be revised based on quotations received from potential suppliers) should be compared. Also, the intangible benefits to be derived warrant a close look, such as receiving information and statistics about the business on a more timely basis. As well, non-cost impacts on the organization (e.g., employee acceptance, discipline imposed by new system) should be considered.

Cost benefit analysis should be approached with a healthy degree of scepticism. Users have a tendency when defining their requirements to trot out every wish and aspiration that occurs to them. While the cost of the new software with all these bells and whistles may still be warranted, there may be buried within it a cost for many additional features that are not really required and whose incremental cost cannot be justified. Thus it is always best when identifying needs to separately document **true** requirements from additional desirable features. In this way the cost of additional features can be separately evaluated. This approach will also be very helpful in evaluating packages. Often a package that cannot meet all desires will indeed fulfil all true requirements plus a considerable number of additional desired features. By considering requirements and desires separately, the significant additional cost of amending packages or creating customer developed applications can often be avoided.

Users also have a tendency to identify more cost savings than they are able or willing in the final analysis to deliver. Thus it is a good discipline to inform users that their budgets will be reduced (or revenue generation targets raised) immediately upon the installation of the new system. When users recognize they will be living with a revised budget that reflects the promised benefits, they will be much more realistic in estimating financial advantages in the first place.

Upon completion, the owner/manager must decide whether or not to continue with the computerization project based on the anticipated costs, savings, and other factors noted above. Even if the decision at this point is to postpone or cancel computerization plans, the information will be useful for identifying and correcting weaknesses in the current systems.

Once the preliminary survey information has been accumulated, it may be included in a request for proposal document (RFP), which is then sent to potential suppliers. This will lead to more complete and more competitive proposals and make it easier to compare and evaluate the proposals received.

A well-prepared request for proposal should include the following information:

- General information about the business and industry.
- Specifics regarding submission of proposals (e.g., timing, number of copies, format).
- Information about current systems.
- Management's information needs for a new system.
- Tentative time schedule.
- Present and anticipated volumes.
- Priority of implementing applications.

- Growth capability required.
- Other specific areas to be addressed:
  - detailed hardware, software costs
  - annual renewal or licence fees
  - payment terms
  - annual maintenance or renewal fees
  - site requirements
  - training costs
  - conversion procedures
  - maintenance costs
  - names and addresses of installed users to act as references
  - warranty arrangements
  - bases upon which charges would be made for modifications at a later date.
  - ownership of the underlying code and access to detailed systems documentation.

Where LAN based accounting packages are being considered, a review of the many magazines devoted to microcomputers and related software packages may be very helpful in developing a list of packages for initial consideration. Articles in these magazines not only list the features of various accounting packages but often compare and contrast different packages in the same way automobile magazines compare performance and features of cars.

There are also a large number of software digests available that list and describe both generic and industry specific software packages and give brief to full descriptions of their functions and features. These digests can be purchased from the publishers or referred to at local public libraries.

From these sources, a short list of possible packages can be developed and then retail stores approached for further information.

Retail computer stores will generally not respond to a request for a proposal, or they will limit their response to providing costs of suggested hardware and packaged software. In this case, the proposed hardware and software then can be compared by actually working through a demonstration package and manuals of instruction for the software and seeing whether the specific requirements can be met. Most computer stores are more than willing to provide this sort of support and assistance. If the demonstration package meets the requirements, then negotiation of price, delivery, training and support can be undertaken with two or three potential suppliers. Any savings generated by finding the "cheapest" solution must be compared to the "support" available from the more comprehensive, full-service dealer.

Evaluation of Proposals

For expensive minicomputer software, evaluation criteria should be established
(and communicated to potential suppliers) to provide a more objective basis for
assessing the strengths and weaknesses in the proposals submitted. The
following sets out the major areas that should be evaluated, and who might carry
out the evaluations.

	Evaluation Performed By
Recommended method of operation	
— Description of hardware (if change is required)	EDP consultant
— Processing characteristics	EDP consultant
Characteristics of application software	
— System design	EDP consultant/ Owner/Manager
— System documentation	EDP consultant/ Owner/Manager
— Programmed controls	EDP consultant
— Technical support and training	Owner/Manager
— Service commitment	Owner/Manager
— Installation support	Owner/Manager
— "Proven" application software package	EDP consultant
— Growth potential of application software	EDP consultant
— Programming language used	EDP consultant
— Delivery date	Owner/Manager
— Program warranty	Owner/Manager
Equipment factors	
— Age and reliability of equipment family	EDP consultant
— Support	EDP consultant
— Service commitment	EDP consultant
— Training	EDP consultant
— Availability of backup	EDP consultant
— Delivery date	Owner/Manager
— Expandability	EDP consultant
— Physical requirements	Owner/Manager
Processing capacities and speeds	
— Number of terminals proposed	EDP consultant
— Printer speed	EDP consultant
— Disk capacity	EDP consultant

	Evaluation Performed By
Other non-cost factors	
— On-site technical expertise required	Owner/Manager
— Reliability and financial stability of supplier	Owner/Manager
— Suggested installation elapsed time	Owner/Manager
One-time costs	
— System purchase or design and installation	Owner/Manager
— Training	Owner/Manager
— Initial supplies	Owner/Manager
Recurring costs*	
— Monthly cost for hardware	Owner/Manager
— Monthly maintenance cost**	Owner/Manager
— Monthly software cost**	Owner/Manager
— Basis upon which requested program changes will be charged for***	

> * **Costs if leased or, if purchased, monthly principal and interest costs.**
> ** **Most suppliers of software packages sell on the basis of an initial one-time fee plus an annual renewal or maintenance fee, often 10-20% each year of the original purchase price.**
> *** **Changes now or in the future will be charged for.**

Contractual Negotiations

As with any business agreement involving significant financial and other commitments, a clear, concise contract between the supplier and the customer is essential. The contract should cover all aspects of the transaction, and should be reviewed by the company's lawyer. The RFP document and supplier's proposal should be included as an integral part of the contract. The contract should provide a clear understanding by both parties of their respective responsibilities and commitments. The contract should address such matters as:

Operating and application software

This section will cover:

1. Requirement that the manufacturer's standard operating software is to be used.
2. The rights of the business in event that the supplier goes out of business, including title or ownership of operating and application software and rights to source code.

20

3. Preparation and approval of detailed system specifications prior to the commencement of any programming (including requested changes).
4. The right to test the system before it is finally accepted.
5. Detailed descriptions of the system documentation and user and operator instructions to be prepared or supplied.
6. Payment arrangements (including annual renewal or maintenance fees).

Computer equipment (where appropriate)

This area should set out:

1. All equipment-related matters indicated in the preceding section on "Evaluation of Proposals".
2. Title or ownership of computer equipment.
3. Payment or financing arrangements.

APPLICATION SOFTWARE DEVELOPMENT, IMPLEMENTATION AND DOCUMENTATION

Due to the rising costs of custom-developed application software and the increasing availability of packages, it is expected that the majority of application software for small computer systems will be either standard application packages or specialized industry systems.

Thus implementation of microcomputer and LAN packages is described first and then certain activities which are appropriate when larger more expensive packages or custom-developed software is acquired is discussed. Lastly, additional consideration for custom-developed software are examined.

Purchase of LAN-based Application Packages

Generally, when purchasing an accounting system to run on a LAN, there will be no direct negotiations with the supplier, nor will a software acquisition contract be negotiated and signed. It is still extremely important, however, to test the application system fully before implementing it. Such software is usually tested by using parallel run procedures, and current accounting systems are kept in place and up-to-date until the software has been proven in its entirety, including monthly or periodic runs and the provision of all management trails.

Of course, the amount of testing to be done will depend to a large extent on how well known and widely used the package under consideration is. Only limited testing may be required for a package that is widely used and has been around for a number of years "with a good reputation". Much more testing will be

21

required for a package from a relatively unknown supplier where few if any people have used it. The many computer magazines available today can be an excellent source of information on the more widely used accounting packages, and often provide comment on their performance and "correctness".

No matter how well known a package is, some testing is always appropriate in that:

- errors could be made by organization's staff in selecting features or options included in the package or in inputting constants and values into the package;
- testing and parallel runs will help the organization's staff become familiar with the package before it is put into regular use; and
- parallel runs can help confirm that the opening data required for the system has been completely and accurately copied over or entered.

The purpose of testing is not just limited to having the user ensure that the package functions correctly, but is an opportunity to verify that all the promised features and functions of the systems are indeed present. In other words, testing helps the user determine that all the functionality he or she was promised was received.

In all circumstances, it is important to ensure that the results produced by the software package being tested are reconciled in detail to those being produced by the manual system. That will provide reasonable assurance that all of the computations, calculations, postings, and summaries being made by the software package under a variety of business circumstances are accurate. For example, assurance would be required that gross payroll and payroll deductions are being correctly calculated in a payroll system, or that extensions, footings, and charges for provincial and federal sales tax are being correctly made on sales invoices. Often, to ensure that the correct calculations are made, the user will have to insert certain values into the program or otherwise provide data to the system at the time it is initially installed. Most LAN-based accounting packages provide the user with a means of printing out, for checking or future reference, the values of various sales tax, volume discounts, and rebate percentages entered into the package at the time of installation. Usually, the packages also provide a means of amending these constants when business circumstances or regulations change.

While the cost of the software may be minor, an inability to produce complete, accurate, and authorized information on a timely basis could seriously damage the business.

Complex Minicomputer Packages and Custom Software

The following additional activities are important when minicomputer packages are being purchased from software suppliers or custom software is written.

User Participation in Specification and Design

This chapter has previously discussed how to define the company's systems requirements. User involvement is essential, and includes both the owner/manager and employees who will be using the new system on a daily basis. The process should never be left to someone, such as a software supplier, who is unlikely to have a detailed knowledge of the business.

Specification of Controls

The use of computerized edit controls to prevent errors during the data entry phase can be extremely important. Such controls should be considered at the design and acquisition stages of applications systems. When considering packages, therefore, edit routines should be evaluated for their effectiveness.

The following controls (which are discussed in detail in Chapter 4) over transactions warrant serious consideration:

- Computer-produced exception reports of unusual transactions of importance to management.
- Edit routines, including such tests as:
  — format checks
  — missing data tests
  — limit or reasonableness checks
  — data field combination or correlation tests
  — duplicate processing checks
  — balancing checks
  — on-line testing for valid reference information such as customer numbers and account numbers.
- Control totalling (provide machine-generated totals used to control and balance data) and production of transaction lists.
- Terminal access controls.
- Password controls.
- Reports of all transactions processed that require authorization or approval.

Another consideration is the ability of the computer system to provide documents or information to management so that the flow of information can be traced through the system. Those documents are generally referred to as the management or audit trail. Some systems will automatically prevent further processing until the appropriate reports have been printed.

Management trails are important for a variety of reasons. They allow individual transactions to be traced through the system to see where and when they were recorded or for totals to be broken down into the individual transactions comprising them. Without such information:

- It will be difficult to correct errors that subsequently come to light.
- Data may not be available to satisfy regulatory authorities such as Revenue Canada.
- Management may not have the information needed to analyze operations.
- If processing is interrupted, it will be difficult to determine which transactions are processed or unprocessed.

Management trails can take many forms, including transaction logs, detailed batch listings, printing of detailed sales or cheque registers. Ideally, management trails will also include the identity of the employee entering the data, both to fix responsibility and to analyze errors by source in order to take steps to reduce them.

Another potentially important factor is the system's capability to provide data for future reference or analysis by management. One example would be the analysis of historical sales in a different sequence than given by current reports. Flexible use of stored data is an important advantage to have in a system. Thus the system should be able to capture and store data at a detail level so that later it can be summarized in many ways.

Testing of Applications Systems Software

For the reasons stated earlier, the user should test all potential applications systems. The testing should include all phases of the system from data collection, data input and processing to production of daily, monthly, and yearly output reports and utilization of such reports. Tests should also include backup and recovery-restart procedures. This testing should be done in addition to any performed by the software supplier.*

---

* Well-known packages which have been modified for a particular business require more testing and custom software requires the most thorough testing.

Two common testing methods are a parallel run and the test pack procedure.

1. A parallel run, as the name implies, involves concurrent data processing using the new applications software system and the system to be replaced. The results of using the two systems are compared and reconciled to determine whether the new system is functioning properly.
2. The test pack procedure involves setting up a separate set of files and input data. The input data is processed against the test files using the program to be tested and the results compared to precalculated results. It is essential that all data types and potential input errors be included in the input data. Test data and files can be retained on a removable disk pack for future use in testing program changes, hence, the name "test pack".

While these testing methods can often be used interchangeably, features of a new system not present in the existing system normally require test data to be developed or alternatively the checking of results by manual redetermination as they cannot be verified by parallel runs.

Conversion from the Existing System to the New Computer-based System

The success of the conversion from an existing system, whether it is a manual or computer-based, to a new computer based system will depend in part on the accuracy of semi-permanent data established for the new system. Semi-permanent data in a sales receivable system includes information such as the customer's name and address, credit limits, product selling prices, discounts, and sales tax rates. All computer systems contain equivalent semi-permanent data.

The importance of ensuring the accuracy of such semi-permanent data can be readily demonstrated by considering the financial effect of selling at incorrect prices or allowing credit to customers in excess of predetermined credit limits.

There are several ways to test the accuracy of the data conversion, including the following:

- Semi-permanent data is printed out and compared to source documents and/or the predecessor system.
- Computerized edit of semi-permanent data using, if appropriate, the predecessor computer system or edit tests such as Social Insurance Number checks, reasonability or range tests, etc.
- Balancing totals and record counts.

25

It is, of course, also of prime importance to enter the correct transaction data and balances for individual customers, suppliers or employees on the data files for any new system. For example, in accounts receivable, it is important to start with the correct balance for all customers.

Usually, it is best to print out the contents of the data files after they have been created and then agree the balances on the printout to those in the existing system. Such procedures will not only avoid financial loss, but also will ensure that the new system is starting with correct amounts so that the results of parallel runs will not be complicated by any errors in opening balances and other transferred data.

Sometimes some or all of the data is transferred from an existing to a new computer system by a specially created computer program. The computer program that does this is usually called a conversion program. This approach avoids the need to re-enter a great deal of data and is usually more accurate as data entry errors are avoided. When conversion programs are used, they should be subject to proper testing by both users and programmers in the same way as any other program. Conversion programs are usually relatively simple but they can contain logic errors nonetheless.

Re-formatting of some data may be required as part of the conversion process. For example, an "A" in a certain field in the old system may indicate that a customer was sales tax exempt, whereas the new system indicates this by placing a "1" in the appropriate field. Or the old system may store dates in the order month, day, and year but the new system uses day, month, and year. Conversion programs usually make such transformations and, of course, they must be done correctly.

Even where conversion programs are used, there may be additional types of data in the new system which were not present in the old. The new data will have to be determined, documented and then key entered. The correct entry of this data should be verified by printing it out and then double checking its accuracy against the source documents.

Recognizing that some errors always creep in over time, many organizations take the opportunity to review all their existing data being converted for errors or omissions. Techniques that can be used to do this include:

- running the data from the old system (after transformation) through the edit routines in the new system may catch some errors;
- searching for blank fields in the data created for the new system, and
- reviewing the data "by eye" for obvious errors.

Obtaining or Creating Adequate Documentation

Documentation is necessary to give users, auditors, and programmers an understanding of the entire system as well as the individual programs within it.

The key elements of system documentation include the following: (Those marked with an asterisk may not be necessary or available when packages are purchased.)

- Index.
- Revision log.*
- General system description.
- General system flowchart, illustrating the flow of data through the system and the interrelation between processing stages.
- List of programs in the system, including a brief description of the purpose of the program.*
- Description of and screen layouts for menus.
- Description and examples of source documents.
- Examples of output reports.
- Tables, constants, or codes used by the system.
- Query procedures.
- File control procedures.
- Security procedures (this section should be restricted to the owner manager).
- Management trails.
- User instructions:
  — data collection and recording procedures
  — security procedures
  — processing
  — edit rules
  — error messages and correction procedures
  — output reports handling,
  — control and balancing procedures
  — month-end and year-end procedures
  — backup procedures
  — restart procedures.

With most microcomputer packages, the trend is to include self-teaching tutorials in the documentation. In some cases, on-line help features are incorporated into the packages and form part of the documentation.

---

* Well-known packages which have been modified for a particular business require more testing and custom software requires the most thorough testing.

Program documentation

Program documentation should include the following (often little or no program documentation is available when packages are acquired):

- Source code listing.*
- If the program is compiled for use, the compilation listing should replace the source code listing.*
- Description of the program's purpose.
- Revision log sheet for the program.*
- Record layouts, including the use and significance of codes, flags, indicators, etc.*
- Report layouts (unless included with systems documentation).*
- Flowcharts or decision tables, or well-annotated, structured program code.*
- List of which programs or systems use output files created by the program.*

In many cases, microcomputer software documentation is limited. Source code listings and record layouts may not be available. Without such information, the programs cannot be readily modified. The owner/manager should be aware of this limitation and ensure that the software package has been reviewed and tested and generally meets the requirements of the business before being accepted.

Additional Considerations for Custom Application Software

Development

User participation, negotiation, approval, testing, and conversion remain essential in the development and implementation of custom software, especially because of the larger expenditures involved and greater likelihood of time and cost overruns.

Custom applications software, whether developed by an outside software company or on-site, will necessitate certain control procedures in addition to those listed earlier.

User participation in the specification and design process must be carefully considered. Experience has indicated that without adequate user involvement at this stage, application systems may well not meet the user's expectations and will probably cost much more than anticipated. If the owner/manager does not have enough experience in the system development process, perhaps an independent consultant should be hired.

The negotiation and approval process should be expanded to provide additional control over the development process. If the system is developed in-house, the owner/manager will not have the protection of a contract to fall back on, and will have to bear the costs for any misunderstandings on the part of the programmer/analyst. The owner/manager should therefore establish minimum standards for the programmer/analyst when designing and programming the system. These standards should ensure the use of accepted programming techniques and the preparation of appropriate documentation.

Testing

Naturally, custom-developed systems need much more thorough and rigorous testing than packages do. With a package, it is possible to ask other users about their experience with it. As well, it is comforting to know that the system has been used successfully elsewhere. This is not, however, true of custom-designed systems or systems to which major modifications have been made for a particular business.

Once the system has been completely tested by those developing and programming it, (be they employees of the company or of outside suppliers) the owner/manager and the user employees should also do testing of their own, as suggested earlier for packages.

Buying and then customizing a package

Generally, it is not possible to ask suppliers of microcomputer-based accounting packages to amend or customize them to the needs of a particular business. The vendors of large-scale and somewhat expensive software packages designed to run on minicomputers are, however, usually willing to modify or change a particular application system to fit the unique requirements of a user.

Caution should be exercised in this area, as often the cost of other than trivial modifications to a reasonably complex package will cost as much as developing a completely customized system.

If a package is purchased and then significantly amended or customized, the user should ensure that appropriate testing and documentation occurs. Normally, this will entail more detailed negotiations and more thorough testing than would be appropriate for an unmodified package, but not as much as might be required for a completely customized system.

Expanding the Number of Applications

In some cases, a business will be adding an additional computer application to an existing system. The main steps in successfully developing a new application system described previously in this chapter apply to this situation. In addition, the ability of computer hardware to service the new application must be considered. Potential problems may include:

- Degradation of on-line response time.
- File space limitations.
- Increased printer run times.
- Lack of sufficient terminals for input.

Any of those problems may prevent completion of processing during a normal business day or answering customer requests on a timely basis.

To illustrate the situation, consider a proposal to increase the living space in a house. The addition of two or three rooms is analogous to the addition of a new computer application system. The problem to be considered in the house expansion is whether the existing heating and air-conditioning or electrical system will be adequate to service the existing house, plus the new addition. If not, heating and cooling may take so long that the entire house may be unpleasant to live in. Similarly, users may be unhappy with an overloaded computer system.

This example illustrates the point that a new computer application system should not be evaluated without considering the potential effect on the total system.

OPERATING SOFTWARE DEVELOPMENT AND IMPLEMENTATION

As stated earlier in this chapter, the acquisition decisions made about operating software (i.e., operating system software and application support software) are interrelated with those made for the purchase of computer hardware and application software.

Operating system software and network operating systems for LANs are programmed sets of routines provided by the equipment manufacturer. Their function is to control all operations of the computer hardware, including the execution of application programs. In addition, the operating system provides job scheduling, input/output control, accounting, memory and storage allocation, assignment, data management, and related services. It also performs common technical functions (e.g., reads/writes for input/output devices). Finally, the operating system controls and monitors the operation of all peripheral devices such as printers, data entry terminals, disk storage units, etc.

Application support software is a term used to describe a variety of programmed routines (normally supplied by the equipment manufacturer) to perform standard recurring functions. The four main categories of application support software are:

- Source language compilers/interpreters.
- General utility programs.
- On-line support software.
- File organization and data management utilities.

Sometimes these functions are included within a particular operating system: for other systems, these functions must be purchased from other suppliers as separate application support programs.

It is rare for anyone to change or modify application support software. Instead, from time to time a decision is made to upgrade to a better type or to an on-line control program, etc. Operating system software, however, can be modified but this tends to be infrequent.

A business with limited EDP staff may have to make any necessary modifications to operating system software. Also, from time to time new, improved versions will be received from the manufacturer and a decision will be needed as to whether to implement it. Application support software will have to be initially chosen by the business and upgraded subsequently as appropriate.

In contrast, where a business has bought an expensive and sophisticated application package, it should be able to look to the supplier for information as to what changes or new versions of operating system software and application support software should be adopted.

Operating System Software

Operating system software operates in the following manner. Each time an application program or a system command requires an input/output or processing (e.g., mathematical, comparison) operation, the operating system performs the function and delivers the result back to the program which asked for it. After the operation has been performed and before the result is returned to the application program or system command, the operating system performs various validity tests to ensure that the results are correct. In this manner, the operating system software ensures that the equipment operates exactly as requested.

31

Experience has indicated that the manufacturer-supplied operating system software for small computer systems is as reliable as those supplied for large mainframe computers.

The role of the owner/manager in each of the two most likely situations, where reliance is placed on third party advisors and where there is limited in-house EDP staff support, is discussed further below.

1. *Dependence on third parties to provide EDP implementation and maintenance skills*

   Under this mode of operation, it is assumed that the owner/manager of the business relies on outside expertise (e.g., an EDP consultant and/or an independent software company) to provide data processing knowledge. Any modifications to the operating system software would be implemented and tested by the independent software company.

   In this situation, the owner/manager may be able to derive some assurance that the operating system controls would not be modified, by-passed, or compromised by company staff, primarily because they are not likely to possess the necessary technical skills. However, even in this mode there may be utilities included in the overall package of programs which could be accidentally or purposefully used to alter stored data without leaving any trace.

   To ensure that modifications to the operating system are properly controlled, the independent software company should ensure that such modifications are properly reviewed, tested, and authorized by them before they are sent to their clients for use. The effectiveness of these procedures may vary significantly between software companies: some are large organizations with well-established and documented standards covering the performance of such operating software maintenance; others are small, with relatively few staff and quite informal procedures. In the latter case, the owner/manager may not be able to ensure that operating system changes are adequately controlled.

2. *Limited in-house EDP staff support mode of operation*

   Here it is assumed that the business has one or more data processing professional(s) on staff performing amongst other duties the functions involving the operating system. Such duties will most often be given to one person who has other conflicting EDP duties (such as developing programs or processing data) which, as explained in Chapter 2, should ideally not be combined in one individual. The owner/manager is totally reliant on the in-house EDP staff to ensure that operating software modifications are properly tested prior to implementation. Appropriate review and authorization procedures may very well not exist.

The practical solution may be to design records and owner/manager controls to recognize that the operating system software and its use are all in the hands of one employee who is fundamentally unsupervised. This is discussed more fully in Chapters 3 to 7.

Application Support Software

The four major functions performed by application support software for either minicomputers or LANs are discussed further below.

1. *Source language compilers and interpreters*

   The primary function of a compiler/interpreter is to prepare a machine language program from source program language statements supplied by a programmer. The difference between a compiler and an interpreter is that the compiler generates a machine language program that can be stored and executed without recompiling while the interpreter performs the translation task each time an application program is executed. There are various compilers/interpreters for small computer systems. The more common ones include BASIC, COBOL, RPG, etc.

2. *General utility programs*

   Equipment manufacturers often supply a variety of utility programs that perform common data processing functions such as sorting, merging, and copying of data files. Such programs are generalized in nature and require a programmer to supply certain parameter statements for the specific application required. Through the use of utility programs, programmers do not have to write a completely new program each time a common function is to be performed. If, for example, a data file is to be sequentially re-ordered, a standard sort utility program can do this; an entirely new program is not necessary. By using a sort utility and providing such parameters as file name, record size, size and location of sort key, etc., the sort program can be written in several minutes rather than several hours.

3. *On-line support software*

   The most common minicomputer configurations available are capable of supporting multiple CRT terminals operating in an interactive or on-line mode. To support such operations, an additional layer of software to control

33

multiple-terminal input and to provide an interface between the terminal and the application software is required. The control-related functions performed by this software include:

- Prompting capabilities (screen formats, messages, etc.).
- Terminal polling features.
- Additional levels of password control (e.g., transactions, functions, menus, programs).
- Extended error recovery capabilities (i.e., ability to recover multiple terminal on-line activities).
- Input transaction logging features.
- Scheduling and queuing of processes requiring the same data.
- Locking out additional access to data already being used.
- Logging of attempted (unsuccessful) accesses via terminals.

4. *File organization and data management utilities*

Software products that perform file organization functions and facilitate data management and retrieval are becoming increasingly common in small computer systems. Several equipment manufacturers now offer database management systems (DBMS) for use on their machines. While still used primarily as a file organization method, the availability of DBMS on small computers will introduce problems of data administration. It must be kept in mind that, historically, effective data administration requires a highly-trained and expensive specialist. Thus, in small business, databases are usually found only in packaged systems where the supplier of an application has built the application to deal with the problems surrounding the database.

Control Considerations over Operating System and Application Support Software (including network operating systems)

The control features available within the operating software will have a significant impact on the overall level of control that might be achieved in the EDP area. If, for example, the operating system software did not support the use of passwords on programs and data files, or the application support software did not allow for proper identification of CRT terminal users, this would be detrimental to achieving proper controls.

In certain cases, control deficiencies in proposed operating system software or in the application support software may preclude further consideration of a specific manufacturer's equipment configuration. Control requirements should, therefore, be defined before any acquisition decisions are made.

Documentation of control features included in the operating system or built into the application to overcome operating system deficiencies should be available. Generally, the documentation supporting small computer operating systems is not as readily available as for mainframe operating systems.

During the acquisition process, the owner/manager should ensure that the operating software being considered contains adequate controls. This may require the assistance of an EDP consultant. In addition, on an ongoing basis, assurance must be obtained that:

- The operating system controls are adequately tested prior to implementation.
- Adequate control is maintained over modifications to the operating system software.
- The controls cannot be readily by-passed or compromised.

These requirements are certainly not unique to the small computer environment, but may be more difficult to meet.

Where there is no EDP expertise available in-house, the effectiveness of operating software controls is highly dependent on the standards and procedures employed by the independent software supplier.

In the limited in-house EDP staff support situation, the data processing expertise and responsibility for operating software will probably be concentrated with non-compatible EDP duties. It will be unlikely that the owner/manager, without help from an outside EDP consultant, will be able to properly review and authorize operating software maintenance.

In designing records controls as discussed in Chapter 3, it is important to keep in mind that operating system and application support software can be misused to make unauthorized or fraudulent changes to stored data or programs. Knowledgeable employees can make such changes without leaving a trace of what has happened. Often, utility programs are used to make unauthorized changes, but other parts of the operating system can be used as well.

SUMMARY

It is important for owner/managers to develop an overall approach to using EDP within the business. This includes making decisions on whether to rely on outside EDP advisors or hiring EDP staff and then formulating system requirements. The effort invested in this stage normally pays off in the selection of a system that best suits a company's requirements and streamlines the day-to-day accounting routine.

Usually it is best to proceed in the following way:

A decision has to be made on whether the business will be writing its own programs or buying packages. As discussed, in most small businesses, packages should be acquired to avoid the cost and complexity of in-house programming. In any event, application packages (or the language that in-house application will be written in) should normally be chosen first. Next, hardware and operating systems can be selected, usually with the help of an external advisor. If the business already owns or has long-term leases for hardware, then packages which operate on that equipment would, of course, be considered.

In choosing hardware and operating systems, the owner/manager needs to consider carefully many technical factors such as speed, disk storage capacity, ability to handle increased volumes by moving to larger computer models, backup and capability of utility programs. For these purposes, the services of an EDP consultant, to help define these technical requirements and then sort through the claims of various suppliers, is normally beneficial.

Application software development, implementation and documentation

Extensive involvement by owner/managers and employees of the company in the detailed determination of application software controls and the testing of application programs is necessary. In addition, successful implementation requires an accurate and complete conversion of semi-permanent and other data from existing to new systems. Also, documentation is important.

If custom application software is acquired, much more attention needs to be paid to detail. Good project management is required to help control the cost of development. Testing should also be more thorough. Often the services of an EDP consultant are needed to help with these aspects.

Operating software development and implementation (including network operating systems)

Operating and application support software are necessary to the efficient operation of computer systems. In a small business, it is often impossible to allocate duties among a limited in-house EDP staff to provide some control against the misuse of this software. Even when the computer system has been bought there may well be utilities present which can be used accidentally or on purpose to alter data without leaving a trail. The key to solving this problem is to bear these risks in mind when designing records controls and when considering which of these controls should be performed directly by the owner/manager.

CHAPTER 2

Non-Processing Controls

INTRODUCTION

This chapter addresses the following non-processing controls:

- Controls related to the organizational structure of the organization (organizational controls).
- Controls related to the maintenance and documentation of computer software (operating software and application software).
- Controls related to recovery or replacement of data or programs stored in the computer in case of accidental loss or destruction of data files, programs or computer equipment.

The controls and procedures discussed in this chapter tend to be preventive in nature — their purpose is to prevent errors rather than detect whether errors have occurred. In most cases, the effectiveness of such preventive controls depends on an adequate separation of duties among employees. These characteristics are not always found in a small business or within a small department of a large organization. The special challenges of the small business frequently include identifying compensating procedures for the following factors:

- Management whose primary focus is not directed towards finance, accounting and control matters.
- Little segregation of functions because of the small number of employees.
- Informally designed procedures with limited documentation.
- Relatively easy access to physical assets by clerical or accounting personnel.
- Informal systems for reporting, analysis, planning and control which depend on the management style of the small business owner/manager.

The introduction of computer-based processing into the small business environment will add the following concerns to that list:

- There may be a further concentration of functions.
- Certain authorization procedures (e.g., authorization of customer shipments based on credit limit tests) may be mechanized.
- There may be a requirement for technical EDP expertise in an area where existing employees' knowledge is likely weak.
- Additional training and supervision of employees will be necessary to provide new skills.

If not properly managed or addressed, the combined impact of the above factors could significantly weaken the effectiveness of non-processing controls. However, these preventive controls are desirable and, in some cases, crucial from an operating efficiency point of view.

ORGANIZATIONAL CONTROLS

Computer-based processing of accounting information has two major impacts on the organizational structure of a company. Specialized skills will be required to some degree and functions will be concentrated. These two impacts will be examined in this chapter. Also, examples of how adequate organizational controls can be exercised are provided.

Requirements for Specialized Skills

For small computer systems, full-time EDP specialists may not be required in-house. If in-house EDP expertise is required, in some cases one person may be able to perform all the necessary functions.

If the decision is made to rely on outside help for the requisite EDP skills, a company can become highly dependent on the data processing expertise of a contract software company and/or an EDP consultant. This reliance in itself can be a source of concern, especially in ensuring the quality and continuity of such support. Use of outside specialists also creates challenges in that:

- It is difficult to exercise control over the data processing function particularly in the enforcement of quality control procedures. No one in the organization may understand the importance of good control.
- EDP technicians from outside organizations will not understand the unique business requirements of the business.

Where the EDP expertise is concentrated in one or two in-house computer personnel, the following factors may cause organizational control problems:

- Once again, the limited data processing knowledge of the owner/manager will make it difficult to exercise effective control over the EDP function. The scope of the data processing activity will not likely justify the cost of highly qualified EDP personnel. As a result, the primary computer resource person for the company may be a programmer/analyst who may not possess the administrative and management skills necessary to provide guidance from a strategic planning and resource allocation perspective.
- Over a period of time, usually a high degree of reliance may be placed on the continuing availability of one or two employees. This leaves the owner/manager vulnerable if that person were to leave.

Concentration of Functions

The computer-based processing of accounting information often results in the concentration of various processing activities that were formerly divided among several employees.

The responsibility for entering data usually rests with clerical staff in the user departments rather than with computer operators. These users are often the people who would have performed the accounting functions in a manual environment. For example, the person who enters accounts receivable accounting transactions on a data entry terminal may be the same accounting clerk who previously made the entries manually in an accounts receivable sub-ledger. In this case, the requirement for segregation of duties is the same as in a manual environment. When a terminal operator is responsible for recording accounting transactions, the minimum requirement for organizational control is that he or she must not also (1) initiate and authorize transactions or (2) have access (direct or indirect) to the related assets.

Data entry functions often extend beyond the accounting group into operating areas. Order-taking and shipping personnel may enter data directly into the computer system using terminals in their work areas. If the same segregation of duties that would normally be maintained in a manual environment is achieved (and proper programmed controls are used to enforce them), the impact on organizational structure for control purposes is minimal. The shipping supervisor who enters shipment data on a data entry terminal is essentially performing the same function as he or she would have in a manual environment (where the shipper would fill out a shipping document and forward it to the accounting department for processing). The data entered on the terminal must be subject to the same or equivalent control as a shipping document would receive in a manual system before entry into the accounting records.

The requirements for organizational control in a small business with automated accounting systems are therefore comparable to the requirements in a manual environment, with the additional consideration that there must be programmed or other controls that either enforce the organizational control plan or compensate for weaknesses in organizational controls.

Segregation of Duties

Organizational controls related to segregation of duties are needed:

1. Within the EDP department or function itself.
2. Between the EDP department or function and noncompatible functions within the organization.
3. Within the source and user departments.

The practicality of achieving such a segregation of duties within the constraints of a small business will most often require implementing alternative controls as discussed below.

1. *Within the EDP department or function itself*

   Traditional texts relating to computer controls recommend the segregation of specific EDP activities within an organization's EDP department. For example, the CICA publication Computer Control Guidelines recommends that the functions of system design and programming should be separated from computer operations.

   Other commonly recommended organizational control techniques (within the EDP function), such as establishing a data control group independent of other operating functions or setting up a computer file library will generally not be practical in the small business environment.

   Organizational controls within the EDP function of small business are examined in two modes of operation as follows:

   • Dependence on third parties for EDP technical support.
   • Limited in-house EDP staff support.

   Dependence on third parties

   The computer system requirements may be such that full-time EDP specialists are not required at all, or EDP activities can be handled by one person. In most cases where the computer system is dependent on third parties for EDP technical support, the responsibility for the systems design and programming functions will be entirely assumed by personnel external to the organization.

40

Because such personnel are independent from the day-to-day operating and accounting activities, there is a tendency to quickly conclude that there is an adequate segregation of duties. This control can be effective if the data entry clerk responsible for operating the computer possesses the required training and technical skills to provide an overall review or check on work done by third parties. If this is not the case, then the organization will inevitably place a great deal of trust and confidence in the outside supplier.

In the absence of any employee with EDP training the only way to review or monitor the work of outside software houses or suppliers is to hire a consultant to do so. This may be appropriate at the time major changes or modification to the system are being made or perhaps once every year or two as a check on the quality of the work.

Limited in-house staff support

Here the system design and programming duties would be the responsibility of the in-house EDP specialists. Operations responsibility would either rest with them or would be carried out by user department personnel. Once again, in theory, an adequate separation of functions appears to exist. However, it is doubtful that the EDP staff's access to the equipment and/or files would be restricted or effectively reviewed or that the user department personnel would have the skills necessary to provide the "effective cross-check" referred to earlier.

Because so few staff are normally involved in the EDP functions, and because training and technical skills of personnel responsible for operations may be limited, it is unlikely that effective organizational controls will exist over the EDP function. As a result, little or no reliance should be placed on such procedures to control, for example, unauthorized program changes or access to computer files. Instead, increased reliance must be placed on detective verification procedures performed by user department personnel and output validation procedures performed by management. These are discussed under records controls, output controls and owner/manager controls in Chapters 3 to 7.

2. *Between the EDP department or function and noncompatible functions within the organization*

In any accounting system, the following functions should always be segregated:

- Initiation and authorization of transactions.
- Recording of transactions.
- Custody of assets.

41

When a separate EDP department is responsible for the processing and recording of data, effective division of initiating and authorizing activities from the recording function is achieved primarily by segregating the EDP department from other areas. Responsibility for the initiation and authorization of transactions is maintained in the user area. Separation of custody of assets from recording can be accomplished the same way. Control over the recording mechanism itself, i.e., the EDP department, is accomplished by establishing input/output controls that ensure the data processed is complete, accurate, and authorized (see Chapters 4 and 6).

If there is no separate EDP staff, computer operations (e.g., backing up files, running control reports, month end routines, etc.) are best assigned to individuals who are not responsible for the other activities mentioned above. If this is not possible, the second best choice is to assign these functions to someone not responsible for recording or custody of assets.

3. *Within the source and user departments*

Organizational controls within source and user departments pose a control problem regardless of whether accounting information is processed manually or by computer. This is not as a result of computer-based processing: it is a problem inherent in the small business environment. Thus, owner/ managers have always put significant emphasis on controlling the results of the accounting process and on their participation in asset protection and comparison controls (see Chapter 7).

In the typical small business system, the responsibility for recording transactions remains in the user area where it always has been. The availability of user-oriented data entry terminals, whether on-line or off-line, facilitates the recording of transaction data by users rather than by specially trained data entry personnel in an organizationally separate department. In addition to the data entry function, other responsibilities are typically given to user department personnel: i.e., error correction, batch control procedures, and basic operating functions. The impact of locating the data entry function and the computer operations function in the user area rather than in a separate EDP area is discussed below.

Illustrations of segregation of duties in businesses

Controls over the initiation, authorization, and recording of transactions are generally discussed under the topic of processing controls. Input/output controls performed by personnel separate from the EDP area constitute one fundamental control of this type. Details of the nature of these controls and other types of controls over processing and recording of data are addressed in Chapters 3 and 4. The responsibility for performing these control procedures, however, is an element of organizational control and therefore is addressed here.

For the purpose of illustration, batch controls are used as a form of input control, although the principles apply to other methods such as the use of transaction lists or registers. The main objective of the process is to ensure the completeness, accuracy, and authorization of the data entered into and processed by the system.

In the ideal situation, the functions of initiation, authorization, recording, and batch control would be completely separated one from another as shown below:

Segregation of Duties

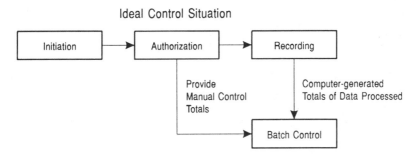

In Case 1, a batch control function exists and is segregated from the initiation, authorization, and recording activities. Batch control procedures include checking that each batch is authorized, reconciling transaction processing totals to predetermined batch control totals, and reconciling master file control totals with processed transaction totals.

In the small business environment, however, such a separation of duties may well be impractical. Some of them, however, can be combined and an adequate, though weaker. separation of duties for control purposes is achieved.

Segregation of Duties — Case 1

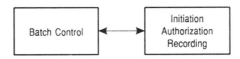

If the three functions of transaction initiation, authorization, and recording are combined. one individual has complete control over the execution of a given transaction. This is obviously undesirable from a control point of view. To provide some control, close supervisory review by the owner/manager would be necessary. Depending on the significance of the specific transaction, the supervisory review may take place during the transaction initiation (preventive) or after the transaction has been completed (detective). Detective controls are the better choice. In certain instances, it may be necessary for the owner/manager to initiate, authorize, and record particularly sensitive transactions. The separate performance of the batch control procedures would still help control the completeness and accuracy of the recorded transactions, but would not provide an adequate level of control over the individual responsible for the three functions of transaction initiation, authorization, and recording. Consequently, Case 1 is not considered to be a good combination of functions.

Segregation of Duties — Case 2

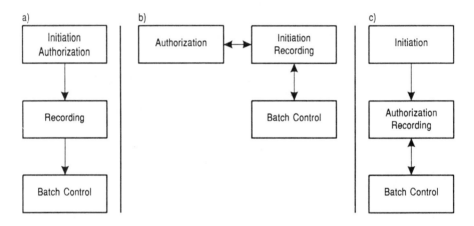

In Case 2, the batch control procedures remain segregated and any two of the three functions of transaction initiation, authorization, and recording are combined. In each situation, an acceptable level of control may be obtained, although a) is generally the most desirable and c) is the least. This is because authorization of certain transactions, such as credit notes or cheques, is tantamount to custody of assets (as receivables or bank balances are thereby reduced). It is always best to segregate recording or accounting activities from custody of assets.

Segregation of Duties — Case 3

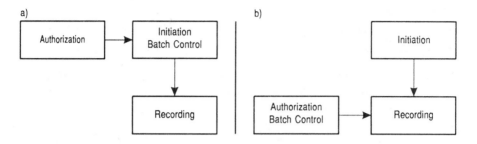

Combining batch control responsibilities with either the transaction initiation or authorization functions would still provide an adequate separation of functions. The batch control procedure should not, however, be combined with the recording function, because that would mean that the individual responsible for the recording function is checking his or her own work. This may be an operating efficiency but not a good control procedure.

Segregation of Duties — Case 4

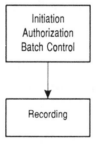

Case 4 maintains the effectiveness of batch controls as a check on the completeness, accuracy, and authorization of recorded data because errors, omissions, and unauthorized transactions made or recorded by the recording individual (terminal operator) would be detected by batch control procedures. There is, however, little control over the individual responsible for transaction initiation and authorization and performing batch control procedures. This individual has almost complete control over the execution of a transaction; therefore, close supervisory review as outlined in Case 1, would be necessary to provide adequate control.

Segregation of Duties — Case 5

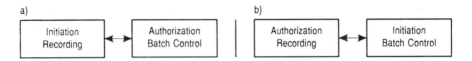

a)

| Initiation Recording | ◄──► | Authorization Batch Control |

b)

| Authorization Recording | ◄──► | Initiation Batch Control |

In both of the Case 5 situations, effective control over the recording (completeness and accuracy) is achieved because the batch control procedures and recording function are separate. In the first situation, authorization is performed during batch control procedures and, in the second situation, during the recording function. Authorization is controlled to a certain degree as in a) it is done separately from the recording function. In case b), the employee doing the batch balancing can see that transactions authorized and recorded were at least initiated by someone else.

As indicated, there are several possible ways to combine certain of the functions of transaction initiation, authorization and recording with the performance of batch controls without losing control over the completeness, accuracy, and authorization of transactions. It should be kept in mind, however, that the combination of any of these functions may weaken control somewhat because some of the "cross-checking" of work by separate individuals has been eliminated.

Automated Controls

One of the major benefits of computer-based processing is the ability to incorporate procedures and obtain information that was previously not available or was too time-consuming to extract from the manual system. In addition to the mechanization of clerical procedures, the computer can be used to incorporate procedures to help ensure the completeness, accuracy and authorization of transactions processed. Basically, however, these controls only provide a degree of protection and usually only against innocent error. They are not a substitute for a proper segregation of duties. Typical procedures that can be programmed in as features of accounting systems are:

1. *Completeness of data:*

   - Standard "fill in the blanks" menus on the data terminal screen for each transaction.
   - Anticipation of remaining transactions (eg., shipping advices being returned for each open order.)

2. *Accuracy of data:*

- Interactive prompting of operators.
- Programmed validation of individual fields against edit rules.
- Validation of combination of entries (e.g., sales personnel to territories).
- On-line reference to semi-permanent data.
- On-line correction of errors.
- Automatic retrieval of semi-permanent data (e.g., prices, addresses).

3. *Authorization of transactions:*

- Passwords on specific systems (e.g., accounts payable. payroll).
- Passwords on specific programs (e.g., process credit notes).
- Passwords on specific transactions (e.g., change credit limit).
- Programmed access control (e.g., read only, read or write).

Assurance must be available that the types of controls discussed above are in place and are operating at all times.

Where third parties provide EDP technical support, this may be accomplished through discussions and confirmation with the outside software company as to whether changes to application or operating software have affected the operation of these controls. In the limited in-house EDP staff support mode, this is difficult to accomplish because of a lack of division of duties and of technically competent supervisory staff to review program changes.

Once again, the answer lies in designing records controls, as discussed in Chapter 3 to incorporate additional controls for each application to offset these problems.

OPERATING SOFTWARE MAINTENANCE

This discussion applies equally to operating systems and related application support software for minicomputers as well as network operating systems for LANs.

Maintenance changes to operating software may be made for several reasons:

- To permit the use of new devices or components of hardware (e.g., to accommodate a different model printer or to facilitate the use of additional main memory of the CPU).
- To introduce modifications to the existing operating software (these are usually referred to as enhancements or new versions of operating system software).
- To correct program errors discovered in the operating software.

- To introduce new utilities or application support software which will enhance operational efficiencies or strengthen controls (eg., better and faster back up routines, utilities that provide further data on computer usage).

Software changes are primarily made by the equipment manufacturer (or operating software supplier if different from the equipment manufacturer). Manufacturers may make the modifications available as individual fixes to the existing operating software and/or provide regular releases of upgraded operating software that incorporate all modifications issued since the last release. These are referred to as new versions and are usually serially numbered such as 1, 2, 3 for each new release.) Similar to the situation with large-scale operating software, most suppliers of operating software for small computer systems recommend a selective implementation of modifications (i.e., only modifications that will have a positive impact on the current operating environment need be introduced). In fact. it is not unusual to have small installations where no modifications to the operating software have been required for several years.

In certain situations. operating software modifications may be initiated by sources other than the original supplier of the software. Most commonly, an outside application software company may make changes to the manufacturer's standard operating software to handle nonstandard equipment configurations or to extend the software capabilities beyond those normally available.

An in-house programmer/analyst may modify the operating software for similar purposes. Operating software modifications of this sort normally result in invalidating the original software suppliers warranty or licence agreement. The use of nonstandard operating software introduces additional risk of inappropriate and/or inadequately tested modifications. The availability of efficient, well-tested standard operating software packages from experienced equipment manufacturers makes the use of nonstandard operating software usually unnecessary and certainly risky. It really should be avoided, except in sophisticated EDP environments.

Expertise Required to Correctly Modify Operating Software

Where the modification comes from the supplier, it may be easy to implement, if instructions on how to load the revised operating programs are provided. However, modifications done directly by in-house personnel are another matter.

The average programmer/analyst working as an application programmer in either the dependence on third parties for EDP technical support or limited in-house EDP staff support modes of operation can easily obtain the technical skills or knowledge required to modify the macro or assembly language statements to effect changes to the operating software. The knowledge required is readily available through courses and reference material supplied by the software supplier. The technical knowledge required to effect software modifications via the executable code version is more detailed and complex.

Control Issues

Whenever changes are made to manufacturer-supplied operating system software or application support software, an additional element of risk is introduced as the modifications may compromise the overall integrity of the software. (This should not be interpreted as a statement that the software supplied by manufacturers is error free in the first place.)

Methods to provide some degree of control

To provide adequate control over maintenance of operating software, the following requirements should be met:

- Changes should be properly authorized (by the owner/manager in consultation with the EDP advisor).
- Changes should be implemented by personnel with no incompatible duties.
- Changes should be adequately tested prior to implementation.
- Changes should be properly documented.

The first two requirements may be difficult to achieve due to the lack of effective organizational control within the small business environment.

The knowledgeable authorization of operating software maintenance changes will require technical knowledge and skill levels beyond those that can be reasonably expected of the owner/manager of a small business. As a result, the owner/manager should obtain outside technical expertise regarding proposed modifications. Except in very unusual circumstances, software modifications should be restricted to those recommended by the equipment manufacturer, or the addition to the system of well known utility programs.

In any event, modified operating systems should be adequately tested and documented before use. While suggested modifications from outside sources will already have been tested by those suppliers, it is usually best to reprocess, as a minimum, one or two days' transactions through the modified system and compare the results with those obtained from the existing system.

Often, companies delay the implementation of new versions of operating systems until these new versions have been used by others and any problems have been corrected by the suppliers. This is an effective approach, providing the new version does not contain new features immediately needed by the company.

Where adequate controls over operating software maintenance do not exist, additional emphasis must be given to processing controls and other procedures features outlined in Chapters 3 to 7.

APPLICATION SOFTWARE MAINTENANCE AND DOCUMENTATION

Application software modification and maintenance are common in both large and small computer systems. For example, payroll programs change when tax rates change, or sales programs change if management requests a new sales report that is currently not produced by the system. It is generally true that, as business owners become more familiar with the information potentially available from data processing systems, they will keep coming up with new ideas for modifications and additions to the information currently produced. Modifications may also be made to systems to "fine tune" them to process information on a more timely basis, or to correct programming errors not detected during the testing phase of systems development.

Making Changes to Application Software

As the computer programs themselves perform important control activities and make many important computations, it is as necessary to control changes to programs as it is to ensure their accurate functioning in the first place.

Other reasons why changes to application software should be controlled include:

- Unauthorized changes may be made for fraudulent purposes.
- Technical changes may improve the operating efficiency of an application program, but may result in a weakening of controls.

Unless users are aware of changes and participate in testing them, programmers could accidentally, or purposefully, incorrectly modify the programs. If changes to application software are not documented, eventually documentation will no longer be useful.

Application Software Changes by an Outside Software Vendor

Sometimes vendors of popular minicomputer and microcomputer software packages will, at their expense, set up user groups so that all users can communicate their need for desired changes and amendments. Participation in such user groups can be a useful means of convincing the supplier that chances and enhancements should be made to a particular software package. User groups also offer an opportunity to share knowledge and experience.

Many packages contain programmed routines or semi-permanent data that require periodic amendments to reflect changes in the law. Examples include payroll packages which need to reflect periodic changes to income tax, Canada pension plan and unemployment insurance deductions. In such cases, the software contract normally provides that the software vendor will make such changes available on a timely basis.

Many software packages are designed so that the business can make the necessary changes itself, using special maintenance or setup screens. For example, it may be necessary to change provincial sales tax rates for certain products from time to time. Although such changes are simple to make, they should be carefully reviewed, controlled, and tested because errors in semi-permanent data (such as sales tax rates) could result in numerous output errors.

Requests to suppliers for specific changes to a package for use only by the requesting company should be avoided. Generally, it is costly to make even a modest change to a package and the supplier will seek to recover all these costs plus a profit margin from the person making the request.

Usually, only suppliers of large and expensive packages will entertain these requests. With "off the shelf" microcomputer packages, effectively there is no way an individual organization can request a change from the supplier.

However, sometimes such special changes are worth the cost. One advantage of using a software supplier to make application software changes is that it will help ensure that all changes are authorized. As the owner/manager will be charged for each change, all changes should be drawn to his or her attention. Naturally, steps should be taken to control the cost of changes. Before the owner/manager gives authorization, the software supplier should be asked for an estimate or if possible, a fixed fee for the cost of making the changes. Of course, the change should be made only if the cost is justifiable.

Often, there may be a temptation to allow a company employee with some EDP knowledge to make changes to a purchased package instead of incurring the costs for having the changes done outside. This temptation becomes especially strong with microcomputer packages when they are written in fairly simple programming languages such as BASIC and the business may well have possession of the BASIC programming code.

These temptations should be resisted. If a business changes or modifies purchased packages, it may later be difficult to bring these changes forward and re-implement them when new, improved versions of the package are made available by the software supplier. In addition, should there be future difficulties with the package. the software supplier may deny assistance in correcting the problems on the grounds that the system has been "tampered with" by the business. This is somewhat analogous to making home repairs on an automobile under warranty.

Application Software Changes Made In-house

Businesses with in-house EDP expertise will, in most cases, make their own changes to application software which they developed in the first place.

In these circumstances, the revised programs should be thoroughly tested by someone other than the person making the changes. In addition, all changes should be approved and documented. All these matters are discussed below.

Testing Changes

Regardless of whether an outside software supplier or the business' own employees change the programs, all modifications to software should be tested before modified software is used, along the lines discussed below. Also, the receipt of a new general version of a package should be treated as an important program change and tested accordingly.

Some software vendors will have quality control procedures over their program changes and how they are to be tested. Other software firms may not have such quality control procedures. In either case, it is unlikely that a small business will possess the technical expertise to determine that changes are proper and have been subjected to adequate testing by the software supplier. Instead, the business should perform its own testing. One way to do this is with "test packs" discussed in Chapter 1 under the heading "Complex Packages and Custom Software-Testing of applications systems software", which contain test input data and test files for trying out the revised programs. The subsequent reports are then compared with. and reconciled to, predetermined results to establish the validity of the change.

Another method used to test software after programs have been changed is to reprocess the previous day's transactions, using copies of backup files created at the beginning of the previous day. The results are compared to that day's processing to help ensure that the change was properly made and that there have been no unexpected side effects, at least in respect of the kind of transactions processed yesterday. It would also be a good idea to re-process special month end routines and reports in the same way.

Where the organization is making its own changes to programs that were developed in house, then more stringent testing is normally required. In fact, if major changes are being made, the revised programs should be as thoroughly tested as the original application (see discussion in Chapter 1 under the heading "Complex Packages and Custom Software").

For changes of a minor nature, some testing will always be required. Its degree should reflect both the complexity of the change and the importance to the business of the program functions being modified. In any event, testing should always include detail testing by the programmer of both the revised program and then the functioning of the overall system with the revised program. Users then should perform their own independent testing to ensure the changes work correctly and as requested.

Documenting Changes

For in-house developed software maintained within the business, documentation should be updated for every system change for all affected areas. The list of suggested documentation contained in Chapter 1 under the heading "Obtaining or Creating Adequate Documentation" should be reviewed to ensure that consideration has been given to all items. In addition, the change should be specifically documented on a program change form, setting out the following information:

- Reason for the change.
- Nature of the change.
- Details of testing performed.
- An indication that the change has been approved by the owner/manager.

In addition, a program change log should be maintained for each system, which should contain the following information:

- Program identification.
- Date the change was implemented.
- Cross-reference to the program change form.

Regardless of who makes the change, the date of such change should be carefully noted and a copy of the programs and files prior to the change kept on file. Data can then be reprocessed using the old correct files and programs if despite all precautions taken, the amended program contains errors and results in incorrect processing.

Authorizing Changes

Small business will find that it will be more difficult to control program changes when they use their own EDP personnel to make the changes. In most small business situations, the systems analyst/programmer will also be the computer operator.

Exhibit 2-1 explains why control over maintenance and modification is difficult to achieve when in-house technical EDP expertise exists. As usual, a response to any weaknesses in such preventive controls consists of strengthening records and owner/manager controls discussed in Chapters 3 to 7.

Control Over Changes

IN-HOUSE EDP EXPERTISE	OUTSIDE SOFTWARE SERVICES USED
Computer system with compilers, utilities and other aids to facilitate changes is available and could be misused.	Computer system may have a compiler, but most utilities can be removed. Programs may be available only in machine code, making it difficult to effect changes.
Program library cannot be restricted to the owner/manager.	Program library could be restricted to the owner/manager.
Documentation may be available at a detailed level on all systems.	Documentation that would aid those planning unauthorized changes can be restricted by the owner/manager and is more limited in any event.
The owner/manager may not have the technical expertise to ensure that changes are adequately tested and documented.	Good software service vendors may have their own quality-control procedures to ensure that testing is complete.
Users might direct requests for changes to the EDP specialist without the approval of the owner/manager.	All changes must be requested by the owner/manager from an outside contractor. The cost of each change will be justified.

Exhibit 2-1

PREVENTION OF RECORD AND EQUIPMENT LOSS

Reasonable steps should be taken by a business to prevent accidental loss or destruction of data files, programs, or computer equipment.

Two things are needed for proper backup. The file itself must be periodically copied and details of transactions processed since the copying took place need to be available. While it is important to control costs, it should be understood that using cheaper tape cassettes or tape drives for making file copies may tie up the computer for long periods of time to accomplish backup procedures. Also. certain more economical tape drives may not be reliable. Therefore, the need for additional disk drives or higher-speed tape devices should be assessed from both operational and backup capability viewpoints.

For example, consider a system that principally operates in a batch update mode with order entry being the only on-line function. Regular backup copies of files for this system should be prepared using the tape cassette drive or other tape drive purchased with the system. The task of regular system backup should be assigned to a specific person and would normally be performed on a daily basis (or sometimes, on a weekly basis). Should a software or human error result in the destruction of a file or program, the backup copy of that system would be restored from tape, and entries from the time the backup copy was created to the time of file loss would be re-entered from source transactions. There might be a problem with the on-line order entry system if the original transaction entries were keyed in from information taken during a telephone call, as no hard-copy information would then be available to re-key the sales orders. The result would be lost sales orders and unhappy customers. This could be prevented by backing up the sales order file much more frequently and ensuring that the system also captures and stores on a separate disk or prints out sales orders which could then be re-entered.

Reconstruction for the order entry part of the on-line system and for all systems in a real-time mode depend on the availability of printouts or machine-sensitive records (e.g., records written out on a separate disk drive) for transactions entered from the time of the last backup to the time of system loss. Most large business data processing systems prepare a computer tape log or journal of all transaction entries to such systems. To help resume operations, the log together with the back copies of files can then be used to restore the system.

Some small computer systems do not have this capability, and alternative procedures will have to be found. One such procedure might be to retain the paper source transactions used for data entry or, if no hard-copy source documents exist (for example, where information is entered directly into the computer from an order received by telephone), to use a terminal that creates its own record of transactions processed. The transactions record may be in hard-copy form or in machine-sensible form, such as on a cassette tape prepared on the data-entry terminal. Where LANs are used, an organization might consider the data duplication or data duplexing capabilities of such systems, as described in Chapter 8.

Two things are needed for proper backup. The file itself must be periodically copied and details of transactions processed since the copying took place need to be available. While it is important to control costs, it should be understood that using cheaper tape cassettes or tape drives for making file copies may tie up the computer for long periods of time to accomplish backup procedures. Also. certain more economical tape drives may not be reliable. Therefore, the need for additional disk drives or higher-speed tape devices should be assessed from both operational and backup capability viewpoints.

For example, consider a system that principally operates in a batch update mode with order entry being the only on-line function. Regular backup copies of files for this system should be prepared using the tape cassette drive or other tape drive purchased with the system. The task of regular system backup should be assigned to a specific person and would normally be performed on a daily basis (or sometimes, on a weekly basis). Should a software or human error result in the destruction of a file or program, the backup copy of that system would be restored from tape, and entries from the time the backup copy was created to the time of file loss would be re-entered from source transactions. There might be a problem with the on-line order entry system if the original transaction entries were keyed in from information taken during a telephone call, as no hard-copy information would then be available to re-key the sales orders. The result would be lost sales orders and unhappy customers. This could be prevented by backing up the sales order file much more frequently and ensuring that the system also captures and stores on a separate disk or prints out sales orders which could then be re-entered.

Reconstruction for the order entry part of the on-line system and for all systems in a real-time mode depend on the availability of printouts or machine-sensitive records (e.g., records written out on a separate disk drive) for transactions entered from the time of the last backup to the time of system loss. Most large business data processing systems prepare a computer tape log or journal of all transaction entries to such systems. To help resume operations, the log together with the back copies of files can then be used to restore the system.

Some small computer systems do not have this capability, and alternative procedures will have to be found. One such procedure might be to retain the paper source transactions used for data entry or, if no hard-copy source documents exist (for example, where information is entered directly into the computer from an order received by telephone), to use a terminal that creates its own record of transactions processed. The transactions record may be in hard-copy form or in machine-sensible form, such as on a cassette tape prepared on the data-entry terminal. Where LANs are used, an organization might consider the data duplication or data duplexing capabilities of such systems, as described in Chapter 8.

Application programs, job control procedures, and backup for semi-permanent data and transactions files are the major elements, but not the only ones required for recovery from a minor file loss. Written procedures, detailing how recovery is to be performed on a step-by-step basis, should also be prepared and tested. Even more importantly, employees should know how frequently to copy each file for backup purposes and how to physically store or capture transaction data which may need to be re-entered.

Preparing a Disaster Plan

The first step in designing a disaster plan is to distinguish between essential and less essential systems. For example, if a disaster occurs, accounts receivable must be restored quickly to protect cash flow. To maintain good employee relations, payroll systems are usually also essential. In contrast, accounts payable systems are often less essential and can be restored more slowly, using a fallback manual system and relying on suppliers to bring urgent problems to the owner/manager's attention until the system is restored.

Thus a good disaster plan distinguishes the systems that must be recovered immediately from those that can wait a while.

A disaster plan turns a potential catastrophe into a manageable business problem, while a minor loss of data requires proper backup procedures for reconstruction of records on site.

A good disaster plan should include the following features:

1. *A secure site should be selected for storage purposes*

   As computer media is subject to deterioration through excessive heat or cold, moisture etc., the physical environment in the off-site location should be carefully determined.

   There should also be good physical safeguards such as fire extinguisher systems to help ensure that the off-site premises will not suffer a disaster.

2. *Off-site storage should be complete*

   A disaster plan is designed to protect against a complete destruction of premises. It is therefore important that all the necessary means to get the computer systems up and running should be stored off site. Items to be so stored include:

   - The operating system and all utilities.
   - All application programs.
   - Copies of all operating instructions and user manuals.

- Sufficient copies of all input forms and output documents (such as blank cheques and invoices) to support operations for a reasonable period of time.
- Recent copies of all master files and transaction files.

As computer media can deteriorate and become unusable, it is a good idea to store two copies of all data and programs in machine readable form. If not replaced on a regular basis (see below), data stored on computer media should be periodically re-copied to ensure that it can always be completely and accurately read.

3. *Items stored off-site should be kept up-to-date*

It will be extremely difficult if not impossible to get systems up and running again if new operating systems or programs or new computer forms have been implemented in the day-to-day environment but only the old, and now no longer used, items are available in off-site storage.

It is a good idea to establish a checklist of items in off-site storage and to review the list periodically to ensure that when changes have occurred in the operating environment, the appropriate changes have been made to the programs, data, forms, and manuals kept off site.

4. *The data files in off-site storage should be kept up-to-date*

Should a disaster occur, it will be necessary to update the master files in off-site storage for transactions which have taken place since the date the information was stored. In other words, if a disaster occurred today and the last data file sent to off-site storage was on the close of business two weeks ago, then it would be necessary to somehow obtain and then re-enter the business transactions for the last two weeks.

This is a very difficult problem to manage as a total disaster in the office premises may destroy the hard copy of all business transactions. Sometimes the transactions can be reconstructed by reference to branch records, records or information in operational departments not affected by the disaster or in the final analysis by contacting employees, customers, and suppliers. The ability to so reconstruct transactions and the loss the business would suffer if it were unable, or only partially able to do so, needs to be taken into account on an application-by-application basis to determine how often information should be sent to off-site storage. For example, it is obviously more important to be able to reconstruct shipping data than to be able to reconstruct accounts payable records. Frequently carrying out a risk assessment to rank the various application programs (and allotted data files) in order of immediate importance to the business, will help the company concentrate on first protecting the most valuable computer files.

Many application systems produce transaction files on disks or tape daily and/or result in printouts listing all transactions. These records can be sent to off-site Storage on a frequent basis and thus be available to update the off-site older copies of master files, should a disaster occur.

On a less frequent basis, the entire master files or data bases can be copied for off-site Storage, at which time the transaction records previously stored can be dispensed with to save storage costs.

5. *Arrangements for backup hardware should be made and kept up-to-date*

It does little good to have all records and systems in off-site storage if there is no hardware on which to run systems until the destroyed hardware is replaced.

Various arrangements can be made for backup hardware for emergency use. Equipment suppliers can be asked to commit contractually to supply backup equipment. Some companies have reciprocal agreements to use each other's equipment should a disaster occur.

Such arrangements should cover all the necessary hardware and peripherals. including sufficient disk and tape storage, modems, printers etc. It is important that these arrangements be kept up-to-date. Another company may upgrade or change its equipment in such a way that your systems will no longer run on them. Equipment suppliers may discontinue the hardware or peripheral equipment you are using and the new equipment might not be able to run your applications.

6. *Disaster arrangements should be tested*

Disaster arrangements should be tested from time to time by obtaining the operating systems, programs, and files from off-site storage and running them on the backup hardware. Only in this way can there be full assurance that the disaster arrangements actually work.

7. *Coverage should be reviewed*

When a disaster strikes, it usually means considerable interruption to the business with resulting loss of revenue, cost of reconstructing records and problems getting systems running again, even where appropriate disaster arrangements have been made.

Thus it is prudent to discuss the coverage available in these areas and related insurance costs with an insurance advisor.

SUMMARY

This chapter dealt with non-processing controls which included controls related to: the organizational structure of the organization, the maintenance and documentation of operating and application software, and recovery or replacement of data and programs stored in the computer in case of accidental loss or destruction of data files, programs, or computer equipment.

Organizational Controls

The primary prerequisite of organizational controls is that there is an adequate segregation of duties between individuals performing noncompatible functions. The typical difficulties in creating such segregation of duties within small businesses requires that less reliance be placed on preventive organizational controls and more reliance be given to detective and other records controls.

Operating Software Maintenance and Documentation

Regardless of whether the mode of operation used is reliance on third parties for EDP support. or limited in-house EDP staff support, the owner/manager should be able to verify that there are appropriate controls over the maintenance of operating software to ensure that:

- Maintenance changes do not compromise or bypass intended controls.
- Maintenance is properly authorized.
- Maintenance changes are adequately tested prior to implementation.
- All maintenance changes are properly documented.

Application Software Maintenance and Documentation

It is necessary for the owner/manager to ensure that:

- All maintenance is properly authorized.
- Maintenance changes do not compromise or bypass intended controls built into the application.
- Maintenance changes are properly documented.

When programming changes are made inside the company, it is much more difficult to ensure that all changes are authorized, free of error, for valid purposes, and free of fraudulent intent. This problem flows from a lack of division of duties because one individual may be doing programming, operating the computer and routinely making use of utility programs that, besides permitting the operator to sort files or copy them for backup, can also make it easy to implement program changes unnoticed by management. In addition, the detail testing which should be performed by programmers prior to acceptance testing performed by users, is quite technical and difficult to review and evaluate.

Where an outside software vendor is used. there is usually less detailed documentation about the system available within the company. In addition, for some packages, the company may have only the machine code available rather than the source language computer statements in easy-to-change languages such as BASIC. At any rate, the owner/manager should authorize and approve the costs of all changes before letting the outside software vendor proceed.

Regardless of where the change is made, all program changes (including new versions of packages) should be thoroughly tested and appropriately documented.

Prevention of record and equipment loss

The risk of and expense related to the recovery from a minor file loss or major facilities destruction must be weighed against the cost of procedures designed to speed recovery and allow processing to resume. For example, the probability that a file containing unpaid invoice records may be destroyed through operator error or machine malfunction is much greater than the probability that the computer system will be completely destroyed by a disaster. Therefore. although it might be prudent to create duplicate copies of computerized accounts receivable information, it does not mean that duplicate computer hardware should be purchased. The cost of creating backup computer files is basically limited to the time required to create the copy, and the cost of arranging back up facilities in case of a disaster is not onerous. Usually these costs are well justified.

CHAPTER 3

Interrelationship of Controls

Previous chapters have dealt with acquisition decisions and non-processing controls. This chapter and the next four chapters look at the controls needed to actually process and balance data; that is, to ensure that transactions (sales orders, cash disbursements, etc.) are completely and accurately recorded and that only authorized transactions are processed. Controls over the integrity and balancing of the resulting computer files are also covered, as are owner/manager controls to protect assets and to periodically compare assets on hand with the books.

These control areas are interrelated because:

- Previous decisions will already have limited the techniques available to control transactions and the resulting computer files.
- Inherent limitations in non-processing controls in most small businesses create a need for compensating records controls and owner./manager controls.

THE EFFECT OF PREVIOUS DECISIONS

The capabilities of accounting packages and related software already chosen will have a significant impact on how controls discussed in Chapters 4 to 7 should be applied and how strong they must be. For example, the acquisition of software which provides for on-line data entry, but which does not accommodate passwords and other control features to restrict access, would make the design of proper records controls more difficult to achieve. Passwords are an important component of a control structure as they support and enforce a proper division of duties. Without them, establishing an adequate control framework will be very difficult and will require active participation by the owner/manager in many of the control activities described in the next four chapters. For this reason, Chapter 1 has emphasized those key control features that companies should search for when buying hardware, software, and accounting packages.

Computer environment (e.g., non-processing) controls in small businesses are often weak for two reasons:

- insufficient personnel to establish an effective segregation of duties (as discussed in Chapter 2); and
- acquisition decisions which limit the opportunities to establish good environment controls (as discussed in Chapter 1).

For example, almost all computers contain utilities which are necessary but can be used purposefully or accidentally to alter stored information including customer balances, pay rates, and programs. Because of staff and knowledge limitations, it is difficult for the small business to ensure such utilities are not improperly used.

Also, decisions have already been made as to whether programs will be developed in-house by company personnel or purchased as packages from outside suppliers. The company may or may not have EDP personnel on its payroll. The potential for programs to be incorrectly altered either accidentally or on purpose, needs to be considered in determining how strong controls over data input and output need to be.

RECORDS, OUTPUT AND OWNER/MANAGER CONTROLS

Records, output and owner/manager controls are the key elements in the system's control framework. The objectives of these controls are to ensure that all transactions are (1) complete, that is, all authorized transactions are processed in their entirety; (2) accurate, that is. the information recorded in the accounts is an accurate reflection of the business transaction that has taken place: (3) authorized, that is, all information recorded is the result of a valid transaction, approved by the owner/manager or his or her designate: and (4) has an adequate management trail, that is, the accounting system should supply sufficient detail to provide information for control purposes and in addition support owner/manager decision making.

Records Controls

Records controls can be subdivided into two distinct types for purposes of an internal control framework:

1. Controls over input;
2. Controls over computations.

Input controls are normally designed to ensure that all data is completely and accurately entered into the computer and has been properly authorized.

In a computerized system, the correctness of computations is normally controlled through systems and program development, and through controlling, changes to software. Examples of computations performed by a computer are footings, extensions, and sales tax computations on sales invoices or calculation of gross wages and the correct posting and summarization of such transactions.

Output Controls

The purpose of output controls is to ensure that output reflects all and only authorized transactions which have been processed by programs which are logically correct. Output controls exist because even with reasonable input controls and controls over program changes, it is still possible for employees to bypass such procedures and accidentally or purposefully alter stored data or programs. Also even with testing, errors can creep into software and may not be discovered until output is reviewed and balanced.

Balance Controls

Such controls are normally applied to an entire balance. For example, a computer-produced report such as an accounts receivable trial balance can be balanced to a manually determined total which has been computed by taking the opening balance and adding or deducting the values of totals for sales, credit notes, cash receipts, and journal entries in the intervening period. It is a strong way of ensuring that the underlying files such as receivables have not been altered in some unauthorized way (such as through utility programs).

Owner/Manager Controls

Owner/manager controls serve to protect assets against loss and theft and to periodically compare assets on hand with those shown on the books. Thus, they can be referred to as asset protection and comparison controls. For example, inventories are physically counted, quantities compared to book records, and differences investigated. Although asset protection and comparison controls are often performed contemporaneously with records or output controls. they are separate and distinct procedures that recognize that accurate records by themselves will not protect assets. Owner/manager controls should be applied to all assets and not just to tangible assets such as inventories and fixed assets. For example, the signing of all cheques by either the owner/manager or, in his or her absence, by two supervisory employees is an effective protection control over the asset "cash in bank". Bank reconciliations compare cash in bank accounts with amounts shown in the books.

Unlike records controls, owner/manager controls usually do not change with the manner in which books and records are kept and are largely unaffected by computerization. However, they are an important part of the overall system of internal controls and are discussed in Chapter 7.

HOW THE CONTROLS INTERRELATE

Exhibit 3-1 illustrates an overall system of internal control which can be useful in creating an overall control framework.

**Overall System of
Internal Control**

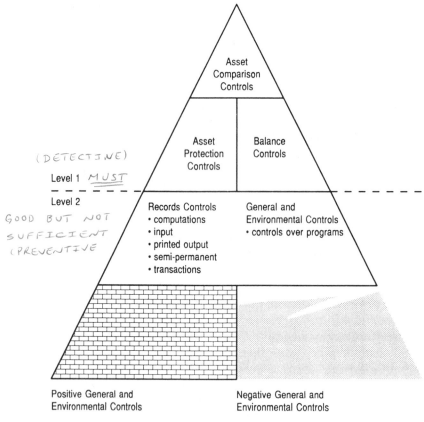

Exhibit 3-1

This exhibit shows two levels of control, level 1 being balance and asset protection and comparison controls and level 2 being all other controls. The distinguishment between these two levels is important as it illustrates the following concepts:

1. No matter how good level 2 controls are, level 1 controls are always required. This recognizes the reality that accounting processes by themselves are never sufficient to protect assets.
2. Many Level 1 controls are detective in nature and can being to light errors or omissions in the accounting records. This will enable accounting records to be corrected, but note that some assets may have already been lost.

Two examples help to illustrate this concept in relation to Level 1 controls: in the first case a loss is incurred with the records then being corrected and in the second case, controls prevent the loss and inaccurate records at the same time.

Example 1 — resulting in a loss

Company X has no password controls and has not installed strong records controls to ensure all shipments are billed or that shipments are recorded and billed accurately. However, inventory counts are taken carefully, differences investigated, and book inventory records adjusted to physical count results.

In this case, unbilled shipments or inaccuracies in billing quantities shipped will come to light if the inventory count is properly performed, summarized, and compared to book records. However, once the errors are detected it may be difficult for the company to determine which customer was incorrectly billed or not billed at all and to recover the additional money from them. Management may be willing to accept this risk provided that inventory counts continue to show little if any loss is being incurred and are performed frequently enough to limit any loss which might occur to an acceptable level. However this is taking a considerable risk.

Example 2 — loss prevented

Company X has only one bookkeeper who enters all data of all types into the computer and has access to all computer software and related utilities. The computer system prints cheques by searching the accounts payable computer files for invoices which are due for payment.

The owner/manager knows that there is no division of duties and the bookkeeper can change computer files readily. The owner/manager therefore personally signs all cheques and examines supporting purchase invoices and related documents when doing so. In this way, any errors in cheques prepared for signature would be caught before any money is lost.

There are two important principles to be drawn from these examples when relying on Level 1 controls to offset weaknesses or limitations in level 2 controls:

1. Will the Level 1 control operate in a manner to prevent any losses occurring in the first place? OR
2. If losses could arise, will the Level 1 control operate soon enough to detect the loss while it is still acceptably small?

Of course, if the owner/manager finds that losses are occurring, he or she should re-assess the need for additional controls at any level and compare the cost of possible additional controls with the potential losses which may otherwise occur.

Illustrations of the accounting process in a computerized environment

As illustrated in Exhibit 3-2, the accounting process in the computerized environment commences with the preparation and entry of transaction input. This input, through program logic, updates semi-permanent and transaction data (accounting records). Program logic produces updated files, accounting reports, documents and other output.

**Accounting
Process**

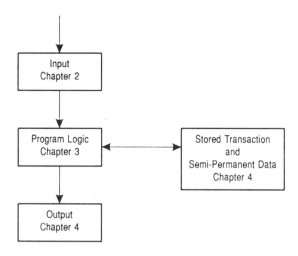

Exhibit 3-2

Exhibit 3-3 illustrates the accounting process for a sales-order entry system. It shows, in summary flowchart form, the activities required to process a sales order.

Exhibit 3-4 breaks down the flowchart to show input, program logic and output for each stage.

This simplified flowchart does not attempt to illustrate all facets of the sales order entry and billings process. For example, back-orders are not dealt with and certain features, such as checking of product availability at the time of order entry, pricing at order entry, etc., which may be common to many systems are not included.

Similarly, any accounting process can be broken down into input, program logic, and output.

Stored data is not treated as a separate item as all stored data was originally input and needs to be accurate and up-to-date. This is explained fully in Chapter 4.

In summary:

1. Input controls relate to:

   • entry of information from documents which are generated directly or indirectly in relation to a business or economic event requiring a record to be made in the books of the business (e.g., sales orders, shipment data).
   • creation and maintenance of semi-permanent data information.

2. General and environmental and program controls relate to:

   • accounting application program logic and proper operation of the computer to ensure that programs take the components of (a) above and prepare output in (c) below in a manner that both properly reflects the transactions which have taken place and the decisions of the owner/manager.

Flowchart of Sales Order Entry in a Computerized Environment

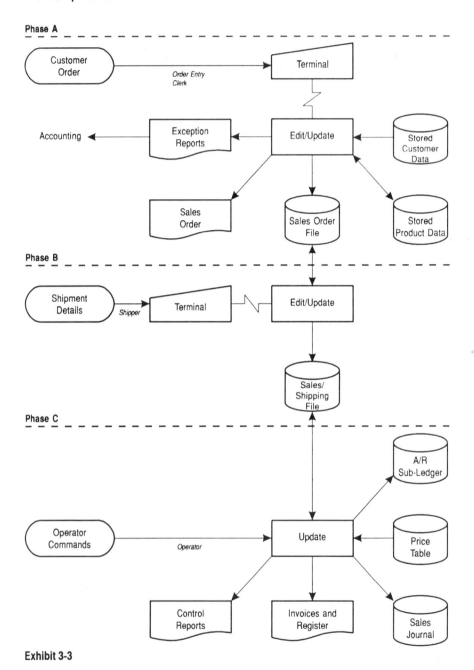

Phase A

Customer Order → *Order Entry Clerk* → Terminal

Accounting ← Exception Reports ← Edit/Update ← Stored Customer Data

Sales Order

Sales Order File

Stored Product Data

Phase B

Shipment Details → *Shipper* → Terminal → Edit/Update

Sales/ Shipping File

Phase C

A/R Sub-Ledger

Operator Commands → *Operator* → Update ← Price Table

Control Reports

Invoices and Register

Sales Journal

Exhibit 3-3

Sales — Order Entry

Phase	Purpose	Input	Program Logic		Output
A	Enter a sales order transaction	Document — sales order information	1)	EDIT sales order	Updated sales order file
		Stored customer data	2)	Updated — add order to sales order file	Sales orders
		Stored product data			Exception reports
B	Record a shipment	Document — sales order signed by shipper	1)	Update — to change status of order to "shipped"	Updated sales order file
		Updated sales order file	2)	Create sales shipping file	Sales/shipping file
C			1)	Change status sales/shipping file to "invoiced"	
		Sales shipping file Price table	2)	Update-Sales Journal file	Updated Sales Journal file and sales/shipping file
	To send invoice to customer for payment	Accounts Receivable sub-ledger	3)	Compose invoice and prepare details for printing	Invoices invoice register control reports
			4)	Accumulate sales invoice details to print sales invoices, invoice register, control reports on total quantities of goods shipped and dollar value of sales invoices produced	
D	To record the sales in the accounting records	Updated sales journal file A/R sub-ledger	1)	Update — A/R sub-ledger	Updated A/R sub-ledger updated sales journal file
			2)	Change status to "posted" on sales journal file	

Exhibit 3-4

3. Output, balance, and owner/manager controls relate to:

- the accounting records (including computer files) and documents of the company primarily through balancing, comparison, and review.

Exhibit 3-5 shows a typical accounting process in a cash disbursements system. Note that Level 1 controls applied by the owner/manager would be important in this instance to offset weaknesses in controls over input and a lack of division of duties.

In theory, a control framework could be developed using essentially Level 2 controls. This system would employ essentially preventive controls over transaction entry. These controls combined with strong controls over program maintenance could, in theory, result in reliable output. However, as is shown in Exhibit 3-5 there are many inputs, programs, and outputs requiring control. Undue emphasis on preventive Level 2 controls in the small business environment may not be the most cost-effective approach because of a number of areas to be controlled. As indicated in Chapter 2, program maintenance controls in most small business environments are limited. In addition, there may be insufficient personnel to create a proper division of duties. Thus, preventive controls in themselves will not necessarily result in an adequate control framework.

Rather than putting total emphasis on preventive Level 2 controls. an owner/manager could arrange to have an accounting clerk gather together supporting purchase orders, receiving reports, and invoices for review at the time the owner/manager signs cheques (the owner/manager may also agree details to the cheque register).

This detective owner/manager procedure will help ensure that only authorized purchases, received by the company and properly invoiced, are paid. This manual procedure, used to detect invalid or incorrect invoices before any cheques are signed, may be the most effective control over cash disbursements. The control framework, then, for this transaction type would place emphasis on detective controls at the time of signing and less emphasis on the extensive use of preventive controls.

Each transaction type should be similarly assessed to achieve a proper balance of Level 1 and Level 2 controls. For example, in the sales order system previously illustrated it would not be appropriate to omit input controls ensuring all shipments are billed on the grounds this might be detected later on through owner/manager review of output.

**Cash Disbursements
Simplified Flowchart**

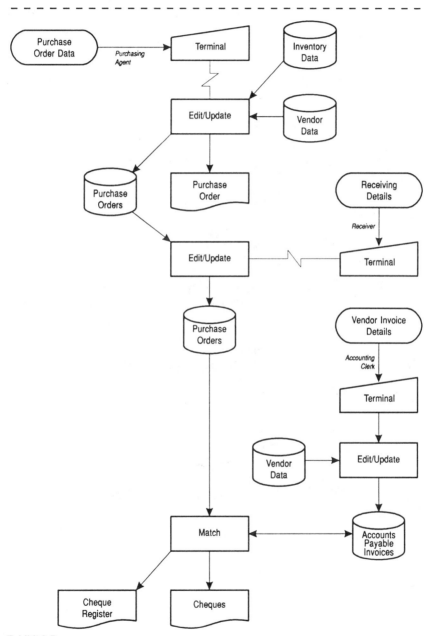

Exhibit 3-5

73

CHAPTER 4

Input Controls

The previous chapter defined input controls as being a part of records controls and relating to:

- entry of information from documents that stem directly or indirectly from a particular business or economic event
- creation and maintenance of semi-permanent data.

Prior to reviewing the steps involved in recording information in a computerized environment and the controls needed at each step, it is important to understand the significance of transactions and semi-permanent data and the different methods of recording transactions.

TRANSACTIONS AND SEMI-PERMANENT DATA

In a manual environment, a voucher of some type is prepared for each business or economic event. Those vouchers are then recorded in the books of original entry and, eventually, in the general ledger. It could be said that the books and records "store" or contain accounting transactions. From those records, information can be summarized and reports prepared.

In a computerized environment, business and economic events are often still written on vouchers, but the vouchers are then recorded on computerized media, which may already contain part of the data related to an individual transaction.

But in a computerized environment, there are two basic types of data: semi-permanent data, and accounting or transaction data.

Semi-permanent Data

Certain information only changes periodically and can be used repetitively. For example, a customer with one address may receive several shipments over a number of months. During this time period, the address remains unchanged.

Data which only changes periodically is called seat-permanent data. For example, customer numbers, customer names, billing addresses, ship to addresses, credit limits and payment terms are all semi-permanent data in an account receivable system.

The storage of semi-permanent data within the computer files has several advantages:

- It reduces the amount of information that must be entered to record each individual accounting transaction. It is not necessary to enter an address with every shipping report; the computer system can find and use the stored customer address.
- It provides a means of editing other data (e.g., a proposed shipment can be checked to see if a stored credit limit would be exceeded).
- It provides information needed by the system for calculations (e.g., stored payment terms are used to calculate cash discounts).

Thus semi-permanent data is used continuously within a computer system.

Semi-permanent data may be recorded as fields within each master record in a file (a common format for customer information such as name, address, and credit limit), or in a separate file as a lookup table (a common format for sales prices wherein each product code and its related sales price are stored in a separate file). In a database, semi-permanent data is stored as data elements under a database management software system. Semi-permanent data such as sales tax rates may be stored in the computer program itself.

All computer applications have semi-permanent data. For example, payroll systems store data on wage rates for each employee and payroll deduction tables. Order and billing systems store data on sales prices and sales tax rates etc.

However, semi-permanent data does change from time to time and transactions need to be processed to keep this data up-to-date. This is accomplished in much the same way as any other transaction.

Accounting or Transaction Data

Accounting or transaction data is data which is usually different for each business or economic event. Instead of being stored in the system for reference, the data is entered for each transaction. Thus, quantities shipped for each shipment, hours worked by each employee, or amounts of each purchase invoice are individually entered.

Normally all data of one type, when converted into machine-readable form, is stored on a separate file, thus creating stored data files of shipments, sales, purchases, etc. These files are similar to books of original entry in a manual system.

As in any accounting system, accounting data is used to update subsidiary ledgers such as accounts receivable, inventories and accounts payable, as well as the general ledger. Thus, accounting data affects the appropriate fields or records on accounts receivable, inventory, accounts payable, and general ledger record files.

If a database management system is used, the various data elements making up accounting data are stored under the control of a data base management software system.

Sometimes information is entered in the computer before any business transaction has been completed. Such temporary data consists of information that will be used to record an accounting transaction as soon as the company's responsibilities are completed. For example, sales orders may initially be entered into a sales order file. As the company has not yet shipped the products, this field does not represent accounting transactions and, thus, does not affect sales, receivables and inventory quantities. When the product is shipped, however, the sales information is used to update the appropriate stored accounting data. The temporary file replaces a physical file of unshipped sales order documents in the manual environment.

The following are typical transactions in a sales/receivables/receipts system maintained on a computer:

Sales, Receivables, Receipts System

Transaction	Updates Accounting Data	Updates Semi-permanent Data
Sales orders	See below	
Shipping information	X	
Credit note information	X	
Cash receipts	X	
Journal entries (write-offs, recoveries)	X	
Add a new customer		X
Delete a customer		X
Change customer information (e.g., credit limit)		X
Add/delete/change sales price table		X
Add/delete/change sales tax rates		X

Sales orders exist as temporary data until the order is shipped, because those orders result in an accounting transaction only after shipment.

For example:

	Temporary Data	Accounting Data
Sales order	X	X on shipment of goods

or

In an accounts payable system:

	Temporary Data	Accounting Data
Purchase order	X	X on receipt of goods

Transactions include information recorded to update/change both accounting data and semi-permanent data. The controls discussed in this chapter need to be applied to all transactions, be they accounting data or transactions to update and maintain the completeness and accuracy of semi-permanent data. These controls also need to be applied to temporary data as such data eventually becomes accounting data.

METHOD OF RECORDING TRANSACTIONS

There are three different methods which can be used to record transactions.

1. Off-line input/batch update
2. On-line input/batch update
3. On-line input/real time update

Off-line/on-line refers to the relationship between the equipment converting data to machine-readable form and the computer itself. For example:

A key tape machine is used to enter information from coding forms onto tape cassettes, which can then be read by the computer at a later time. Because there is no link between the key tape machine and the computer, this process is referred to as off-line data entry.

A terminal, located in the originating department, is used to enter a transaction into the computer. Or a microcomputer, linked to a LAN, is used to accomplish this. Because there is a direct link between the terminal and the computer, this process is referred to as on-line data entry.

Batch/real-time refers to the method of updating data already, stored in the computer, either periodically after several transactions have taken place (batch) or instantaneously after only one transaction (real time) has occurred.

As the control techniques for each of the above modes of data entry differ, it is important to review each method in some detail. To aid this process, Exhibits 4-1, 4-2 and 4-3 outline the general tasks required to enter information in each mode.

Because off-line batch processing is not prevalent in the small business environment, the controls over this mode of data entry will not be dealt with in this publication. Most small computer systems are designed for on-line data entry, with either real-time or batch update. To some extent, the move away from off-line batch update has paralleled the development of small computer systems.

In the following discussions it will be assumed that information will be entered on-line and file updates occur either in batch or real time modes.

Some systems provide for the keying of information onto diskettes. At a later time, the diskette is used to enter the batch of transactions and update stored data. Frequently, these data entry devices are not physically connected to the mainframe and the stored data. Such systems are quite similar to on-line data entry batch update if the data entry devices contain programs to edit the data as it is entered and also contain file copies for semi-permanent data needed during the edit process. The features normally inherent in on-line data entry are thus present and, for the purposes of this text, these systems will be treated as on-line data entry with batch update.

On-line Entry Batch Update

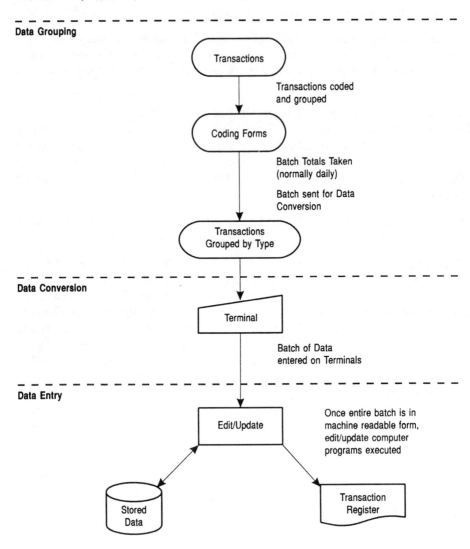

Data Grouping

Transactions

Transactions coded
and grouped

Coding Forms

Batch Totals Taken
(normally daily)

Batch sent for Data
Conversion

Transactions
Grouped by Type

Data Conversion

Terminal

Batch of Data
entered on Terminals

Data Entry

Edit/Update

Once entire batch is in
machine readable form,
edit/update computer
programs executed

Stored
Data

Transaction
Register

Exhibit 4-1

Off-line Entry Batch Update

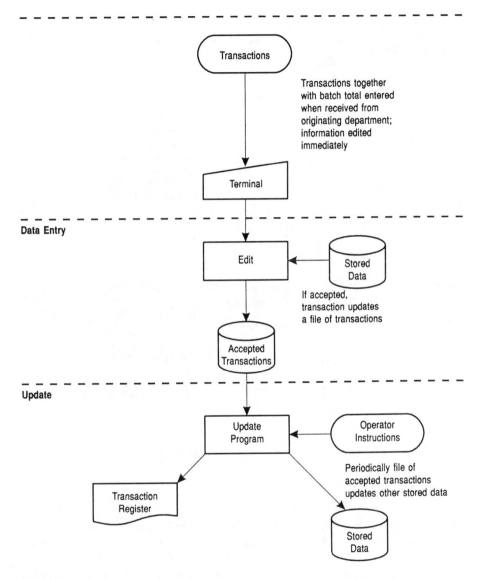

Transactions

Transactions together
with batch total entered
when received from
originating department;
information edited
immediately

Terminal

Data Entry

Edit

Stored
Data

If accepted,
transaction updates
a file of transactions

Accepted
Transactions

Update

Update
Program

Operator
Instructions

Periodically file of
accepted transactions
updates other stored data

Transaction
Register

Stored
Data

Exhibit 4-2

On-line Data Entry
Real Time Update

Data Entry and Update

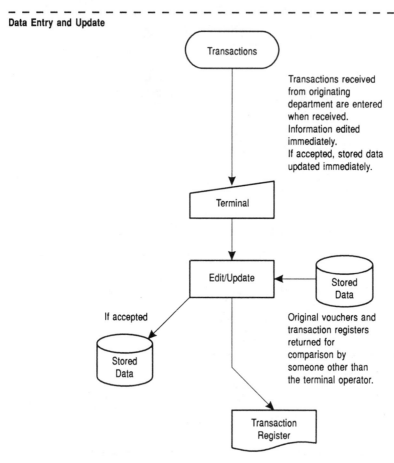

Transactions

Transactions received
from originating
department are entered
when received.
Information edited
immediately.
If accepted, stored data
updated immediately.

Terminal

Edit/Update

Stored
Data

If accepted

Original vouchers and
transaction registers
returned for
comparison by
someone other than
the terminal operator.

Stored
Data

Transaction
Register

Exhibit 4-3

Once a computer is installed and on-line data entry begins, the accounting records will, of course, be maintained in a computerized form. Because all grouping, posting, and summarizing is now computerized, user data entry procedures must be adequately controlled. Traditional manual controls over the recording process, such as use of subsidiary ledgers and control accounts each posted by independent sources, no longer exist and should be replaced by other controls discussed later.

Responsibility for data entry is usually dispersed throughout the company. Data entry frequently takes place in the area where the transaction originates. For example:

- Sales order personnel enter sales orders
- Shippers enter shipment information
- Accounting clerks enter cash receipts, journal entries, etc.

As a result, numerous individuals potentially have access to the accounting records, making input controls and passwords all the more essential.

INPUT CONTROLS

The process of entering a transaction in a computerized environment normally commences with the data entry clerk receiving a source document and keying in the information on the terminal required to record the transaction. This process updates (either simultaneously or by later batch) the data already stored. Because, in many cases, the entry of transaction information results in further business activity or has an impact on other transactions, it is important that transaction information be entered completely and accurately and that only authorized transactions are entered. Consider the following examples:

- Entering a sales order can result in shipment of goods (accounting data).
- Entry of a wage rate increase will eventually result in higher pay cheques (semi-permanent data).
- Entry of sales price changes will affect the pricing of future invoices (semipermanent data).

Although many of those events will subsequently be carefully scrutinized by the owner/manager (see Chapters 6 and 7), a system of internal control should not rely solely on one type of control to detect all previous inaccuracies, or incomplete or unauthorized transactions. For this reason, the data entry or input process is controlled using:

- Source document procedures
- Semi-permanent data
- Edit routines
- Batch totals
- Transaction totals or transaction lists
- Terminal access controls.

Exhibit 4-4 illustrates the main components of the data entry process and the related control areas.

It is also necessary to control data entry activities and access to the data entry device. Exhibit 4-5 illustrates the major control techniques often used.

Segregation of duties will help ensure that only authorized personnel can enter transactions and that those individuals do not have conflicting responsibilities. Terminal access controls seek to ensure that only authorized operators can use terminals and that they can use them only to enter the particular transaction types for which they have been assigned responsibility.

Source Documents

In a manual environment, transactions often originate in operating areas and, once authorized, are sent to the accounting area for recording. In a computerized environment, the operating areas may often enter their own transactions through their computer terminals. Because transaction documents are handled by fewer people in such an environment, less emphasis on procedures prior to data entry is necessary. The following procedures do, however, remain important. (It should be remembered that transactions include items affecting both accounting data and semi-permanent data.):

1. *Authorization of significant input transactions by operating management,* for example, by having operating management review and initial source documents. The individual reconciling transaction totals or reviewing transaction lists (as discussed later in this chapter) can review source documents to ensure that they were all properly authorized.

   In a small business environment, the authorization process can be made more efficient by providing:

   - Computer-produced exception reports of significant transactions for owner/management review.
   - Programmed authorization routines, such as checking sales orders to ensure that the customer's authorization credit limit is not exceeded.

Data Entry Process

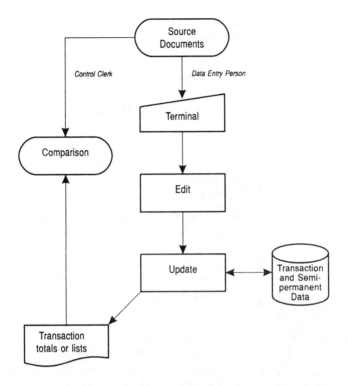

Exhibit 4-4

Data Entry Control Technique

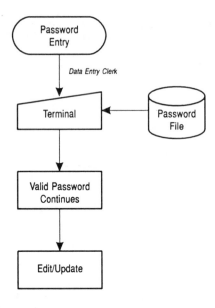

Exhibit 4-5

2. *Use of standard, numerically, sequenced input forms, controlled by the users.* Use of sequenced forms provides the opportunity to either manually or by computer program identify breaks in numerical sequence that may stem from forms being misplaced and, as a result, transactions going unrecorded.

   Access to unused forms should be appropriately controlled commensurate with their importance.

3. *To prevent duplicate entry, source documents should be cancelled by the data entry clerk immediately after entering the transaction.* In some circumstances, there may not be a source document. This frequently occurs when sales orders are entered as a result of a telephone call from a customer. This should not create additional control concerns; however, it must be remembered that the lack of a source document does not eliminate the need to approve the transaction. For example, in the case of telephoned orders, prudent business practice would suggest as a minimum that large orders be printed out for owner/manager approval before being accepted and be confirmed in writing prior to shipment. Computerized routines can also ensure that accepted sales orders will not cause credit limits to be exceeded.

Use of Semi-permanent Data

As previously stated, some semi-permanent data stored in the computer files reduces the amount of information that needs to be entered for a particular transaction. As less information is entered for each transaction, efficiency improves while the likelihood of error is reduced.

Also, the computer system can display the stored semi-permanent data to the terminal operator while a transaction is being recorded. This can help the operator detect any errors which may exist.

An example of how a sales order could be entered is provided in Exhibit 4-6.

A typical sales order has the following information:

* customer number
+ customer name
+ customer address
+ ship to address
z current date
* shipment date
+ freight terms
z sales order number
* product code
* product size
+ product description
* quantity ordered

* *information that required entry*
+ *semi-permanent data*
z *data generated by a program which thus does not have to be entered*

Clearly the amount of data requiring entry by the terminal operator has been greatly reduced through the storage and use of semi-permanent data.

Edit Routines

The purpose of an edit routine is to validate the transaction input to the extent possible to prevent inaccurate or incomplete data from being accepted for processing. As transaction information is entered, the appropriate application program performs tests for format, logical relationship, reasonableness, etc., as applicable. Edits are a part of an application program and, as such, should be part of the design requirements or acquisition criteria.

Terminal Operators	Response by the Computer System	Semi-permanent Data Accessed
— enter customer number	— search stored data for customer number	— customer data
	— if match found, display customer name and address on terminal screen	
— agree name to sales order		
— enters ship date	— error message if date is "impossible" or in an incorrect format	
— enters product code	— search product semi-permanent data for product code	— product data
	— if match found, display product description	
— agree product description to sales order		
— enter quantity	— format check	
	— reasonableness check	
	— inventory availability and message displayed as required	
— after all products entered, enters total quantity	— computes total quantity and compares to total entered	
	— reports and requires any imbalance to be corrected before entry can be further processed	
	Entering a sales order	

Exhibit 4-6

The following are examples of edit routines (it should be noted that edit routines cannot catch all kinds of errors and that it remains important to ensure source documents are correct and to check output):

1. *Format checks.* These ensure that each field contains either numeric or alphabetic data, depending on its designated function. For example, because a pay rate would generally be numeric, the presence of alphabetic characters suggest an entry or coding error and is therefore flagged as an error.

2. *Missing field tests.* This edit procedure ensures that all relevant fields for the transaction type have been entered. For example. when adding a new customer to the customer master file, it would be anticipated that customer number, name, address, ship to address, payment terms, credit limit, etc., are to be entered. The absence of one of these fields results in the transaction being rejected.

3. *Limit or reasonableness checks.* These will ensure that the information is within management-defined limits. They will reject a transaction when, for example, hourly pay rates exceed a specified maximum, sales order quantities exceed a predetermined maximum, or pay rate increases are too high in comparison to existing pay rates. Such routines can catch only grossly incorrect amounts or quantities; plausible but incorrect amounts will not be caught by the edit routines.

4. *Data field combination or correlation tests.* These compare data in different fields for reasonableness or correctness based on internal mathematical relationships. An example might be a check digit calculation for employee social security numbers, or normal hours worked plus overtime hours must equal total hours worked.

5. *Record matching*, which will check input transactions against related semipermanent data. For example, entering a customer number triggers a search for the number in previously stored data. If the number is not present, an error has occurred. Usually the related data is displayed to the terminal operator for visual verification, e.g., if the operator enters what he or she believes to be Mr. Korloff's number, the system should respond with Mr. Korloff's name which the operator can then compare to the source document. Alternatively, the system can require both the number and the name to be entered and match both of them to stored data. This is a more reliable approach, as it does not rely on the operator.

6. *Duplicate processing checks* to identify input of duplicate sequence numbers. The idea here is to verify, for example, that only one time card per employee has been entered.

7. *Balancing checks* to ensure that certain transactions balance to zero or totals agree to input totals. For example, journal entry debits should equal credits.

As another example, on entry of sales order details, total sales order quantity is computed and entered by the data entry clerk for comparison by the program with the total of quantities entered for individual products.

When errors are identified by the various edit routines, the data entry person normally cannot proceed until they are corrected. When an error occurs because of incorrect keying, the terminal operator can simply correct it and proceed. Where the error results from a source document error, the operator may correct the source document if the operator's responsibilities include initiation of that transaction. Where the operator does not initiate the transaction, it should be returned to the originator for correction. Some systems provide for the listing on a suspense file of transactions that were started but not completed. Transactions not re-entered are listed in a report for follow-up. This is a good control feature as it provides a means for checking that transactions rejected by edits are eventually re-entered.

As a further control, some computer systems have additional edit routines which "reports" unusual values but, because the value could be correct, allow processing to continue. Reports produced by these routines are called "exception reports". They should be closely reviewed by the owner/manager or the owner/manager's designate as they may well disclose errors which require corrective action. Even if the transactions are correct, such exception reports can be a source of good business information.

Prompt follow-up of reports is extremely important in real time systems. For example, flagging a customer order as exceeding the established credit limit is not an effective control if the transaction is allowed to update the sales order file. By the time the report is reviewed, the sales order may have been filled and shipped.

Edit routines are also useful in identifying keying errors. They will not, however, in themselves ensure that the information entered is correct. For example, a format check will reveal that the date entered is numeric but will not necessarily reveal that the date entered is not correct.

An edit routine cannot be designed to discover situations where invalid but correctly formatted and plausible information is entered. A quantity of 50 entered as 500, for example, cannot be detected by edit routines unless 500 is an exceptionally and unusually large quantity (reasonableness check).

Edit routines cannot be solely relied on to ensure that the entry of data is performed accurately.

Transaction Control Procedures

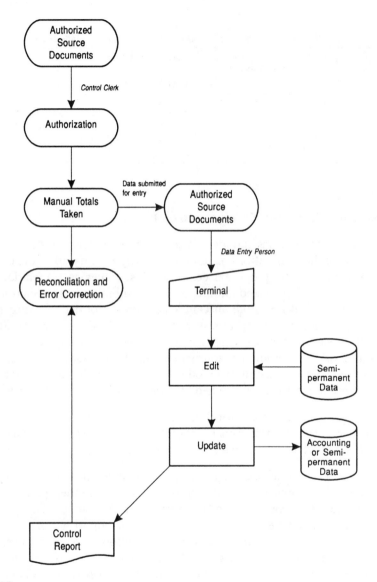

Exhibit 4-7

91

Control Log — Cash Receipt Transactions

Sequence No.	Date	Data Entry Person Identification	Total Per Source Documents	Total Per Control Report	Differences	Reviewed By
7	Jan 30/xx	J. Doe – Terminal 4	22,436.50	22,436.50	0	O/M
8		J. Smith – Terminal 1-2	19,438.60	19,238.60	$200.00[1]	O/M

[1] Customer X cash input of $200, rejected due to wrong coding of customer number
Re-entered Feb. 1/xx No. 10

Exhibit 4-8

Transaction Totals (or Batch Controls)

As discussed, edit routines can identify gross errors in quantities or dollar data but, because of their limitations, cannot necessarily identify all errors occurring as part of the data entry process. Because of this, values on source documents should be carefully checked before they are submitted. Transaction totals should be developed for all significant accounting information being entered. Normally, in an accounting environment, significant information is quantitative; that is, it may involve quantity ordered, hours worked, pay rates, sales prices, or dollar amount of journal entries. It does not necessarily have to be money but can be quantities or other numbers which can be totalled. For example, shipments are often batched by adding up total units shipped, etc.

In developing transaction total procedures, the first step is for the owner/manager to identify for each transaction type the significant quantitative information to be controlled by a transaction or batch total.

Transaction totals are developed by having someone other than the data entry clerk review the source documents for authorization and then prepare manual transaction totals for the significant information. As part of the updating of accounting or semi-permanent data, a control report is printed giving transaction totals for the same significant information. The control person then compares the computerized totals with the manual totals, reconciles differences, identifies errors, and ensures that the errors are corrected. The details of the manual and computerized totals, reconciliations, etc., are normally recorded in a log book, which should be reviewed periodically by the owner/manager (see example in Exhibit 4-8). Errors identified are sent back for correction to the person who originated the entry. The control person ensures that the correction is made. The log book also helps to ensure that rejected transactions are eventually corrected and recorded by supplying a cross-reference to where such transactions (which caused a difference between manually and computer produced control totals) have been re-submitted and recorded.

Error correction procedures will depend on the design of the application system. Corrections should be entered, however, in the normal input stream and be subject to the same control procedures as any other transaction.

Exhibit 4-7 provides an illustration of the transaction control procedures.

Transaction total procedures are a strong control because they determine whether the information that should have been entered has, in fact, been entered and used to update the applicable accounting or semi-permanent data.

In a batch environment, transaction totals are referred to as batch control procedures. Totals in the batch environment are easier to establish because transactions are grouped by type and each group is identified and totalled. In the on-line environment, transactions tend to be entered on a continuous basis. Transaction totals can be established, however, in the following two ways:

1. *On-line data entry — batch update.* Manual control totals are established by someone not involved in data entry. Separate control totals should be established for each terminal and each transaction type. At the end of each day, the computer program reads through the items accumulated in the transaction file and, after updating the stored data, prepares a control report showing daily transaction totals by terminal and transaction type.

2. *On-line date entry — real-time update.* Procedures are similar to the above except that the system must be designed to maintain a transaction log file that records all transactions entered for each shift's or day's processing. Control reports can then be prepared by the computer showing control totals by day or shift for comparison with predetermined manual control totals established on the same basis.

In all cases, the computer system must be capable of listing details for all transactions entered into the system as this information will often be required to investigate differences arising between control report totals and manually predetermined totals.

In most cases, it is more efficient to clear control totals on a batch-to-batch basis even for an on-line real-time system. The operator would have a group of, say, 50 items for entry with a predetermined control total. This total would be entered into the computer at the start of the batch as a control total. Once the 50 items have been entered, the computer would compare the pre-entered control total to the total of amounts actually entered. If the amount agrees, the operator is allowed to progress to the next batch. If the control totals do not agree, the operator must be able to produce a listing of the current batch, either directly on the screen or in printed format. This listing can be compared to the original transactions. If the error is a result of an incorrect manual batch total, the operator, perhaps with the authorization of the supervisor, would revise the original control total. If the error is, in fact, an entry error, the particular transaction line number must be corrected. The batch could then be completed and the next batch started.

Once a batch has been cleared, the computer should not allow the modification of a transaction already subjected to this control procedure. Subsequent corrections should be made by separate reversing or correcting entries that are subject to the same controls as the original entries, including appropriate approvals. At the end of the day, the computer produces a control log similar to the one above which is balanced to the original manual control totals by someone other than the terminal operator. In these circumstances, original control totals still need to be agreed to computer-produced control reports or logs by someone other than the terminal operator to ensure the operator has only recorded authorized transactions.

Transaction Lists

Transaction total and transaction list procedures are normally substitutes for each other. They, too, require assigning someone other than the data entry clerk to check details on the transaction list. As with transaction totals, errors are identified and corrected and source documents can be scrutinized for proper authorization.

Exhibits 4-9 and 4-10 provide illustrations of the transaction list control procedure.

Transaction List Control Procedure

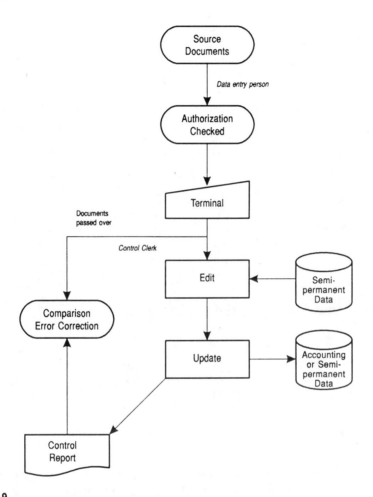

Exhibit 4-9

```
                    PAYROLL SEMI-PERMANENT DATA

                         TRANSACTION LIST

                     Month of September 19XX


                         - Terminal 5
                         - J.Brown
```

Transaction Type	No.	Name	Old Payrate	New Payrate	Change in Payrate	Social Insurance Number	Sex	Dept. No.
01 Wage Rate Change	1543	Green	20,000	25,000	5,000	—	—	—
04 New Employee	1672	Grey	0	15,000	15,000	421-673-234	M	—
05 Termi- nations	0674	Lawrie	35,000	0	[35,000]	—	—	—
06 Change Depart- ment Code	0742	Allin	—	—	—	—	—	746

Totals by Transaction Type	Numbers	Dollars
01	1	$ 5,000
04	1	15,000
05	1	[35,000]
Net Payrate Change		[15,000]
Old Payrate Total		167,000
New Payrate Total		$152,000

Exhibit 4-10

Transaction lists have the advantage of being able to check all fields for accuracy rather than just the quantitative amounts used for control total purposes. However, a major disadvantage is the time required and the need to rely on the diligence of the person performing the comparison. Errors in quantitative fields are more readily identified under transaction totals by out-of balance conditions.

Because transaction lists can be effective when the transaction volume is small, they are frequently used to control transactions prepared to update semi-permanent data, as shown in Exhibit 4-10. Also, a detailed transaction listing is similar to a book of original entry and can constitute an important part of the management trail.

Proper use of source documents, edit routines, and transaction totals or transaction lists will help ensure that information is completely and accurately entered and that only authorized transactions are processed. It is also important, however, to restrict terminal access to those authorized to use them and to ensure proper segregation of duties among terminal operation and other functions.

Legal Access Controls

As illustrated in Exhibit 4-11 terminals can, unless controlled, provide access to all company records and programs on the computer.

As data entry terminals are frequently dispersed throughout the company, anyone with access to a terminal could conceivably obtain access to, and possibly change, company records or programs. It is, therefore, extremely important to implement terminal access controls to effectively limit the use of terminals to only those individuals authorized by the company to access the predefined types of information. This helps to enforce an effective segregation of duties.

Most manufacturers provide terminal access security by way of a password protection system. Technically this is often referred to as "Logical Access Controls". This is illustrated in Exhibit 4-12.

To gain access, the user enters his or her user identification (user ID) and a password. The password is compared with the passwords on the password file for that user ID. If there is a match, the user is assumed to be an authorized user and is allowed to continue based on the level of password. If there is no match, the user cannot continue. A single password could provide access only to the total system. For most employees, passwords should be refined to allow access only by application (e.g., a user can access only accounts receivable) or by type of data or function (the user can access only semi-permanent data or record cash receipts). In other words, a password should only allow an employee to perform functions required by his or her job description.

Password control can be provided by the operating system, the application programs, or both. In fact, usually both the operating system and the application system are involved in enforcing a division of duties with passwords.

The operating system (or network operating system on a LAN) examines passwords and locks would be entrants out of the entire computer system if the valid password for that user ID is not supplied. The operating system can usually also restrict a user to a specific application system, such as sales and receivables, accounts payable, payroll, etc. The operating system can also restrict whether an individual user can write on computer files or only read information for each specific application. Generally, to further restrict the capabilities of a user within an application system, the application system itself must support an appropriate use of passwords. For example, in an integrated sales and receivables system, it is desirable to segregate the ability to record cash receipts from the ability to record credit notes. The application system would examine the password submitted and then present the owner of that password with a menu only containing those choices or functions that are authorized for the individual.

Depending on the design on the systems involved, one password may be sufficient for both purposes. In this case, after performing its checking the operating system hands over the password to the application system for further analysis as described above. In other computer environments the user must enter a second password after getting access the application and when prompted to do so by the application software. The important thing to remember is that logical access controls are generally needed at the application system level as well. The way an application is able to divide up and restrict access to its various functions should be an important selection criterion.

Other techniques to limit access include use of keys or badges that are physically inserted into the terminal for identification.

**Terminal Access Control
Uncontrolled**

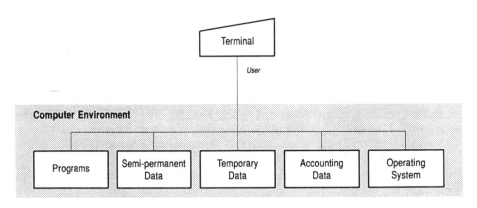

Exhibit 4-11

**Terminal Access Control
Controlled**

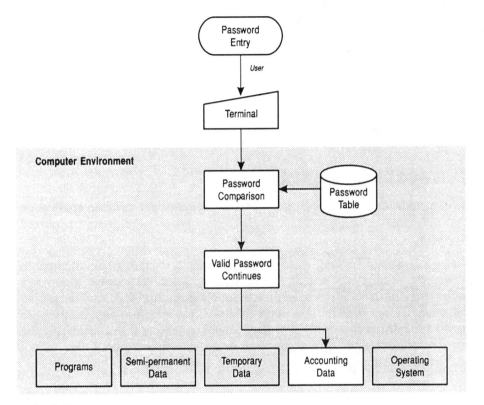

Exhibit 4-12

In deciding how to limit access to or via terminals, it should be recognized that the use of keys, badges, or passwords will not provide absolute security against non-authorized personnel as these can be used by anyone if they are deliberately, or inadvertently made available or disclosed. Using passwords in combination with locks or badges provides a greater level of security.

To establish effective logical access controls, the following should be considered:

1. Who should have access? Access should be limited to individuals who perform data entry functions or individuals who have a need to use company records for enquiry purposes. Access should not be permitted to any individual who does not have a preauthorized requirement.

2. What access should be permitted? Any employee's password should permit that employee to perform only those functions or access data commensurate with the employee's duties.
3. Responsibility for control of the password system. The owner/manager should determine who should have access to the system and determine what each individual should have access to. The owner/manager should also define password control procedures and directly maintain and control the password file (or delegate this to some employee who acts as the system administrator).
4. As previously stressed, employees who have access to or custody of assets and those who check batch control reports or transaction lists should not have passwords which allow them to record transactions.

PASSWORD CHARACTERISTICS

Most manufacturers or suppliers of operating systems and software application packages provide for a reasonable degree of flexibility in designing a password structure.

Passwords should be long enough so that random or systematic attempts to access the accounting records by entering a series of possible passwords (searching for a valid password) are time-consuming and would lead to detection. On the other hand, a password that is too long may force employees to record their passwords because they cannot remember them, increasing the chances of detection. In normal circumstances, a password of five or six characters should provide a sufficient degree of security.

To develop an effective terminal access control framework, the following areas should be addressed and the control techniques provided carefully considered.

Assigning of Passwords

- The owner/manager should be the only person who can assign an individual his or her original password.
- The owner/manager assigns a password only to users who have authorized data entry or enquiry responsibilities.
- A password should permit individuals to only record certain transaction types or access data in their area of responsibility.
- An original password should be communicated to users verbally (and never in writing).
- Users should be informed of the requirement to keep passwords confidential since they will be held responsible for all transactions recorded or changes made through it.

- Passwords should be assigned on an individual basis (global passwords should be avoided).

Use of Passwords

- Users commit passwords to memory and do not keep a written record.
- Terminal password entry procedures inhibit printing of the password or display of a password on a terminal screen.
- Passwords are not printed out on reports.
- Users have a limited number of attempts to enter a password (say three attempts) and, if not successful, further entries from that terminal are prohibited until action is taken by supervisory personnel. Alternatively, users are given a fixed length of time (say 15 seconds) to enter a valid password.
- Users are required to change their password frequently. This feature is available on some systems. For example, after a password has been active for a defined period (say, 45 days), at the time of sign-on by the users, the terminal asks the user to change the password. Processing cannot continue until this is done.
- Users sign off each time they leave the terminal. Some systems provide for automatic sign-off if the terminal is inactive for a specified period of time (say, two minutes).
- Users keep passwords confidential.
- Users design passwords that are random and do not contain employee initials, numbers, etc.

Changes of Employee Status

The passwords for users leaving the company or whose job responsibilities have changed are deleted from the password file.

Inactive passwords are flagged for review by the owner/manager. Some manufacturers provide for automatic deletion of inactive passwords.

Password Files

The owner/manager should have the responsibility to assign original passwords and maintain the password file. Alternatively, the actual maintenance (but not authority to authorize passwords and their functions) should be delegated to the systems administrator.

The password file, if possible, should be encrypted, protected by a password or otherwise protected from access by all users other than the owner/manager, or systems administrator.

- The password file should be updated only by the owner/manager or the systems administrator.
- The owner/manager should periodically scan the password file to ensure that only authorized users are present and that access rights allocated to each user remain appropriate.
- The owner/manager should review reports of terminal activities and invalid access attempts.

The above discussions apply both to minicomputers and LANs. Chapter 8 provides additional commentary as to how the security features in LAN network operating systems may be effectively used.

Additional challenges arise when dial up ports are installed which permit users to dial in from outside the office. As dial up ports are most prevalent in the LAN environment, additional controls for dial up ports have been described in Chapter 8 the concepts however would apply to any computer. Chapter 9 contains information on security procedures for individual microcomputers.

SEGREGATION OF DUTIES

In any control environment, one of the most important control procedures is to provide for an adequate segregation of duties. The idea is to structure each individual's job responsibilities so that one individual will not have custody of an asset and initiate and record transactions that affect the accounting records for that asset.

As has been mentioned, the introduction of on-line data entry normally results in a dispersion of the data entry function. As a result, segregation of duties can become more difficult. This is illustrated in Exhibit 4-13.

In the manual environment, the recording process is separated from authorization and custody of assets. The only potential area of concern is that the same individual in the operating area could both authorize transactions and have custody of assets. This concern is normally alleviated by either segregating the two responsibilities amongst personnel in the operating area or by having someone in the office closely review and approve all recorded transactions.

The following summarizes organizational control issues discussed in greater depth in Chapter 2.

In the computerized environment, initiation and authorization, recording, and custody of physical assets may be centralized in the user area. To achieve the ideal division of duties, a user who operates the data entry terminal should not have responsibility for initiation or authorization of transactions or have custody of the related assets. Data entry personnel should also not be responsible for batch balancing or checking transaction lists. It is acceptable, however, for those who initiate and authorize transactions to assume responsibility for balancing or checking transaction controls or transaction lists. The minimum acceptable level of segregation is to divide duties into the following three areas:

1. Initiating and recording transactions on the terminal
2. Authorizing transactions and transaction control balancing procedures
3. Having custody of assets.

Such segregation of duties preserves the arrangements needed in any system of internal control, be it manual or computerized. It recognizes that those entering data via a terminal are recording accounting transactions and, thus, should not have custody of assets. Custody of assets extends beyond physical custody to having effective custody by being able to approve a release or reduction of assets through, for example, signing cheques or approving credit notes. Division of duties is more completely discussed in Chapter 2.

In most computer systems today, general ledger control accounts are automatically updated by computer programs. Thus, the alternate procedures of transaction totals or transaction lists are used to help ensure the completeness, accuracy, and authorization of data. Like the control account procedures they replace, those controls should be performed by someone other than the employees responsible for the recording function (e.g., terminal operators) to provide an independent check on what terminal operators have actually entered.

It is not sufficient, however, to merely allocate responsibilities to achieve the minimum standards of segregation. To ensure that personnel granted access to a terminal use that terminal for only authorized purposes, controls must be implemented to restrict each individual's access to computer functions. As mentioned previously, a terminal, unless controlled, can be used to change programs, enter all transaction types, and change stored data.

Location of Data Entry and Other Functions

(A) Manual environment

Operating Area	Accounting Area
— Authorization of transactions	
— Execution of business transactions	— Recording of business transactions
— Custody of assets	— Controls over the data recording process
	— Control over the integrity, completeness and accuracy of the accounting records

(B) Computerized environment

— Authorization of transactions	— Control over the integrity, completeness and accuracy of the accounting records
— Execution of business transactions	
— Custody of assets	
— Recording of business transactions	

Recordkeeping Area

— automatic execution of the recording function

Exhibit 4-13

The password file, therefore should indicate the functions and resources (often phrased in terms of menu options) that each password can have access to. On entry of the user's password, the user can only carry out the functions that have been preauthorized in the password file.

Limiting functions by the use of passwords can also be achieved in the following three ways:

1. *Restrict the terminal.* The functions available on each terminal can be restricted. For example, cash receipts. and only cash receipts, can be entered into the terminal allocated to the cash receipts clerk. The cash receipts clerk's password will activate only this terminal.
2. *Use of menus.* On sign-on, the user by entering his or her password is offered a menu of authorized activities. For example, the cash receipts clerk may have a menu that allows that person to enter cash receipts, run the transaction control report, or read the accounts receivable master file, but do nothing else.
3. *Resource restrictions.* Resource restrictions are normally associated with stored data and program libraries. There are several levels of resource restriction. For areas where they are not responsible for recording data, accounting and operating users should only be provided "read" access, and only if they have a genuine information need. Read access allows the user to read stored data or programs but not to change their contents.

Using one, or a combination, of these techniques to restrict user capabilities is essential for proper segregation of duties. It is equally essential to ensure that any on-line data entry facilities have access control capabilities.

Many accounting packages are almost totally menu-driven. The user turns on the machine in the morning, and after entering a password, the application menu appears. The user does not have to work at all with the operating system and, in fact, knowledge of the function and capabilities of the operating system can be limited by restricting the operator's access to the operating system manuals and diskettes. The application package itself can have built-in capabilities that restrict the user to only the menu items associated with the user's passwords.

SUMMARY

Input controls are an important part of an overall control structure to ensure the completeness, accuracy, and authorization of data. They consist primarily of procedures to prepare and authorize correct source documents, organize them into batches, record them on terminals and compare, or balance computer reports of transactions recorded to original documents or control totals. These procedures should be applied to both transactions and changes to semi-permanent data.

As has been indicated, it is frequently not possible to establish a complete segregation of duties in the small business environment. Nevertheless, a company should attempt to segregate duties as much as possible, considering how many employees it has.

CHAPTER 5

Management Trails and Computer Operations Controls

In a well-controlled environment, strong controls over the authorization and the recording of transactions (input controls) combined with strong controls over program logic maintenance and development can help ensure complete, accurate, and authorized output. However, the right programs need to be run against the correct files, backup files need to be made, and all the output required needs to be printed. Management trails which provide the information needed for management and legislative purposes need to be created and kept on file.

Operations controls serve to accomplish these goals.

MANAGEMENT TRAILS

A management trail is important for the following reasons:

1. To provide information for control purposes.
2. To provide information for management decisions.
3. To satisfy legislative requirements.

It is important for reports to be prepared in sufficient detail so that management could, at a later date, follow each transaction through the various states of processing from the origination of the source document to each output document.

It should also be possible to identify individual items making up computer totals and to evaluate the accuracy of computations by having available details of all items used in the computational process.

Control procedures to achieve these goals would include the following:

- Ensuring that each transaction entered appears on a control report indicating who entered the data.

- Providing a unique identifier for each transaction, by use of terminal numbers, dates, etc., to facilitate tracing to and from computer output.
- Having daily or periodic printouts of transaction totals or transaction list reports, including edit and exception reports.
- Reporting stored semi-permanent data control totals, and periodically listing all semi-permanent data.
- Providing detail reports that facilitate checking of computations.
- Formulating clearly defined retention policies for source documents, printouts and master accounting and semi-permanent data in machine-readable form.

Output reflects the information base of the company. This information is crucial for the running of a business because it enables the owner/manager to analyze past activities and compare them to budgets, as well as providing a historical base for decision making. Reports should, therefore, contain sufficient detail to satisfy owner/manager information requirements.

Business records are necessary to satisfy the applicable corporations acts, income and sales tax acts, consumer protection acts, etc. The legislative requirements should be addressed when application packages are acquired or developed. Retention policies covering all data in machine-readable form and printouts of the management trails, which ensure adherence to these legislative requirements, need to be developed. Because this is such a complex area, professional advice will probably be needed.

COMPUTER OPERATIONS CONTROLS

These controls help ensure that the management trail discussed above is created, printed reports needed for input and output control activities are produced, files are copied for backup purposes, and the correct files are processed by programs.

In discussing these controls, it is important to draw a distinction between system imposed controls and controls which are designed into the programs by an applications programmer. System controls are features of the operating system, whereas application controls are included in application programs.

System Controls

The major purpose of these controls is to help ensure that data is being processed against the correct computer file and that files needed for backup purposes are not prematurely erased. For example, if sales transactions are posted daily, it is important that those for November 23 be processed against the sales and accounts receivable files as they stood at the close of business on November 22, and that the backup files for November 21 are not used in error. Some systems have software procedures which help to avoid these kinds of problems.

Most small computer operating systems maintain only the name, date, and physical size for each file in disk storage. The disk volume itself usually has a name and volume identification recorded on it. Depending on the system, only certain users (executing certain programs) may access certain data files or disk volumes.

Larger systems and more powerful small computers often have disk volumes labelled with volume identification, volume name, and serial number. When a disk pack is mounted, this information is printed on the console or is entered into a log file. On such systems, the following file information may be present: file name, file space (start and end), creation date, expiry date or retention period, and cycle. By using this information, the system can help guarantee access to the requested data provided the user has the proper authorization. It is important, however, to realize that the application software must be programmed to print this date and the user must examine the log or console listing for improper volume usage.

Magnetic tape is seldom used in today's small computer systems except for backup purposes. When it is present, tape labelling should be used. Typical information includes a tape volume label followed by file headers and trailers.

The tape volume label would contain name, volume identification, and creation date. Each file header would contain file name, creation date, expiry date or retention period, and cycle. File trailer records usually contain the number of records in the file.

The operating system itself will prevent deletion of an unexpired file, if that feature exists.

Controls within the Application Software

Several controls features may be implemented through the application software. In some cases, an application control cannot be used because of a missing element in the operating system. However, many small computer systems will support the following application controls:

Start of Day Routine

- open all proper files for daily processing
- check process dates; prints messages if process date is not one day greater than the previous day's closing date

- clear monthly figures on the Control Record if starting a new month
- print control report showing daily and monthly controls.

End of Day Routine

- close all files after completion of processing
- print daily control reports providing totals on amounts, number of transactions entered, quantities, etc., which are generated for manual balancing purposes to the originating source documents
- clear daily files on Control Record after successful printing of reports
- set Control Report Indicator, and
- back up all data files.

Transaction Control

- print detail management trails for all transactions processed
- flag gaps in transaction sequence numbers (if used), and
- provide summary information.

Control Record

- contain daily and monthly totals for number of transactions, amounts, and quantities by application and the integration thereof with other applications.

The above control functions are taken from an actual application. In addition, the following procedures should be computerized, or handled manually based on control output:

- specification of proper procedure if a fault is detected
- abort, restore start of day files, reprocess daily transactions to date, and
- report discrepancies for investigation.

The operator may almost totally rely on the application software for the daily processing routine. The terminal operator is responsible for the actual operating of the computer plus the entry updating and summarization of accounting data. A good application program should provide facilities to ensure that the management trail and control reports are available. The program, for example, could prevent a month-end update from occurring unless all appropriate transaction journals or listings had been printed. The program could also prevent daily processing until a backup of the data files, as they exist immediately before the update, is taken.

Operations controls that are either built into the application or are part of an operating system can significantly improve the general reliability and operating integrity of a small computer. Unfortunately, many software packages do not fully use the capabilities of the operating system to facilitate good operations controls.

In this situation, one can only rely on the operator to see that all necessary reports are produced and all files backed up on a regular basis. To help ensure that these important activities take place, there should be written instructions for the operator to follow. Also, the work of operators should be carefully supervised to help ensure that all necessary operations activities are performed. The use of daily, weekly, and monthly checklists of operations activities, signed by the operator as each task is performed and periodically reviewed by the owner/manager, can be of considerable assistance.

SUMMARY

While technical in nature, these controls are very important. Unless they are in place, transactions can be processed against old accounting files rather than current files, and cause serious confusion in the accounting records. Important management trails and control reports will not be printed and checked. Backup copies of important files will not be made and this could result in the loss of critical data if the current file were lost or damaged and there was no backup copy from which it could be re-created.

Often professional advice is needed to establish appropriate controls in this technical area.

CHAPTER 6

Output Controls

In a computerized environment, output may include the following:

- Negotiable instruments, such as cheques.
- Management reports, such as sales by product line.
- Accounting reports, such as general ledgers, trial balances, subsidiary ledgers, listings and control reports.
- Documents such as financial statements, invoices, and customer statements.

All output is the product of transaction input plus program logic. For example, cash receipts, sales and miscellaneous adjustment transactions are entered as transactions and are then posted by application program logic to the accounts receivable stored data. Further program logic then produces an aged trial balance of accounts receivable (output). Thus, the completeness and accuracy of output reports largely depends on input controls and controls over program logic. As previously pointed out, the control over application program maintenance and development is frequently limited in the small business environment. Also, powerful utilities which can alter data or programs without leaving a trace often exist. This can result in:

- Unauthorized or incorrect alterations to existing programs.
- Unauthorized or incorrect changes to semi-permanent or accounting data.

This in turn can result in a serious loss of money by accident or through fraud.

Also, controls over input, including transaction totals, terminal access procedures and segregation of duties are necessary to ensure that all transaction input is authorized and completely and accurately processed. These controls are often difficult to implement in small businesses, with the result that accounting or semi-permanent data can occasionally be incomplete, inaccurate, or unauthorized.

As well, computer environment controls often are weak in the small business environment. The weaknesses can give EDP and other personnel the opportunity to alter program logic and the contents of stored data, either on purpose or by accident.

Inaccuracies introduced into the computer process as a result of the above weaknesses will ultimately be reflected in output. As output represents the end of the information recording process, proper controls over output represents an excellent opportunity to detect errors previously introduced but as yet undiscovered.

Clearly, output controls are an essential element in any control framework. The output control procedures suggested in this chapter are neither time consuming nor complex and, thus, are particularly appropriate for a smaller business. It should be noted, however, that output controls will not detect all types of errors introduced into the recording process. For example, transactions not entered, incorrect information in fields not subject to stored data controls as discussed below, and incorrect information in source documents usually cannot be detected by output controls.

No output document should be accepted as valid until one or more of the following checks has been made:

- the file from which it has been drawn has been subjected to balance controls
- it has been reviewed by the owner/manager or senior personnel for obvious errors or inconsistencies
- in some circumstances, a periodic test check of calculations has been made.

BALANCE CONTROLS OVER STORED DATA

In a manual environment, subsidiary ledgers are controlled by a general ledger control account which contains a summary of all entries in a subsidiary ledger. That account should always be equal to the sum of all accounts in the subsidiary ledgers. If the control account is posted from a source independent of the subsidiary ledger, the control account provides an effective check on the subsidiary ledger. In a computerized environment, however, subsidiary ledgers and the general ledger accounts are, in many applications, simultaneously updated from the same source. As a result, the control account is no longer an effective control.

The control can be re-established by using input control reports to build up a control total to which the output can be agreed. This is accomplished by establishing and maintaining control totals over stored data for both semi-permanent and accounting data. Such totals could be developed as follows:

Opening control total over stored data (beginning of the month in many cases)

Plus/Minus:	Transactions entered affecting the applicable stored data (totals from transaction control logs or transaction list reports)
Equals:	Closing control total over stored data (end of the month).

The manually prepared control total can then be reconciled to totals prepared on computer or reflected in computer-produced reports. This control procedure gives the user an independent check to help ensure that all authorized entries — and only authorized entries — have been processed. It also would likely disclose, through an out-of-balance condition, that an incorrect master file was used to process a particular group of transactions (as discussed in the previous chapter) or if a utility had been used to directly and incorrectly alter the contents of the master file.

Control totals should be developed along the following lines for both accounting data and semi-permanent data.

Accounting Data

A company would normally establish control totals over all files that act as subsidiary ledgers (e.g., accounts receivable, accounts payable, inventory, fixed assets, etc.) and files that are accumulations of one transaction type (e.g., sales history files, etc.). For example, an accounts receivable control total could be developed as follows:

Opening Accounts Receivable balance December 1, 19XX

Plus:	Total of December sales transactions[*]
Minus:	Total of December cash receipts transactions[*]
Plus/minus:	Miscellaneous adjustment transactions[*]
Equals:	Closing Accounts Receivable balance December 31,19XX (for agreement with computer-produced accounts receivable trial balance or any other analysis of receivables).

---

[*] Obtained from transaction control log totals or list

Sales might be controlled as follows:

> Opening gross sales balance year to date December 1, 19XX
> Plus: Total of December sales transactions as above
> Equals: Closing gross sales balance December 31, 19XX (for agreement with computer-produced sales summary)

The manual totals so developed are agreed to computer-produced general ledger account balances, aged trial balances, management reports, etc. before they are used.

Semi-permanent Data

Because many kinds of semi-permanent data are of continuing importance for use in editing, building transactions, valuing transactions, and providing details for documents and reports, it is essential that they be maintained in a controlled environment. Use of control totals over semi-permanent data is an important element in this environment. Unlike accounting data, semi-permanent data usually cannot be balanced to business records (trial balances, etc.). Often, special output reports need to be prepared showing, for example, the number and total value of prices in a price table or wage rates in a wage table for balancing purposes.

Manual control totals can be determined from the transaction lists originally used to control the input. In many cases, control totals will be balanced for both dollar values and item counts (called hash totals). In other instances, balancing only by dollar values will be sufficient.

For example, a price table (showing prices for each product code) could be controlled by maintaining control totals over the number of prices on the table (item count) and the total of all prices (dollar value). These totals would be developed manually as follows:

Opening:	No. of prices on table December 1	from
Plus:	No. of prices added in December	semi-permanent
Minus:	No. of prices deleted in December	data change
Closing:	No. of prices on table December 31	transactions shown
		on control logs or
		transaction lists

*   *   *   *

Opening:	Price total December 1	from
Plus:	Total of prices added in December	semi-permanent
Minus:	Total of prices deleted in December	data change
Closing:	Price total December 31	transactions shown
		on control logs or
		transaction lists

NOTE: A price adjustment in this example is effected by a deletion followed by an addition.

The manual totals can then be agreed to a computer control report providing price table totals and item counts to help ensure that unauthorized, incorrect or missing additions and deletions are detected.

Also, semi-permanent data can be periodically printed out in its entirety for review at a supervisory or owner/manager level. This type of review is most effective where there is not a large volume of items in the file.

Whether or not all of these techniques are required is a matter of judgment, and that judgment should be made separately for each semi-permanent data item of accounting significance. For example, most companies would probably want to apply all three techniques to stored sales prices as any errors in them could have significant financial implications. On the other hand, many companies find that a periodic printout and review of stored customer credit limits is a sufficient control for this data element. The following factors can be helpful determining the degree of control required:

- The frequency of additions, deletions and changes to the semi-permanent data. Generally, the fewer the changes, the less control is required.
- The dollar value of the accounting transactions that make use of the semipermanent data. The higher the dollar value, generally the more control is required.
- The number of semi-permanent data items. Where the items are numerous, a periodic printout and review of them tends to be less effective.

117

- Any seasonal fluctuations in amendments to the semi-permanent data. Some data elements, such as wage rates, may have virtually a 100% change rate once a year, which needs to be carefully controlled. Throughout the rest of the year, changes may be infrequent and thus less control is required.
- Because development of control totals over stored data is an important control feature, the individual who maintains these totals should be independent of the data entry function and should not have custody of assets. The build-up of the control actuals and balancing to computerized totals should be recorded in a log and subject to periodic review by a supervisory employee or by the owner/manager.

SUPERVISOR OR OWNER/MANAGER REVIEW OF OUTPUT

Output should not be used until the computerized accounting and semi-permanent data have been balanced. Once they are balanced the reports, instruments and documents should be subject to critical review by a supervisor, owner/manager or other knowledgeable employee. The nature of the review will depend on the nature of the output. For example, negotiable instruments such as cheques should be agreed to source documents prior to signature. Some output will be subject to independent confirmation (bank reconciliations, inventory counts, customer statements, etc.). The significance of these procedures is outlined in Chapter 7. Other output, such as revenue and expense details in the general ledger or sales invoices cannot be verified in this manner. The supervisor or owner/manager — who has an intimate knowledge of the business — can often effectively perform a detailed review of these items.

PERIODIC TEST CHECK OF CALCULATIONS

One of the control procedures outlined in Chapter 5 was to provide details of information used for computations by the computer program. User personnel can use such details to periodically test-check programmed computations. The frequency of test checking will depend on:

- The sensitivity of the calculation
- The complexity of the calculation
- The degree of control over program development and maintenance
- Frequency of program changes
- Recency of program changes.

Examples of computations that may require periodic testing would include inventory costing, gross wage calculations, and computations on sales invoices.

Even where the chance of error is slight, a testing of computations, at least to some minor extent, should be carefully considered because the financial consequences of undetected computational errors can quickly accumulate to a significant dollar amount.

SUMMARY

Output controls are simple and cost effective techniques which should be applied before any output is used or distributed. While they would not detect all kinds of errors, they are often effective in detecting unauthorized changes to stored data which can so easily occur and which otherwise might go unnoticed.

CHAPTER 7

Asset Protection and Comparison Controls

Books and records by themselves do not provide any protection over a company's assets. No matter how complete, accurate, and authorized records may be, it would still be possible, in the absence of other controls, for assets to be stolen, lost, or misplaced.

For those reasons, asset protection controls are required. As their primary function is to protect assets, they are separate and distinct from the controls discussed in earlier chapters that relate to the completeness, accuracy, and authorization of books and records. Asset protection controls function on a day-to-day basis, often at the same time as the other controls.

The final and most important group of controls required consists of comparison controls. Their purpose is to determine whether or not any assets have been lost or stolen and take corrective action or to determine whether there are any errors in the accounting records and correct them. They include procedures such as taking a physical inventory and comparing the results to book records and bank reconciliations which compare cash in the bank with accounts recorded in the company's books and records. These controls function on a periodic basis.

Comparison controls can be thought of as the keystone or final method of proof in any system of internal control. On the other hand, records controls exist to ensure complete, accurate, and authorized books and records. On the other hand, asset protection controls help ensure that a company's assets are not lost, misplaced or stolen. In theory, a comparison of assets on hand with the books and records should never disclose any differences. In practice, however, differences almost always exist, as all systems of internal control have inherent limitations and are designed with cost effectiveness relationships in mind; that is, the owner/manager thinks it is better to incur a modest loss than to spend more than the amount of the potential loss to prevent it.

Where a comparison discloses significant differences, they need to be carefully investigated to determine whether they are primarily due to errors in the books and records or whether any assets have been lost, misplaced, or stolen. If accounting errors caused the differences, they should he corrected and steps taken to strengthen the internal accounting controls to prevent an unacceptable level of inaccuracies or incompleteness in the records. If they are the result of assets being lost or stolen, steps should be taken to determine how that occurred and then to strengthen the internal controls to make sure it does not happen again. A more frequent comparison in the future would also be advisable until differences settle down to an acceptable level.

Controls over books and records, controls to protect assets, and controls to make comparisons are all interrelated. Books and records help safeguard assets by providing a source against which assets on hand can be compared (this was the major purpose of accounting for many centuries). Asset protection controls depend, in general, on the availability of documentary evidence supplied by the accounting process (for example, goods should be released for shipment only when a properly approved shipping order has been presented and cheques should be signed only after supporting vouchers have been reviewed). Finally, comparison controls serve to compare assets on hand with the books and records.

Asset protection and comparison controls, to be effective, depend upon an appropriate division of duties which is discussed in detail later on in this chapter. Exhibit 7-1 shows in general terms the overall division of duties which provides for the strongest system of internal control.

Both asset protection and comparison controls are basically unaffected by the methods used to keep books and records and usually take the same form in both manual and computerized environments. These controls have been used in small businesses for many years, and the techniques required are usually well known and understood by owner/managers. As they are principally detective in nature, they can often effectively serve as compensating controls for absent or weak preventive controls. However, it should be recognized that unacceptably large losses could be incurred if such detective controls were applied too infrequently or if preventive controls were so weak that large losses could occur over a short time.

For all these reasons, asset protection and comparison controls have an exceedingly important role to play in the overall systems of internal control for a small business. They will be often used to offset or compensate for weaknesses in other controls discussed in Chapter 2 and for a lack of division of duties over the preparation and conversion of input or the balancing of output as discussed earlier in Chapters 4 and 6.

It should be kept in mind that it is better to prevent errors in the first place than to detect them later on. Thus, an adequate system of asset protection and comparison controls is not a reason to eliminate the important controls over records described elsewhere in this publication.

BASIC NATURE OF ASSET PROTECTION CONTROLS

All of a company's assets need to be protected, not just those of a physical nature such as inventory or fixed assets. Procedures are required to safeguard cash in banks and currency receipts. Accounts receivable need to be protected against unauthorized or incorrect write-offs or credit notes.

Assets need to be protected against a range of risks such as fraud by company employees or third parties, accidental loss or misplacement, and loss by fire. While the precise nature of the controls used will vary from asset to asset, the techniques employed will be of the following:

- Ensuring proper division of duties between those having custody or access to assets and those who keep books and records.

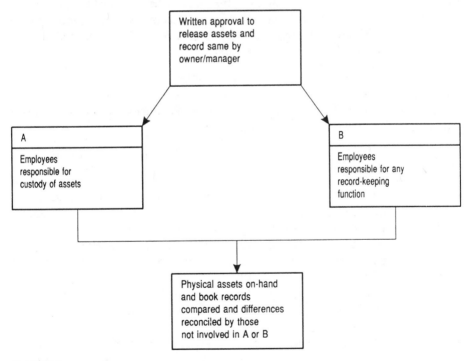

Exhibit 7-1

123

- Having custodians (often the owner/manager) release assets only after they have carefully reviewed appropriate documentation.
- Providing, where appropriate, joint access to assets by two employees.
- Implementing appropriate physical safeguards to protect assets against unauthorized access.
- Reviewing the adequacy of insurance coverage on a regular basis.

Each of these techniques is discussed below.

Division of Duties

The effectiveness of using books and records to verify that all the company's assets are accounted for is, for the most part, impaired if physical custody over assets and the ability to make entries in the books and records are in the hands of one employee. This is the primary reason why accountants have always stressed the necessity of dividing custody of assets from record-keeping activities.

It is important to realize that custody does not mean just physical control; any person who has the authority to reduce or release an asset has effective custody over that particular asset. For example, employees who are able to sign cheques have effective custody over the company's bank accounts. Those who are able to approve credit notes or journal entries to reduce accounts receivable have effective custody of the accounts receivable.

Even when a company has only a small number of employees, it is usually possible to divide duties involving custody of assets and the authority to record entries or otherwise affect books and records. This division of duties should be a priority to any other division of duties suggested.

Responsibility for the custody of assets might be allocated as follows in a typical small business:

- Cash. All cheques are signed by the owner/manager or, in his or her absence, by two other employees not involved in record-keeping (which includes data entry).
- Cash receipts. Mail is opened by the owner/manager or an employee who does not have other accounting responsibilities. Cash receipts should be directly deposited in the bank, with only remittance advices or photocopies of the cheques being given to accounting employees.
- Investments. All transactions should be approved by the owner/manager.
- Accounts receivable. All credit notes and journal entries are approved in writing by the owner/manager.
- Inventories. Wherever possible, one employee should perform warehousing functions, picking orders and delivering them to the shipping bay. Another employee acting as shipper is then responsible for double-counting the goods, preparing the shipping report and loading the goods onto common carriers.

Those involved in shipping should have no accounting duties: they are merely to report shipments made, either on paper or by computer terminal, for updating records.

- Payroll bank accounts. Payroll cheques are signed by the owner/manager. who should question any employee's name he or she does not recognize. In larger enterprises, payroll cheques are distributed by personnel who have no authority to authorize or record payroll changes and who are not involved in payroll or payroll bank reconciliation procedures.

Review of Appropriate Documentation

For effective protection, those having custody of assets should obtain and review appropriate documentary evidence before releasing any asset. Without this safeguard, asset protection controls serve little or no purpose. For example, a shipper should make sure that the shipping order is valid, and initialled as required by company procedures before shipping any items to a customer. Owner/managers or others signing cheques should obtain and review underlying supporting documents such as purchase invoices, purchase orders, and receiving reports before signing cheques.

Depending on the strength of other controls in the overall internal control system, cheque signers may also wish to do an approximate addition of the amounts on purchase invoices and compare their result to the amount appearing on the face of the cheque and compare the name of payees to that shown on the invoices.

Joint Custody Over Assets

Where assets, either because of their nature or value (for example, any small but valuable inventory or fixed asset items), are vulnerable to theft or physical loss, joint custody is appropriate.

Similarly, unless the owner/manager is also the one signing the cheques, banking resolutions should require the signature of two employees before the cheque is honored by the bank. The bank would be instructed not to cash cheques made payable to the company but to instead require their deposit. A withdrawal of the funds would, of course, be possible only with the joint signature.

Where currency receipts are involved, proper point of sale controls should exist including the use of registers which record the total of cash sales in a way that cannot be altered by cashiers. The use of retail inventory methods and related controls should be carefully considered.

Physical Safeguards

Physical safeguards are the oldest internal controls used by companies and include safety deposit boxes, locks, fences, guards, etc. In designing a system of physical safeguards, the following factors should be taken into account:

- Not just physical assets such as inventories need safeguarding. The books and records also constitute an asset and need protection. For example, if accounts receivable records are lost or destroyed, the company could suffer a significant monetary loss.
- Physical safeguards exist to keep people outside the company from getting access to the company's assets. They also exist to fix responsibility to a particular company employee. For example, an employee responsible for the custody of valuable inventories cannot be held responsible for any shortages if the inventory was stored in a place where other employees could easily obtain access to it.
- Blank forms should be physically safeguarded. Blank cheques, credit notes and journal vouchers should all be carefully controlled as they could be used to obtain unauthorized release of assets.
- The computer equipment, terminals, software and files should also be physically safeguarded. as these are important assets and also because uncontrolled access to them provides an opportunity to make unauthorized changes to stored data.

Insurance Coverage

Insurance is part of an effective overall system of internal control. The purpose of insurance is not only to protect against loss from employee theft (through bonding) but also against loss by outside theft, fire, etc. Insurance should not only be considered for physical assets such as inventories and fixed assets, but also for potential losses of other assets if the books and records were destroyed.

Insurance should not be considered as a replacement for an adequate system of internal control. Unless the system of internal control is adequate to detect that a loss has, in fact, taken place and to provide sufficient documentary evidence to support a claim, insurance is useless. It does little good to take a physical inventory of valuable items on hand for the purpose of detecting shortages unless accurate records are available to determine what inventories should be physically present.

THE FINAL CHECK

Comparison controls act as the final detective control to determine whether there are any errors or omissions in the books of account and/or whether any assets have been stolen, lost or misplaced.

Comparison controls should not be limited to inventories and fixed assets, but should encompass almost all assets owned by a company. For example, a bank reconciliation constitutes a comparison of cash in the bank (according to the bank's records) with that shown in the company's books. Reconciling items other than timing differences require investigation and can disclose errors or omissions in the company's books or items recorded incorrectly by the bank. Similarly, if a company sends out accounts receivable statements and the customers complain, it is likely that there is a difference between the real asset (what the customer is apparently willing to pay) and the books and records.

While the precise nature of comparison controls will vary from asset to asset and company to company, the following techniques are often useful in applying such controls:

- Making comparisons with sufficient frequency so that losses, errors, or theft of assets would be disclosed before they become unacceptably large.
- Differences should be investigated by, or under the supervision of, employees who are not responsible for the custody of assets or the maintenance of books and records on a day-today basis.
- Differences should be adequately investigated to determine their cause and correct errors or omissions in the books of accounts. In addition, appropriate steps should be taken to prevent further unacceptable errors in the books and records and/or to prevent a further loss of assets.

These techniques are discussed below.

Frequent Comparisons

Many factors need to be considered in determining how frequently assets on hand need to be compared with the books and records. Factors the owner/manager should assess include:

- The comparative strengths of other aspects of the overall system of internal control, especially records controls and asset protection controls.
- The nature of the asset in question and whether it is relatively vulnerable to loss or pilferage.
- Prior experience.

Division of Duties

The major purpose of comparison controls is to periodically compare assets on hand with the books and records. If the comparison or reconciliation were performed by someone responsible for either custody or record-keeping over the assets in question, results could be biased either by accident or on purpose to hide errors in either the books or the assets. Personnel having custody or record-keeping responsibilities for assets other than those under consideration can, however, assist in the comparison process. For example, employees who keep inventory records could reconcile the bank account and cheque signers could assist in physical inventory taking.

Sometimes, it is impractical or impossible to divide duties as suggested above. In such circumstances, supervisory personnel or the owner/manager should closely supervise the work. It may also be necessary to test or spot check the work being performed.

For the same reasons, differences disclosed by the comparison process should be investigated wherever possible by employees who normally do not have custody or record-keeping responsibilities over the assets in question.

To divide duties appropriately and to ensure that differences are investigated by appropriate personnel or the owner/manager, the following comparisons are often carried out by the people indicated:

- *Bank reconciliations* (including payroll bank accounts). Bank reconciliations are prepared by someone who is not involved in handling cash receipts, signing cheques or recording cheques in the accounting system. The bank reconciliation is reviewed and approved in writing by the owner/manager, who should investigate unusual items to determine their cause and to ensure that the books of account or the bank's records are adjusted as necessary.
- *Accounts receivable*. Accounts receivable statements are usually printed on computer by someone not normally involved in recording entries that affect customers' accounts. Complaints by customers are referred to supervisory personnel or the owner/manager for investigation and disposition.
- *Physical count of in inventories or fixed assets*. Physical counts should be taken under the close supervision of the owner/manager or supervisory personnel. If someone who keeps inventory or fixed asset records, or who normally has custody of the assets, participates in the count that person should be only one of at least two employees making up each count team. Differences between physical count results and book records should be investigated by supervisory personnel, and the owner/manager should review and approve any adjustments to the books of account to reflect physical count results.

Investigating Differences

Due to inherent limitations of any system of internal control and cost effectiveness considerations taken into account when the system was designed, certain differences can always be expected from the comparison process. If the differences are normal, it will only be necessary, after review by the owner/manager, to adjust the books and records appropriately.

In considering whether differences warrant further investigation, individual differences and not just the net value of differences should be considered. For example, the overall difference in physical inventory results might be quite small. That small net difference could, however, include certain items where counted quantities exceed book amounts offset by other cases where book records show much greater quantities than the physical count. Such differences should be investigated as the former might be due to errors in the books and records and the latter due to inventory loss or theft.

Where differences are considered to be more than what is normal or acceptable, their causes should be determined and additional internal control procedures implemented, either to further ensure the completeness and accuracy of books and records or to protect assets. Assets on hand should then be compared with the books and records more frequently over the next few months until there is reasonable assurance that the problems have been corrected.

AN EXAMPLE

The following example illustrates one possible use of asset protection and comparison controls as part of an overall system of internal control:

Company X recently acquired its first computer. One application is an accounts payable system, which also updates raw materials inventory records to show quantities on hand for production purposes. The computer hardware and the accounts payable application system have been bought from a software supplier. As Company X did not have sufficient computerized systems to warrant the hiring of a programmer/analyst, no in-house expertise was available at the time the computer system was acquired to assist in testing it. The owner/manager did, however. go through some test transactions and results with representatives of the software supply house. He also spoke to other users of the system who informed him that the system accurately processed and recorded transactions. Also, he had his staff re-process transactions for the previous week and agreed all the computer-produced output to the results produced originally by the manual system.

Prior to computerization, the accounting staff consisted of a general accountant and an accounting clerk. The accounting clerk was trained to operate the computer terminal and now uses it to record purchase orders and receiving reports forwarded by the purchasing and receiving departments. The clerk also uses the terminal to record purchase invoices as they are received from vendors.

Company management has not considered it necessary to develop batch control or similar input control procedures over receiving reports, purchase orders, or purchase invoices as they are reasonably sure that they can count on suppliers complaining if purchase invoices are not paid for in a reasonable length of time, when it is still possible to make an appropriate investigation.

The system does, however, require the approval of the owner/manager before a new vendor (supplier) can be added to the accounts payable master file. This approval is required because the owner/manager wishes to make sure that his purchasing department is dealing only with suppliers with whom he is familiar.

On a weekly basis, the owner/manager receives a program generated control report listing all of the new vendors added to the accounts payable master file, and he reviews and initials this list as evidence that he has approved them all. From time to time, however, business is done with a supplier with whom repeat business is not anticipated. The system records purchase invoices for such temporary suppliers as "vendor 9999 miscellaneous" and permits the terminal operator to designate the name of the supplier for each purchase invoice that will appear on the cheque.

Edit routines help monitor the accuracy of quantities entered for receiving reports and purchase orders and for quantities and dollars on purchase invoices. The terminal operator has to enter in the quantity and, where appropriate, the dollar amounts for each individual item on the receiving report, purchase order, or purchase invoice. The operator also has to enter a total of the items and dollar values involved for each individual voucher. The computer program adds together the quantities and dollars as appropriate and compares the computed total by voucher with the total entered by the terminal operator. If the two totals do not agree, an edit message appears stating that an error has occurred requiring a re-entry of the voucher in question.

The correct entering of accounting distributions (making sure the correct account is debited) is controlled by visual verification procedures. The account number to which a purchase invoice is to be charged is indicated by the general accountant on the purchase invoice, along with the name or description of the account. When the terminal operator enters the account number into the computer terminal, the program finds the name in the computer files for that account number and displays it on the terminal operator's screen (input edit control). The terminal operator compares the name on the screen with the description entered by the general accountant on the purchase invoice, thus determining whether the original coding plus his or her entry of the number were correct. Any differences not due to key entry errors are referred to the general accountant for correction.

The computer system generates the following output:

- A list of differences between prices on purchase orders and purchase invoices for review and action by the purchasing department and the owner/manager.
- A listing of older purchase orders where goods are overdue from suppliers.
- A listing of rejected (unprocessed) purchase invoices rejected because quantities received were less than invoiced or because there is no receiving report.
- On a daily basis, general account cheques to pay purchase invoices due today (at which time the amount due to each vendor on the accounts payable master file is appropriately reduced by the computer program).
- On a monthly basis, an accounts payable distribution summary showing the debits to the various accounts representing the recording of all purchase invoices entered and accepted during the month.
- An accounts payable trial balance by supplier showing each individual purchase invoice outstanding (e.g., entered but not yet paid).
- A list of open receiving reports recorded but for which no purchase invoice has yet been entered and, thus, no entry made in accounts payable or the general ledger.

On a monthly basis, the owner/manager reviews the accounts payable trial balance for unusual suppliers or amounts owing. In addition, the general accountant reviews open receiving reports and records by journal entry an estimate representing the amounts due to suppliers for goods received for which, as yet, no purchase invoice has been recorded.

Such a system of internal control represents a reasonable and cost effective approach over payables for many smaller companies. In certain respects, however, it fails to reflect the following internal control standards described in this publication:

- There has been very limited testing of the accounts payable application programs.
- As batch control totals or transaction lists are not used, there is no check by another employee of the work of the terminal operator. Thus, the terminal operator could either accidentally or purposefully record purchases or enter receiving reports or purchase orders even where no properly approved document is provided.

- Although the owner/manager exercises effective output application controls over the addition of new vendors to the accounts payable master file, the existence of a miscellaneous supplier would permit the terminal operator to record transactions for non-existent suppliers.
- Because of the inadequate testing procedures, there is little assurance that program-performed accounting computations of major importance are correct. For example, under certain conditions, the computer system might incorrectly accumulate individual purchase invoices and arrive at an incorrect total, which then appears on a cheque. Or possibly the program under certain conditions might fail to detect a difference between goods received and goods invoiced.

The inclusion of the following asset protection and comparison controls in the overall system of internal controls could help compensate for the above problems:

- All cheques are signed by the owner/manager only upon submission of the related purchase invoices, together with receiving reports and purchase orders which have been agreed to the purchase invoice by the chief accountant. The owner/manager ensures that the name of the payee on the cheque corresponds with the name of the supplier on the purchase invoice and, furthermore, compares in rough total the total dollar value of the purchase invoices with the amount on the cheque. The owner/manager also investigates any suppliers or purchases that appear unusual and warrant further investigation.
- Differences between monthly counts of raw materials on hand and quantities as recorded in the perpetual records maintained on computer are carefully investigated. As a result, errors due to the incorrect or incomplete recording of receiving reports and purchases might come to management's attention and corrective action could be taken. The nature of the company's business (metal extrusion) is such that pilferage or loss of raw materials is very unlikely.
- Bank reconciliations are performed by the general accountant who has nothing to do with the recording of purchase invoices, receiving reports, and purchase orders that cause the computer system to generate and then record general account cheques. The bank reconciliation is approved in writing by the owner/manager who carefully reviews reconciling items.

It should be noted that accounts payable systems provide the greatest opportunity to use asset protection and comparison controls to offset control deficiencies elsewhere. This occurs because a business can always rely on its suppliers to bring to their attention unpaid purchase invoices and, thus, the system does not have to stringently control the completeness of recording. If a similar example were given for sales and receivables, the completeness of billing is a far more important issue and more attention would have to be given to preventing incomplete or inaccurate processing of shipments in the first place. Customer dissatisfaction and financial loss could both occur if such errors were found only at a later date.

SUMMARY

Computer systems can and should be acquired to produce many positive benefits to the business, including more timely and more complete information useful in running the business.

However, they should not be used as an excuse to eliminate necessary control procedures on the false assumption that computers do not make mistakes. Computers can be accidentally, or purposefully, misused by those programming them, operating them, or entering data into them. Regardless of how the records are kept, assets still need to be protected and the possibility of losses having occurred investigated through comparison procedures.

CHAPTER 8

Local Area Networks

INTRODUCTION

This chapter is a supplement to the previous chapters one through seven, revisiting the issues raised therein from the perspective of a local area network.

Local area networks, which tie together microcomputers and enable users to share files and resources, are now a viable alternative for organizations that might otherwise require a minicomputer. Departments in large companies can now consider LANs instead of a mainframe for new departmental systems.

This chapter describes local area networks and discusses those features to be considered in deciding to acquire them and the steps for successfully implementing them. Controls important to their ongoing operation are also discussed.

WHAT IS A LOCAL AREA NETWORK?

A local area network (or LAN) can be thought of as part of the operating system. Its function is to tie together a number of microcomputers so they can share resources and to enable users of those microcomputers (or workstations) to share the same programs and work on the same files. In other words, it can enable a number of users to work on the same application at the same time, e.g., several employees could use their microcomputers to perform functions of shipping, billing, and invoicing in a sales/order entry system.

A LAN can support multiple users on one application in much the way that a minicomputer does. As always, the application itself also has to be designed to support multiple users.

On a LAN, each user has a microcomputer (sometimes called an intelligent workstation) which can be used as a stand alone device to perform all the tasks that microcomputers perform. When it is tied into the network, it can use programs and files stored on the network.

For example, an employee might use his microcomputer to connect with the LAN and use the sales/order entry system to record sales orders. Later, that same employee might sign-off the LAN and use the same microcomputer and the word processing package on its own hard disk to create a document.

Alternatively, the word processing package might reside on the network and the user would use the LAN to access the software, create the document, and store it on the network. This approach might be used when there is a desire to share the document in electronic form with others. Indeed, the LAN might contain an electronic mail package so the document could be sent electronically to the recipient.

The major difference between a LAN and a minicomputer resides in the power and functions put into the hands of each user on a minicomputer, generally each terminal can only be used as a "door" to the minicomputer itself, using software and files resident on the mini. In a LAN environment, each workstation can be used like a terminal to a minicomputer, while at the same time, each workstation is a microcomputer and can have its own programs and files, and by itself perform all the tasks a microcomputer is used for.

THE STRUCTURE OF A LOCAL AREA NETWORK

Exhibit 8-1 portrays a typical structure for a local area network.

The centre of a LAN is usually a large, powerful microcomputer that acts as the "network server" for the network. Usually, to ensure availability, quickness of response and to enhance security, the microcomputer used as the network server is dedicated, e.g., it is not used for any other purpose. As the network server is a microcomputer, it needs an operating system like any other computer.

The heart of a LAN is its network operating system (or NOS), purchased from a LAN supplier. Residing on the network server, the NOS manages and controls all access to the network's shared programs and files resident on the network server and creates the communications bridges to and from the workstations. To enable this to occur, a special board containing additional operating systems software is installed in each workstation. These boards are usually supplied by the LAN vendor, or alternatively they can be purchased from a microcomputer retail store.

Naturally, cabling is required to physically connect everything together. There are a variety of cabling systems and the one chosen must be compatible with the NOS and the boards chosen. Some network systems only support or work with one cabling system, whereas others may support two or more.

Exhibit 8-1 illustrates a typical LAN. Provided they have been given rights and passwords to do so, any user at any workstation can access programs and data on the network server. In addition, programs resident on each workstation usually can process shared data resident on the network server and store additional files there. Conversely, programs resident on the LAN can be used to process files on the hard disk of the microcomputer acting as a workstation.

Structure of a Local Area Network

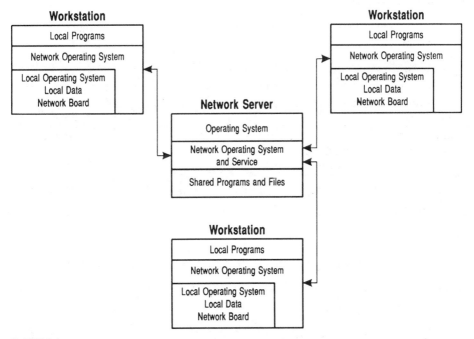

Exhibit 8-1

Also LANs can be connected to each other through gateways to form wide area networks covering many locations, including third parties. If a company has two or more LANs in one building, they can be connected to form one large LAN these connections are sometimes called backbones or bridges. These arrangements require a level of cost, complexity and technical support normally not available in small organizations, but which is needed in larger organizations when tieing many LANs together.

REASONS FOR ACQUIRING LOCAL AREA NETWORKS

Organizations can acquire local area networks for one or more of the following reasons:

137

To share peripherals:

In the past, LANs were usually acquired so that expensive printers and other peripheral devices could be shared by many users. Today, few organizations acquire LANs just for this purpose. With the decreasing cost of printers and hard drives and the increasing complexity of LANs, their acquisition solely for this purpose is usually not cost justified.

To support office automation:

In many offices, there is a desire to share files and information through office automation products and this can be effectively supported by a LAN.

Firstly, by creating a LAN and buying network versions of programs such as word processing, databases, spreadsheets, and graphics presentation software, an organization can ensure that the same programs are used throughout by all employees. This may reduce the costs of acquiring software, make it easier to train and support users, and most importantly, ensure that documents and information can be shared and re-used.

Furthermore, information stored on the LAN such as budgets, correspondence, form letters, and financial models can be shared by all users having access rights to them. Electronic mail can be installed to enable employees to communicate quicker and more efficiently.

To support the major corporate systems of the organization:

Corporate systems are those systems on which the organization depends to manage, conduct, and report on its operations. Thus all financial systems such as payroll, general ledger, sales and receivables etc. are corporate systems. Often there are many operational systems that are corporate in nature such as personnel, marketing, and purchasing systems.

Except in the smallest of organizations, corporate systems need to support several users, e.g., they need to be multi-user systems.

LANs CAN SERVE AS A BASE FOR CORPORATE SYSTEMS

Today there is a wide choice of packaged software with LAN versions to support multiple users in an environment which provides for good control over logical access. The programs and data can reside on the network server, thus setting the scene for good back-up and disaster recovery arrangements.

138

Deciding on whether to acquire a local area network:

As pointed out in Chapter 1, usually the first decision to be made is to determine the needs of the organization, e.g., what is the application software which the business requires and what are the packages that best meet the needs of the business? As NOS and the LANs they create are really just operating systems the features and benefits they provide should be considered in concert with the business needs.

It is also important to bear in mind that not all microcomputer programs will run on a network allowing multiple users. A special network version of programs is typically needed that will support multiple users.

With these thoughts in mind, all the discussions on the inter-relationships between hardware, operating systems and application software in Chapter 1 apply.

However, the existence of LANs brings additional considerations into play as now minicomputers and LANs can be looked on as competing alternatives. The office automation needs of the business now also play a bigger role in this decision making process.

COMPARING MINICOMPUTERS AND LOCAL AREA NETWORKS:

Exhibit 8-2 summarizes the differences between minicomputers and LANs. Each of the factors in the exhibit is discussed below.

Comparison of Minicomputers and Local Area Networks

Factor	Local Area Network	Minicomputer
Cost	Lower	Higher
Ability to Process Large Volumes	Lower	Higher
Availability of Financial Application Packages	Good	Good
Availability of Third Party Support	Poor	Varies from poor to excellent
Need for In-house Technical Staff	High	Low to high
Training Tools and Courses	Good	Good
Availability of Good Office Automation Software	Good	Limited
Need for Special Environment	Almost none	Medium to high
Logical Security	Good	Good to very good
Continuity of Processing and Disaster Recovery	Relatively simple	Can be more complex

Exhibit 8-2

Cost:

As a generality, hardware, operating systems, and packaged application software are often a lot cheaper for a LAN than for a minicomputer. While minicomputer capacity and software sophistication at the higher end of the market may be better than for LANs, the cost differential is often not warranted.

Furthermore, the organization may need microcomputers for a wide variety of reasons. By installing a LAN, there can be double value for money. The microcomputer and the LAN together can support the organization's corporate systems as well as office automation activities. The microcomputers are still available as such for a host of other tasks.

Ability to process large volumes:

Given the power of larger microcomputers and the continually increasing features of packages that run on LANs, most smaller organizations can satisfy their requirements through LAN hardware and software.

If you intend to process thousands of transactions a day and need over say 1 gigabyte (or one thousand megabytes) of storage, then perhaps a minicomputer is required. To put this in context, 5,000 customer records each containing 2,000 characters of information is only 10MB. And the program might require another 1-2MB. This is only a fraction of a gigabyte leaving lots of room for many other systems of similar size.

With larger microcomputers having at least 8-16MB of memory and 32 bit processors, processing power certainly compares with all but the largest of minicomputers. Thus, unless there are a great number of users trying to access a system at once, a LAN built around appropriately powerful microcomputers should provide the processing power and response times required.

Availability of financial application packages:

Today there is a wide variety of good financial application packages that will run on a LAN. Indeed, the choices are almost as wide as for minicomputers.

There is really no need today to think of LANs as a second class choice due to a lack of good software. Many of the packages for LANs contain a wide variety of features that allow the purchaser a wide variety of choices in installing the system.

Most LAN based application packages are "off the shelf" products — e.g., they can be bought from a store or ordered through the mail at prices ranging from a few hundred to three or four thousand dollars for multi-user versions and site licenses. Because the software supplier is selling an off the shelf product at a comparatively low price, indeed it will be very hard, if not impossible, to get the supplier to make special amendments or changes to the software. However, a good deal of tailoring is possible through selecting from the many alternatives the better packages offer.

For minicomputer packages, the supplier is usually selling a much more expensive package using a one to one sales approach with a limited number of customers. Thus these suppliers are generally willing to entertain requests for special changes or amendments over and above the alternatives built into the software.

As noted earlier in the book, special amendments or tailoring of software products should be approached with caution. Even minor amendments can be very expensive and the additional functionality required may not be worth the cost.

Of course, it is possible to create custom developed software to run on a LAN just as it is for any computer. Indeed, some very impressive programming languages and tools have been developed for the microcomputer market.

Availability of third party support:

In this area, LANs are very different from minicomputers.

In a LAN environment, the organization is generally forced to deal with many ultimate suppliers. The hardware is purchased from one supplier, normally a retail chain. There is another group of suppliers who create the network operating systems, or the LAN itself. These are purchased directly "through the mail" from the network supplier or once again purchased through a retail chain.

The application software is purchased through the mail from another group of suppliers or from the same retail store.

Thus, the organization may be faced with buying the hardware, network operating systems, and application software from three different sets of suppliers, either directly or through a retail store. It is important to note that the suppliers and the stores are really in the business of selling off the shelf products and provide only limited advice and support.

Thus, the organization is faced with four major challenges:

- Determining whether the hardware, operating software and application software will work together and whether there is enough capacity to meet needs;
- Connecting and integrating the hardware, network operating system and the application system;
- Ensuring that the features of the network operating system are properly used to ensure security (sometimes called logical security) as well as back-up and recovery; and
- Supporting users and their constant requests for help as the local area network is used.

While the suppliers of network operating systems have hot line support numbers, sometimes the only help available is over the phone. The support for LANs available through third parties such as retail chains is growing, but can vary significantly in quality.

Often the support available is technical in nature, relating to the installation of the network or in dealing with technical questions on the NOS. The suppliers are least capable when advice is being sought on business solutions and answering questions on which application solution might be best for a particular organization. Thus, it is difficult for smaller organizations to receive an overall integrated service from one third party.

Also, suppliers are often not conversant with internal controls or risk management requirements. The organization itself must be particularly vigilant to ensure that the controls in earlier chapters in this book are put into place and that the software is designed and implemented in such a way that a proper environment for good control is established. This includes the proper installation and ongoing maintenance of user IDs and passwords to support good logical security.

Many firms of chartered accountants are stepping into this area, offering services to help organizations to select hardware, LANs and application programs, doing the initial software installation, and providing support.

With minicomputers, there are many suppliers called original equipment manufacturers or OEMS who will act as a sole source supplier and provide the application packages as well as the minicomputer and its associated operating systems. They have personnel that are available to work at the organization's premises to install and implement all the equipment and software. Their personnel are available after installation to help support and maintain the ongoing use of the systems. However, as mentioned elsewhere in this book, the cost of such services can be significant, especially when seeking amendments or changes to packaged applications.

Even if the organization buys its minicomputer and related operating systems directly from the hardware manufacturer and its application packages from the software house, at least there are only two suppliers to deal with. Usually all these suppliers will have trained personnel who, if necessary, will come on-site to provide direct support.

Need for in-house technical staff:

As discussed above, there is limited support available in the market to help impartially select, implement, and operate a LAN. A variety of suppliers need to be dealt with and the hardware, network operating system, and application programs need to be connected so they will work together.

Even after implementation, a host of duties must be performed to maintain the system and support the users.

It would be highly unusual for an organization to install and rely on a LAN without having a qualified network manager to perform all these functions. The network manager, in a sense, operates as a systems programmer, initially installing and then managing and maintaining the network operating system. He or she also acts as a supporter for all users — answering their questions about how to use the network, getting the network back up when it crashes, helping with requests for disk space or access to printers etc. This person also establishes and maintains user IDs and passwords in accordance with policies and approvals set down by management.

An organization should not use a LAN for corporate systems unless it is willing to have a network manager, and except in the smallest organizations, this will probably be a full time job. In fact, if you have more than say 30 – 40 users, two people may be required in the network management function.

When minicomputers are used, contractual arrangements can be made with suppliers to perform many of the equivalent functions and thus the need to dedicate a full time employee to these tasks is optional. Instead, one employee as part of his or her job can be designated to back up files and print off reports daily, with other functions generally being performed by third parties.

Training tools and courses for network managers:

Fortunately, most major suppliers of network operating systems make available good, if somewhat expensive, courses as to how their product can be used to install and maintain LANs. Organizations having an employee who is already computer literate with a good base of technical skills can turn this individual into a network manager by providing one to two weeks of classroom training.

With the widespread use of LANs, there are now larger numbers of trained and experienced individuals who can be hired as network managers. Network management is an important function and should **not** be assigned to a secretary or someone else in the organization on the grounds they have "some micro" knowledge or happen to be available.

Availability of good office automation software:

Chapter 10 reviews in detail the kinds of office automation software that are available and the business needs which they can fill. Office automation software includes:

- electronic mail
- word processing
- desktop publishing
- spreadsheets
- project management

and many other products. All these products produce documents that people want to share or store for re-use in machine readable form.

Without doubt, microcomputer software is better in these areas and less expensive than their equivalents on minicomputers. Thus an organization may want to acquire a LAN to support office automation. If a minicomputer is chosen for financial or other corporate systems, then an organization may end up with both a minicomputer and a LAN! In this environment, users will then want to download data from the minicomputer to their microcomputers and the LAN for a wide variety of purposes. This will add another layer of complexity and costs as efforts are made to tie the microcomputers and the minicomputers together.

The key point here is that all the information technology needs of the business should be addressed and considered as a whole before making major acquisition decisions. LANs may often offer the most cost effective solution as they can support traditional application systems, office automation requirements and provide individuals with microcomputers, all driven off the same set of hardware.

Need for a special physical environment:

While it may be desirable to lock up a network server in a separate area for security reasons, LANs, like all microcomputers, do not need any special environment.

Security:

As discussed in a later section of this chapter, most network operating systems provide for a good level of password security. It should provide adequate protection for most organizations if the features are properly utilized.

Of course, the password security features should be assessed as part of the acquisition process as outlined in Chapter 1.

Continuity of processing and disaster recovery:

If anything, it is easier to counter these risks in a LAN environment than for minicomputers. Microcomputers and the network operating systems boards are off the shelf merchandise and can easily be replaced. Minicomputers are far more specialized and have much longer lead times for replacement.

SUMMARY RE ACQUISITION DECISIONS

On balance, LANs have much to offer in comparison with minicomputers. The hardware and software generally cost far less. There is a much greater variety of office automation software available for LANs. This allows an organization to put all of its software on one configuration and avoids the problem of uploading and downloading data to and from microcomputers and minicomputers. The microcomputers on the LAN can serve as personal workstations as well as terminals to the network, thus providing much greater use and return on investment for the microcomputers the organization would own in any event.

With a LAN, the organization may be able to meet all of its processing needs on one set of hardware. In fact, if a minicomputer is acquired for financial systems, at a later date a LAN may be needed in any event to support shared word processing, electronic mail, project management software, spreadsheets for financial modelling, and other purposes. Employees will want to download data from the minicomputer. Running both minicomputers and LANs and transferring data from one to the other adds a lot of administration and cost.

The major drawback to a LAN is the need to have a trained and qualified network manager. As previously mentioned, in the minicomputer environment, there is a goodly amount of external support available from the hardware supplier, the OEM, or the software vendor. In the LAN environment, the organization has to really look to its own internal resources to manage and maintain the LAN and must be comfortable with its ability to do so.

NON PROCESSING CONTROLS

The major impact of LANs on non processing controls, as discussed in Chapter 2, is the introduction of the network manager as part of or in some cases the entirety of a small EDP department within the company. To understand this impact, it is first necessary to review the functions of the network operating system and the typical roles and responsibilities of a network manager.

The Functions of a Network Operating System (NOS)

It may be useful to refer back to exhibit 8-1 in reading this section.

The network operating system (NOS) sold by the LAN supplier is effectively an extension of a microcomputer disk operating system, or DOS. In fact it can be thought of as being wedged between the overall operating system and the files and programs maintained by the network on the network server microcomputer.

Many people refer to the shared programs and files managed by the NOS as being resident on a "network server". These shared data files and programs reside in directories or subdirectories in just the same way as any files do on any microcomputer. The network server is also where the NOS itself resides.

It is equally important to note that other programs and data (illustrated in exhibit 8-1 as local programs and data) not defined as part of the file server are **not** under the control of the NOS.

In addition to the NOS sitting on the network server, special network boards need to be installed in each microcomputer or workstation in the LAN to communicate or talk with the network server and each other, as well as to access peripherals such as printers.

Thus the purpose of the NOS is to:

- provide the necessary communications so that all the microcomputers and devices on the LAN can "talk" to each other;
- act as a gateway to manage all access to the shared files or programs resident on the file server;
- provide the capability to implement passwords to control access to and use of all shared programs and data;
- provide the capabilities to both back up and restore shared programs and data, (important activities for prevention of loss of data and disaster recovery); and
- provide the network manager with software tools to help set up and manage the LAN, including the ability to add new users, workstations and printers, change passwords, allocate and manage storage space on the file server, etc.

The Duties of a Network Manager

Effectively the network manager acts as both a systems programmer and a chief operator. He or she sets up the LAN in the first place, makes changes or amendments as required, supports users as they encounter difficulties, and is responsible for backing up the system. In chronological sequence in an organization acquiring and implementing a LAN, the network manager would be involved as follows:

At acquisition:

- assist the owner manager in the selection of a LAN and related microcomputers and printers;
- physically install the cables and the network boards;
- prepare an implementation plan, including plans for security, back up and disaster recovery.

During implementation:

- install the network operating system itself;
- copy and install all the application software and files to be shared on the network server;

147

- set up the initial passwords and user IDs for all users;
- train all users in how to use the LAN.

On an ongoing basis:

- provide support to all users as required;
- maintain the network, including adding users and workstations, managing and adding memory or storage capacity and new versions of application programs, and maintaining passwords;
- ensure that files and programs are backed up as required on a daily, weekly and monthly basis;
- install new versions of the network operating system;
- manage the relationships with hardware and software suppliers, including services and control of costs.

Against this background, it is now possible to discuss the non processing controls in Chapter 2 from the perspective of a LAN.

Organizational Controls

REQUIREMENTS FOR SPECIALIZED SKILLS

The point has already been made that a trained network manager is really essential for an organization with a LAN. Thus there will be an EDP department consisting of the network manager and perhaps other employees.

Naturally, the organization and the owner manager are highly dependent on the network manager. Maintaining the network could be a problem if the network manager were to leave. Thus, it may be appropriate to provide some training or familiarity with LAN software to other employees. Alternatively, contingency arrangements can be made with the company's firm of Chartered Accountants or some other outsider to provide temporary support.

CONCENTRATION OF FUNCTIONS AND DIVISIONS OF DUTIES

All of the thoughts set forth in Chapter 2 apply in the LAN environment, keeping in mind that the existence of a network manager is equivalent to having a small in-house EDP department.

Thus, the network manager should not have any accounting duties and should **not** be involved in initiating, authorizing, or recording any financial transactions. Similarly, accounting and other personnel should not have access to the NOS itself and should not in any way be able to change any passwords except their own individual passwords.

The network manager, like a systems programmer, has virtually unlimited access to all the financial system programs and data files. While in theory one could involve the owner manager or some other employee in reviewing and approving the activities of the network manager, in reality this would not really provide any effective control.

As suggested in Chapter 2, the practical response is to design records controls, output controls, and owner manager controls discussed in Chapters 3 to 7, to take into account the ability of the network manager to make unauthorized changes to financial programs and data.

Password capabilities exist in NOS in order to enforce a proper division of duties and prevent unauthorized changes to programs and data. Because microcomputer operating systems have little or no password support capabilities, NOS provide additional security routines. It is the responsibility of the network manager to effectively install and maintain the passwords. The NOS can do this as it is designed to sit between the overall operating system and the shared files and programs on the file server.

The **goal** is to ensure that financial data can only be accessed or changed by **authorized** users using **authorized** programs. At the same time, the security features should be used to ensure that only the network manager and perhaps one or two other designated individuals can add or change programs on the file server. This is illustrated in exhibit 8-3.

The Ideal Password Control Structure

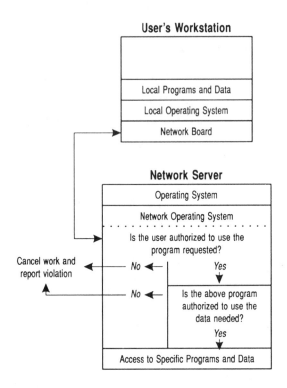

Exhibit 8-3

While not implemented in exactly the way illustrated, most logical security systems on mainframes and minicomputers can be set up to ensure that **both** the user and the **program** being used are being authorized to work on the data. This prevents users from changing or reading say financial data except through the application system. The application system is designed to provide control reports, batch control totals, etc., and thus the activities of the user are controlled.

Unfortunately the way LAN security usually works is not quite this good. With NOS, a user's password normally has to be defined in such a way that it gives the user the right to the program as well as the data which the program itself uses to perform its task.

For example, suppose a user has as his job the recording of cash receipts from customers. The user's password has to allow the user the right to execute the accounts receivable programs. Because the user is recording cash receipts and posting them to accounts receivable, **his** password has to grant the ability to **write** on the accounts receivable file.

150

The Typical LAN Password Control Structure

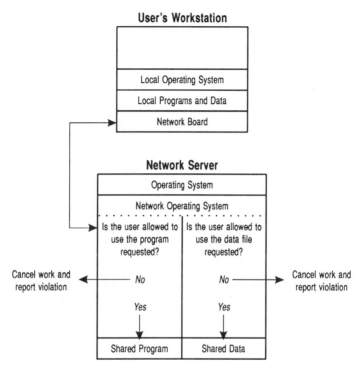

Exhibit 8-4

This kind of password protection is quite impressive in itself. It can be used to prevent anyone who is unauthorized from using the accounts receivable program or indeed any other program on the file server. In addition, any user who is not involved in accounts receivable activities can be denied any access to the accounts receivable files.

Indeed, LAN security is usually even deeper than this brief discussion indicates. Access to files can be restricted to read only access and programs can be protected from change by allowing the user only to execute them. This level of control may be sufficient for many organizations.

However, in the presence of a **sophisticated** and **highly** computer literate user, there is a major hole as users rather than programs must be given access to data.

To go back to the previous example, the user has been given the privilege of writing on the accounts receivable file for the very good reason that his job using the accounts receivable application requires him to do this. But there is nothing preventing him from using **any** program which may be resident on say

151

his own workstation hard disk to write on or alter the accounts receivable file. Obviously using a text editor or other utility to figure out the layout of the receivables file and then changing it requires a considerable amount of computer knowledge.

A further barrier can be created in many NOS if the NOS can be so set to deny any user the right to read the file names in any directory or sub directory. It is indeed very hard if not impossible to alter files with other programs if you don't even know their names. If a NOS provides this feature, it is good to make use of it.

The major concept is that NOS can provide good or very good security over unauthorized use or access to programs and data stored on the file server. It is a fairly time consuming and indeed technical task to originally set up and maintain appropriate logical security structures. The owner/manager should be generally familiar with the level of security that is being achieved and indeed discuss his requirements in a general way with the network manager. These activities can best be done by having the network manager draw up a security plan, working in conjunction with the owner/manager. The security plan would:

- identify who should have access to the NOS itself, and be able to perform network manager functions;
- identify all the files being kept on the LAN and the degree of security each set of files requires given its confidentiality and the damage which could occur if unauthorized changes were made;
- document the access rights that each group of users require (so that **all** other access rights can be denied);
- set forth policies and procedures over the use and maintenance of passwords to be followed by all users.

PREVENTION OF RECORD AND EQUIPMENT LOSS AND PLANNING AGAINST MINOR LOSS OF STORED DATA

Most NOS provide a means whereby the network manager can back up all shared programs and files from the file server onto some other medium, often a tape drive.

It is important to note that the network manager can only back up the files managed by the network. Programs and files on individual microcomputers will not be covered under these procedures. This is discussed further in the next chapter on end user computing.

Most network managers back up daily any files which have been changed during the day. These back up files are then either stored in a fire proof cabinet somewhere else in the office premises or sent to some offsite storage location.

It is a good idea to back up the entire system of every shared program and file as well as the NOS itself on a weekly or, at an absolute minimum, a monthly basis. These total system back ups should then be sent to off premises storage as part of overall disaster recovery arrangements.

In effecting these arrangements, licensing agreements with software suppliers should, of course, be respected. Most software licenses provide that programs may be copied for back up and disaster recovery purposes, although some of them may state that only one such copy may be kept. In this case, the program copies should be kept in off premises storage. The other backup routines would then focus on the data files.

Naturally, any loss of data, no matter how minor, and the time necessary to restore it is disruptive to the conduct of business. Some companies are so dependent on access to their data and computer resources that they would want to avoid even an interruption of a few hours that might be necessary say to restore some corrupted files.

Some LAN suppliers provide or support the use of features of considerable sophistication to guard against these possibilities. Obviously the cost of these extra features needs to be weighed and considered. Such features include:

- Boxes which guard against power surges or brown outs. Such changes in electrical power could otherwise interfere with processing or corrupt files.
- Uninterruptible power supplies, which not only deal with the above power fluctuations but also provide battery support for short periods of time if the electrical supply is unavailable.
- Data duplication capabilities. An extra copy of all data files being worked on is automatically created and kept up to date in real time on a separate disk drive in the network server. Thus, if a data file is accidentally destroyed, the second hard disk can be used.
- Server duplexing capabilities. This is the "cadillac" of arrangements against any minor interruptions. The LAN keeps an extra complete copy of the entire NOS and all of its shared files and programs up to date and in real time available on a duplicate microcomputer. Should the network server have a hardware failure or a hard disk crash, then it is only necessary to switch to the other microcomputer and use it.

Remember that data duplication and server duplexing exist to guard against problems caused by temporary disruptions or minor losses of data programs. Disaster recovery arrangements are still required!

All Other Control Areas

As NOS are really just extensions of operating systems, all other areas of internal control over applications and procedures to ensure that data captured is complete, accurate, and authorized really remain unchanged.

Thus, all the discussions in Chapters 3 to 7 remain appropriate whether or not a LAN is used.

CHAPTER 9

End User and Personal Computing

INTRODUCTION

End user computing refers to the use of computer software or systems where the end user, rather than the EDP department, is responsible for selecting, implementing, **or** maintaining the software. The term is also used to cover those situations where the user makes use of the features of certain packages such as Lotus 1-2-3 to write his or her own reports or to perform financial analysis. In some circumstances, a user may even write his or her own program using a computer language such as BASIC or C to perform a task unique to his or her own job responsibilities.

PURPOSE OF THIS CHAPTER AND ITS RELATIONSHIP TO THE BOOK AS A WHOLE

In the context of a large organization, a department or a division within that organization often creates its own computer systems that are unique or separate from the enterprise wide corporate systems. As it is the department or division that is acquiring and supporting the system, such departmental systems can be properly referred to as end user computing, even though such systems may be quite large and sophisticated and run on minicomputers or local area networks.

Such large organizations should create overall policies and standards for the proper management and control of such larger scale and sophisticated end user computing. The department or division can then use the first eight chapters of this book as a guide to acquiring, implementing, and using such systems within the context of organizational policies and procedures. Indeed, employees charged with developing such policies and procedures may find this entire book useful in designing them. In this context, the book can be read thinking of the department head as the owner manager and the information systems department as an outside supplier.

This particular chapter focuses on end user computing in the more narrow sense of the personal use of software on a microcomputer to perform individual tasks, including the creation of reports and the use of spreadsheets to create financial models or to perform financial analysis. To distinguish between end user computing involving departmental or divisional systems, individual use of programs and software will be referred to in this chapter as "personal computing".

The way in which software is acquired or used, rather than the software itself or the machine on which it resides, is what defines the difference between personal computing and the use of corporate or "official" systems.

For example, an individual may use his workstation to record cash receipts. This is not personal computing as the application software resident on the microcomputer or a local area network is part of the financial systems of the organization. The software has been designed and is supported by either the organization's EDP department or some outside supplier. The person designated by the organization such as the overall computer operator or the network manager is responsible for backing up the files and seeing to disaster recovery arrangements.

On the other end of the scale, the same individual may be using a spreadsheet package to create a financial model for decision making purposes. This is personal computing because it is the individual creating the template who is responsible for the correctness of the logic in it. This key fact does not change even if the spreadsheet package is located on the LAN and the individual stores the template or file on the network server. However, the personal computing responsibility of the individual would be even greater if he had selected and purchased the spreadsheet package and stored it and the template on his or her own machine. In this case, the user would also be responsible for back up arrangements over both the spreadsheet package and the files it uses. Also, this individual might be responsible for deciding whether or not a new version of the spreadsheet software should be purchased and whether it is compatible with the hardware and the operating system in his personal computer.

The principles set forth below for personal computing are applicable to all applications including office automation activities described in Chapter 10.

SETTING POLICIES AND STANDARDS

Standards over personal computing are important for several reasons:

- A lack of standards can lead to a proliferation of hardware and software, increasing costs and complicating support;
- Without them, it may be difficult or impossible for users to share data in electronic form;
- Any plans for office automation may be frustrated or complicated by a proliferation of hardware and software;
- Without standards, there is a greater chance of incorrect programs which generate inaccurate information. This in turn can lead to poor or incorrect decisions;
- Unless users are aware of the need to back up files and programs, important information can be lost;
- If users are not provided with appropriate training and/or support, then use of computers may be inefficient and non productive and
- Lack of regard for licensing arrangements with software suppliers can cause disputes difficulties, and litigation.

For these and other reasons, every organization should make some basic decisions on personal computing and ensure that all employees are aware of the resulting policies and standards. The areas in which policies and standards are usually required are set forth below.

The Use of Personal Computing Should be Appropriately Restricted

Personal computing should really be restricted to those circumstances where there are genuine individual needs. Where several people have similar needs an overall solution for the organization should be sought.

Thus, any corporate or financial system should be selected, implemented and maintained for the organization as a whole. Also, every effort should be made to support office automation activities on an organization wide basis.

Common Software Should be Used Wherever Possible

One major purpose of office automation is to allow people to share information and documents. This requires a common choice and use of software for word processing, spreadsheets and desk top publishing. Indeed, as pointed out in Chapter 10, it is useful to be able to pass files from one of these software products to another.

Common office automation software is desirable even when the software is to be used on an individual basis to create documents and files. The need to share these documents and files will almost inevitably arise. Also, without common software, it will be far more difficult to support the user in the sense of providing training or help.

Set a Standard for Hardware and Peripherals

Every organization should avoid a proliferation of hardware and peripheral brands wherever possible. Failure to do so only results in having equipment that may not talk to each other or where additional layers of software and complexity are required to overcome this problem. It also makes it much more difficult to provide support to users in setting up and using printers and other peripherals and in getting service from a wider variety of suppliers.

Microcomputers are multi purpose devices and can be used both as personal workstations as well as terminals to a LAN or a minicomputer. Where LANs or minicomputers already exist, standards are obviously required to ensure that microcomputers can be used for both purposes.

Even in organizations currently without LANs and minicomputers, hardware standardization is important. If a proliferation of hardware is allowed to arise, it may be much harder in the future to install LANs and get all of the hardware working together. Indeed, in many cases it might be necessary to replace hardware to achieve future office automation objectives.

In setting hardware standards, the claims of manufacturers that their equipment is compatible with or a clone to that of some other manufacturer have to be carefully reviewed and assessed. Very small differences in the hardware or their operating systems can be very significant. Situations can arise where two different computers are currently able to use a particular software package of the same type and exchange the resulting files. However, at a later date, when a more complex package is acquired which fully stresses hardware and operating systems features, compatibility breaks down.

The safest approach is to choose one major hardware vendor that fully and contractually supports the compatibility amongst its various models. Thus, the needs of individuals, some of whom want desktop models, others of whom want portables and others of whom want the newer and smaller "notebook" models can be more safely accommodated.

The minimum size and power of microcomputers should also be set. Once again, this reflects that microcomputers are multi purpose devices and the user today who wants a stand alone machine may tomorrow need to connect it to a LAN.

It can be costly to upgrade or replace hardware that rapidly becomes inadequate for a user's expanding needs. Thus, in setting standards it is desirable to consider future needs and the cost of purchasing extra computing power today to accommodate future requirements at an overall lower cost. Some of the technical factors to be considered are:

Memory Size

Is the size of the RAM (random access memory) sufficient to cover the personal computing requirements? In the future, the users may want to use more sophisticated programs or packages that require more memory. Or, they may wish to make use of sophisticated operating systems which allow several programs to run at once and cut and paste and move data back and forth between applications. Such capabilities need a lot of memory. These new features are discussed more fully in Chapter 10.

Processing Speed

Slower chips may not provide the kind of speed and processing power to support the more demanding applications mentioned above. The applications could run so slowly that the user would find the delay unacceptable.

Expansion Slots

The use of LANs, electronic mail, enhanced graphics and other software often require additional physical boards to be installed in the microcomputer. There may not be enough expansion slots in the microcomputer to meet all these future needs.

Amount Of Disk Space

The user may want to store increasingly large amounts of programs and data on his or her personal machine. Usually it is better to buy a larger hard drive now than to upgrade it in the future. This is true for all microcomputers, be they desktop, portable, or laptop.

Portability vs Ergonomics

Some employees may want equipment they can take home with them or transport with them when they go out of town on business.

Today both laptops and notebook computers are lightweight and can run on batteries as well as normal electric current. They have sufficient power to support most personal computing needs, with easily 2-4MB of memory and over 40MB of hard disk storage.

The trade off is that these portable machines usually have screens that are harder to read and smaller keyboards than their desktop equivalents. Thus, while an employee may gain the benefits of portability, he or she will find some inconvenience in the office, especially if heavy use is made of the machine.

Create the Policies and Acquire the Necessary Resources to Support Users to the Greatest Possible Extent

Employees are most productive when they are employing their specialized skills and knowledge and are focused directly on the key elements of their job. Thus, while it is reasonable to expect that employees should become skilled and literate computer users, everything possible should be done so that employees do not have to learn **technical** computer and information systems skills.

Thus, all reasonable steps should be taken to provide effective support for personal computing. As previously mentioned, this is a lot easier to do when hardware standards are in place and the same software is being used throughout the organization. In these circumstances, one individual can be assigned to find training for all users for the word processing, spreadsheet and other packages selected. This training can range all the way from attendance at recommended outside courses through to the provision of good books and guides as to how to use the software in question.

The designated individual or individuals can also be responsible for helping the users make best use of the features of the software packages selected and be a source of advice and troubleshooting when problems arise. This "local coach" role is different from the support provided by the network manager as in this case we are supporting the software and the word processing or spreadsheet package itself rather than focusing on the technical problems of supporting and accessing any local area network.

If a LAN exists, other opportunities exist to support users in the area of back up and recovery. Users can be provided with private directories on the network server to store their programs and files. In this way, all users' programs and files are backed up whenever the network manager performs daily and monthly back up routines.

Respecting the Conditions of Software Licenses

The vast majority of microcomputer software is sold under licensing conditions which limit the duplication, copying or additional use of the software product. Obviously, these conditions should be respected and the use of "pirate software" or unauthorized software copies should be prohibited.

Many organizations have issued policies in this regard reminding employees that licensing agreements should always be respected. Some companies have even gone as far as to make the use of pirated software grounds for dismissal. These companies may also examine software on employees' machines to determine that only authorized and properly purchased software is being used.

The above policies are more than good business ethics. Pirated or unauthorized copies or versions of software are a major source of computer viruses. One of the best protections against a virus is to ensure that all company personnel only use or install authorized software purchased from a well known supplier in its original box and packaging.

Internal Controls and Personal Computing

No matter how much effort is spent in supporting and helping users, there is almost always a remaining element of personal computing. Users will almost inevitably want to create their own programs from time to time and create and store files on their own microcomputer.

The information so produced is of importance to the organization. If the reports produced are wrong due to faulty logic or data or files stored in microcomputers are lost, the organization does suffer some damage. Thus, it is important to put some controls in place over both programs and data resulting from personal computing. Both these subjects are discussed below.

Controls Over Programs

First of all, it is important to remember that spreadsheet templates or the use of report generators are computer programs in a very real sense. They contain logic and formulae and if these are incorrect, then the results will be wrong.

Thus, spreadsheet and report generation programs, like all computer programs, should be tested before they are used.

The Degree of Testing Required

The efforts and thoroughness of the testing process should be commensurate with the importance of the results or output which will be produced. The following factors can be reviewed in assessing the amount of testing required:

- the more important the results of the program are, then the more thorough the testing should be;
- the level of testing should increase with the complexity of the logic in the program; simple programs involving little computation require less testing than programs involving many formulae or computations;
- if the resulting program or output is to be used by many people, then testing should be more thorough than when the programs and the results are to be used only by the individual creating the program. In the latter case, the individual in question is more familiar with the situation and can more readily spot obvious errors in the output. The individual is also more familiar with the limitations on completeness and accuracy of the data;
- if the output of the program can be verified or substantiated by comparison with other data generated by other programs, then less testing may be required.

Testing Procedures

Depending on the above circumstances, one or usually more of the following procedures should be used to test programs. For ease of reference, the procedures below are listed in order of the amount of time and effort they normally require, starting with the least time consuming:

- agree the results with overall totals or results produced by other programs;
- print out all the formulae or calculations in the program and review them (there is software for spreadsheets which do this). This review is usually more effective if it is performed by someone other than the individual writing the program;

- write the program in such a way that individual data elements have to be individually entered as well as the total of the items (or conversely ensure that the program logic examines all records whether or not they are selected and compares a computed total of all items with a control total). Put routines in the program to check that the total of the detail equals the total manually entered and report any difference as an error. This approach is useful in verifying both program logic and the data;
- create some simple test data for a spreadsheet, calculate the results which should occur, enter the test data in the spreadsheet, and compare the results. For a report generation program, obtain a small extract or sample of records from the file covering all possible variations. Predetermine the results manually, run the program against the test file, and compare results.

Program Documentation

The need for program documentation can be assessed in a similar manner to the need for testing. Once again, the nature and amount of program documentation required can vary widely.

It is rare for a template or report generation routine to be used only once and/or only by one individual. Thus it is rare for a situation to arise where no documentation at all is required.

Documentation can be thought of as serving three basic purposes:

- the creation of documentation puts a discipline on the programmer to be thorough, thus reducing the likelihood of programming errors. It also supports and eases the testing process, especially when another individual is involved;
- it can help ensure that the user of the program output understands the nature and limitation of the data in the reports. This can be done either by providing the user of the program with a copy of the written description of the purpose and nature of the program or ensuring some summary comments along these lines are printed by the program on each output report;
- it helps preserve the re-use or amendment of the program for other purposes at future dates.

Generally, program documentation should include the following elements:

- the nature and purpose of the program;
- name of author, and dated list of revisions and enhancements;
- a description of the data used by the program and from where it was obtained;
- a listing of all computations or selections made by the program and their purposes;

- a description of any edit routines in the program, especially those that balance the sum of detail elements to overall control totals;
- a description of the contents and purpose of each output report.

Depending on the amount of documentation required, often the template or program itself can contain most or all of the documentation required.

With a spreadsheet or a program, additional comments lines can be written to explain the purpose of each formulae or routine right in program or template itself. If properly written, these program lines are ignored as part of the program when it is run but they still appear as part of the template or on the program listing when it is printed.

As previously mentioned, the output of each program should contain sufficient information or descriptions to allow the reader both to understand the content of the report and any limitations on the data.

A Final Thought on Personal Programming

While occasions will arise when users may want or need to write their own spreadsheet programs or create their own reports using corporate databases and report generation software, it is good business sense to appropriately restrict these activities. After all, the typical user is usually not a skilled programmer and it can take a long time for him or her to create (and test) programs.

This can deflect the user from other activities where his or her talents can be more productively used. Also, the risk of programming errors increase when users, with little technical skills, start writing quite complex programs.

The following guidelines should assist in appropriately restricting "personal programming":

- consider assigning either the EDP department or some designated employee to assist users in creating programs (including spreadsheets). With a greater knowledge of the software and of technical EDP matters, the assigned individuals can help ensure that programs are correct and documented and assist in developing the program in less time.
- really complex programs should be developed by a professional programmer, not a user. This advice equally applies to spreadsheets.
- if users are creating programs which are to be run monthly or on a regular basis, why not make a program change request and have the program created and run as part of the regular EDP operations?
- if users are generating a lot of reports and analysis using corporate data, this can be a sign that the application programs are not meeting the needs of the organization. Furthermore, there is a danger that several users will generate

their own but different ad hoc financial reports and meetings will degenerate into discussions as to whose data is correct rather than focus on solving the business problem.

In these circumstances, the need to replace or appropriately modify the application systems to better meet the information needs of the organization should be considered.

Controls over Data

For the purpose of this section, data should be viewed as any file that an individual might want to store. Thus, it would include for example, a word processing document containing data, a spreadsheet or information downloaded from financial systems for analysis.

Correctness of Data

We discussed above how incorrect programs can lead to incorrect information and thus incorrect management decisions. This is also true of data, which if it is incomplete or inaccurate, can, of course, lead to false information and incorrect decisions. In the personal computing environment, the individual has to take responsibility for data as well as for programs.

The initial file of data to be downloaded (eg., extracted from) corporate and financial systems of the organization should be sufficiently complete and accurate as a result of internal controls surrounding such systems. However, the individual needs to make sure that all the relevant data has been extracted and that the correct version of the files in the corporate system have been used. In other words, incorrect extraction or use of incorrect versions of data files needs to be avoided.

Perhaps the most effective way of checking that the correct data has been obtained is to balance it in total against some other report that has already been produced. Thus, a report analyzing all sales by province could be tied into the monthly sales report or the income statement. A report designed to list all customers having balances over $1,000 should also include a program-generated total for all accounts under $1,000, enabling the individual to tie the overall total into say the accounts receivable trial balance.

Not all data entered into spreadsheets or reports comes from official corporate systems. Often the individual will supply some of the data himself. For example, a report on wage costs might contain a cost summary drawn or built from a corporate system together with a notation of number of the employees per department gathered or obtained by the individual from other sources. In many cases, the additional data may be quite soft, e.g., estimates of market share, prices being charged by competitors, etc.

Thus individuals may create reports containing a wide variety of data quality ranging all the way from "hard" data from corporate systems through to "soft" data which are in fact "educated guesses". Where the quality of the data or lack thereof is not otherwise obvious, it is a very good idea to put a note right on the report spelling out any limitations on the data.

One good way of conveying precision is to give ranges instead of a specific number. If a report states a competitor price for wholesale lots of x is $4.36 per unit, the reader receives an impression of accuracy. If the report states the price is somewhere between $3.75 and $4.50, a more reasonable view of data quality is portrayed.

Protecting Confidentiality

If the previous suggestions made in this book are followed then there should be reasonable assurance that confidential data stored in minicomputers or on the network server in a LAN is protected from unauthorized access by anyone not having permission to see it.

A challenge arises from the tendency of many individuals to want to keep copies of confidential data on their own microcomputers. This may be because they consider the data so confidential that they want to avoid even the network manager or computer operator being able to view it. Far more frequently, it is because the individual wants to work on the computer files at home or away from the office. This is a rapidly growing trend as more and more knowledge workers are acquiring portable and notebook personal computers.

When data and the programs to read them sit on portable microcomputers there is a considerable risk that confidentiality can be lost. The damage can be extensive as today's portable computers can contain easily 40MB or the equivalent of 12,000 pages of information. It is not just budgets and summary information we need to guard; the microcomputer may contain all of the organization's detailed sales and cost data.

There are several simple and effective steps which can be taken to help guard this data:

- If data is extremely confidential, don't put it on the hard disk. Instead keep the file on a floppy diskette. Guard the floppy diskette by locking it up in your desk drawer. In other words, guard the file just the way you would guard a very important confidential document or printout.

- Guard your personal computer in the same way you would guard your briefcase.
- There are computer programs which you can buy which sit on the hard disk and ask for a password before any files can be read off it. Some of these products will cause the hard disk to be disabled after say three invalid attempts have been made to enter the password. A special diskette provided with the package then must be used to reset the password and thus access the hard disk. Alternatively, some of these products include an extra board in the microcomputer which interprets a password entered by the user. In the absence of the password, information on the hard disk cannot be accessed. Obviously, if these approaches are used, there has to be good backing up of files (see below).
- Put reasonable restrictions on the nature and amount of data which can be stored on personal computers.

Of course, the ultimate safeguard is to use encryption software. In this process, every file is encrypted by a special piece of software before it is written to any kind of disk or tape. A special password or key is required to be entered before any files are decrypted and then available for use. Thus, if the microcomputer is lost, the encrypted files on it are still safe.

Encryption, of course, consumes processing time and makes the microcomputer run less efficiently. The software to do the encryption has to be purchased and supported and people need to be trained in its use.

Hardware boards are also available to do encryption, and because they provide their own additional CPU, there is little if any degradation in performance. However, this is a more expensive solution.

While encryption packages have been available for microcomputers (and thus LANs as well) for quite a period of time, to date few organizations have gone to this extent. It would certainly make good sense to provide reasonable protection by other means before proceeding to this ultimate step.

DIAL-UP PORTS

Many organizations have added dial-up telephone lines to their LANs so that individuals can access programs and files when they are at home or away on business. The most common reason for doing so is to provide access to electronic mail.

167

In considering dial-up ports, it is important to consider that dial-up lines often work at low transmission speeds. Thus, while it may make sense to support electronic mail in this manner, the use of more powerful software that requires a lot of data to be transmitted to and from the remote microcomputer can result in unacceptably slow responses from the user's perspective.

The most crucial concern in dial-up access is to maintain control of access to the programs and files on the LAN. Without dial-up ports, someone trying to penetrate a LAN not only has to overcome LAN security but also has to be in an organization's premises and be physically connected to the LAN. When there are dial-up ports, then the penetrator can be located literally anywhere in the world, as long as he or she knows the telephone number to call.

Experience has shown that it is very hard to protect telephone numbers and this cannot be counted on as a defence. In fact, some hackers have written software to dial telephone numbers randomly and then record those where there is the special beep present which is generated by the dial-up facilities. Hackers have also created electronic bulletin boards on which they share telephone numbers to dial into LANs and Data Centres.

Thus before dial-up ports are installed, the organization should ensure that there are adequate features in its LAN security, these features have been adequately installed, and they are being properly maintained.

Some organizations have installed additional protection by using answer back software on their LAN. This software stores a telephone number in relation to each password. When an employee calls in to connect to the LAN, the answerback software intercepts the call and asks for the password. Once a valid password is entered, the software then interrupts the call and dials back the phone number stored in relation to that password. Thus the user must be using the phone for which the number has been stored.

This approach can add a useful additional layer of security. As always it adds additional costs and administration not the least of which can be maintaining the phone number associated with each password. This can be especially difficult for those executives moving around from office to office or city to city who continually want to have the phone number changed.

As an alternative, some organizations put their electronic mail on a separate file server and install dial-up software so that it can only access the machine containing electronic mail. Thus, if a hacker does break in, only the electronic mail is at risk.

There are two additional steps that can be taken to protect LANs when dial-up ports exist.

Firstly, a special modem can be purchased to control the dial up ports. These modems contain a switch which can only be activated by the correct entry of a four or five character password by the person signing in. If this password is successfully entered, the user is then able to connect to the LAN and then enter his or her normal password to perform functions.

As a result, an extra password layer is added, in that the user must have a password to get past the modem and talk to the network and then enter passwords as normally required to access programs or files stored on the LAN. Obviously this extra layer of password protection provides additional security.

As an additional precaution, it is good to set quite tight limits on the number of password attempts which can be invalid before the user is thrown off the system. This concept would apply both to the password required for the switch on the modem as well as the password to actually access programs or files on the network.

One particular problem with dial-up ports is that the dial up port itself is effectively defined as a "user" to the network operating system. Thus, throwing a user off the network due to exceeding the number of permitted logon attempts may disable the dial-up port for all users.

Obviously, an appropriate balance between security and accessibility is required here. If we set the number of attempted violations too low, based on the configuration on our system we can end up all too frequently with the dial-up port being unavailable to one or more legitimate users. On the other hand, we have to recognize that hacking threats are real and it is not necessarily a bad thing if hacking attempts result in a shutdown of the dial-up port. Indeed if there is no shutdown, a hacker can sign in numerous times, even though he fails at each time to enter a valid password and gets thrown out. Simply another telephone call gives another series of attempts.

The use of encryption software can also be a good defense. The great advantage of encryption is that if someone gets through all the user id and password screens which are created, the data is still unusable to the penetrator in the absence of knowing the seed or word necessary for decryption. As previously stated, the use of encryption software does involve some overhead in that additional computer processing cycles are used to both encrypt and decrypt the files.

In summary, an organization needs to understand that creating dial-up ports to a local area network seriously increases the risk of unauthorized access and alteration to programs and data. A careful analysis should be made of the additional steps which may be necessary to offset this increased risk. It is generally advisable to implement at least one of the three techniques described above, being the use of modems with switches and additional passwords, the use of dial back facilities, or the encryption of information on the files.

BACKUP AND DISASTER RECOVERY

Where an individual stores programs or data on the hard disk of his microcomputer, then he or she must take responsibility for performing back up procedures over these files.

Where a LAN exists, it is best to encourage individuals to store copies of all files that have been changed during the day on the LAN's network server. In this way, there will be two copies of all files (one on the microcomputer hard disk and one on the LAN). Each user is provided with a separate storage area or private directory on the LAN that no other user is given access to. Further protection is provided as the network manager will have procedures to backup all files on the network server.

It is best to provide each user with a special program or batch routine to do this backup. In this way, the user only has to invoke this program at the end of the day to create the backup. At the same time, users need to be reminded to erase old files out of their private areas on the network server when they are no longer required, and this should be monitored by the network manager. Unless this is done, the amount of disk space required by the network will grow unreasonably large.

In summary, whenever a LAN exists, it is a good practice to ask users to store all of their data on the LAN rather than the hard disk on their own microcomputer. In this way, backup and recovery is automatically dealt with by the network manager. However, there will be circumstances where users have information that is so confidential that they do not wish to risk putting it on the LAN. After all, even in the best managed LANs where logical security has been properly installed and maintained there will be network managers who have access to all data.

In other situations, users may be taking their portable microcomputers home or out of town and creating additional data while not in the office. In this case, there is a risk of the data being lost if the hard disk in their microcomputer was damaged or crashed before the information could be transferred over to the LAN. In all the above cases, it would be good to provide the users with routines as described below to enable them to permanently or temporarily backup their files which are not stored on the LAN file server.

In the above circumstances or where there is no LAN, each user will have to look after his own backup. The following procedures should help each user to do this:

- store copies of all programs in their original containers in a location elsewhere in the office.
- provide pre-programmed routines which the users can simply execute to backup all files that have changed during the day at the end of each day and to backup all files say weekly or monthly. The backed up files are written from the hard disk on the microcomputer to diskettes.
- consider the need to store copies of key files outside the office say on a weekly or monthly basis as protection against a disaster.

Where a LAN exists, the disaster recovery plan should cover all of the microcomputer hardware which is normally attached to the network. This plan should be extended to cover any additional portable computers used solely for personal computing.

When individuals have key files stored on their own microcomputer and use their own microcomputers to access files on the LAN on which they are really dependent, the unavailability of their machine even for a few hours can be a real disaster from their point of view.

Breakdowns in microcomputers and their disk drives are rare today but over any lengthy period of time where there are a number of users, some breakdown is almost inevitable.

Some organizations keep one or two additional microcomputers around to provide for this eventuality. If portable microcomputers are used for this purpose, they can serve double duty as loaners for those who want to work at home during the evening or while they are away on business trips. Also, many microcomputer stores will enter arrangements ahead of time whereby microcomputers can be rented by the day or the week while broken hardware is being repaired.

CHAPTER 10

Office Automation

INTRODUCTION

There are almost as many definitions of office automation as there are people using it. Basically, office automation products exist to support the performance of tasks rather than functions. Thus, office automation includes word processing, desktop publishing and electronic mail and may be used by many people throughout the organization. Of course, these office automation activities may interrelate with functional systems such as general ledgers and other financial systems. This interrelationship arises when individuals want to make use of information contained in functional systems by transferring it to office automation products to create reports or other common files for access across the organization.

As implied by its name, office automation seeks to automate tasks within the office and this presupposes that the software and the resulting files or reports can be shared in electronic form by many individuals. Thus, the use of office automation products normally presupposes the existence of a local area network or a minicomputer with a number of terminals to provide the communications necessary to allow such sharing to take place.

Purpose of this Chapter

Most of the controls needed over office automation products have already been addressed in other chapters. Chapter 1 discusses the acquisition of hardware, software and operating systems. Chapter 8 addresses local area networks which are normally the vehicle through which office automation products are implemented. Chapter 9 discusses end user computing from the point of view of an individual making use of both office automation products located on a local area network and personal computing tools.

Thus, the primary purpose of this chapter is to pull together and re-emphasize key control and management decisions in respect of office automation. The chapter then continues to describe some of the major tasks which can be supported by office automation software and briefly describes their most desirable features.

A REVIEW OF KEY CONTROL CONSIDERATIONS

Acquisition

As pointed out in Chapter 1, office automation needs should be addressed as part of the total information technology strategy for an organization. An overall strategy is required both so that information can be shared across corporate and office automation systems as well as to ensure that users are adequately supported in the use of the products. Users require support and education not only from a technical point of view in the use of their microcomputer and its interface with corporate systems but also in the use of the office automation products themselves.

As pointed out in Chapter 8, the choice of office automation products available on a LAN is much richer and less costly than that provided on minicomputers. Thus, office automation usually includes the acquisition and implementation of a LAN. As discussed in Chapter 8, if a LAN is not purchased for the financial and corporate systems, the organization may need a LAN for office automation in any event.

Thus, for all these reasons, it is highly important that the overall information processing needs of an organization be looked at and planned for on an overall basis.

This overall planning perspective is not only important in acquiring the correct hardware, operating systems, and application technologies but also in establishing organizational structures and staffing. When an organization has a variety of office automation products which employees count on daily to perform their tasks, clearly the organization must have in-house appropriate support to users both in respect of the network and to provide guidance and advice on the office automation tools. In fact, the more successful the implementation of office automation products is, the more essential it becomes that quick and reliable support be available in-house. As more and more information becomes stored and shared in electronic form, employees must be assured access to the software and the files in order to perform their jobs. Even minor interruptions to the availability of programs and files or a knowledge on how to use them to get a report printed or formatted can become critical.

As local area network hardware and software and office automation products are generally purchased "off the shelf" from retail stores, fundamentally an organization must look to its own resources to provide the prompt support that is required.

OPERATING SYSTEMS FOR OFFICE AUTOMATION PRODUCTS

There are new operating systems now available called graphical user interfaces or GUI's which can greatly enhance the use of office automation products. GUI's have been available for a number of years with some functionality in the Apple operating systems and are now becoming wide spread on DOS and IBM type products. The capabilities of the GUI's are expanding.

Fundamentally, GUI's can provide one or more of the following capabilities:

- They permit a user to have two or more applications running at the same time. Thus, a user can switch from application to application without having to exit one application and save the files in use before switching over to the next application.
- GUI software provides the user with the ability to "cut" a portion of a document or file from one application and then "paste" that document into a file or document from another application. Thus, for example, part or all of a spreadsheet could be cut and inserted into a word processing document.
- Dynamic linkages between files, so that data from one file and application can be cut and pasted into the other and the two files then become linked together. This is referred to as dynamic data exchange or DDE. Subsequently, when a change is made to the linked area in either file, the other file is automatically updated.

All these functions are discussed below.

Using Several Applications at Once

Most GUI operating systems support the capability of having two or more applications actively in use and "on the screen" at the same time. This can save a great deal of time. If a user is working on a spreadsheet and wishes to see a word processing document or add a sentence to it, the word processing software and the associated files can be activated without having to exit the spreadsheet application and saving its files. Furthermore, both the word processing document and the spreadsheet can be overlapped on the screen so the user can toggle back from one to the other and work on both documents at the same time. Some GUI's allow the user to split the screen and see the spreadsheet in one area of the screen and the word processing document in the other.

In such an environment, the GUI operating system will remind the user to shut down or exit each application and save the related files before exiting the operating system or shutting off the computer. Of course, if the user forgets to properly exit all applications or there is a power interruption, there is a risk that files that have been changed will not be saved.

Cutting and Pasting

Cutting and pasting often involves two documents. If one of the documents is changed by the user, the other document will not reflect this change.

For example, suppose a graph from a spreadsheet package was cut and then pasted into a letter stored as a word processing file. Subsequently changing the spreadsheet would **not** cause the graph in the letter to be updated. Also, if there is a need to change the graph in the letter, it will be necessary to go back to the spreadsheet file, update it and then re-paste the graph.

All of this can require careful control of a composite document that contains pieces which have originated or been pasted from several other files.

Dynamic Data Exchange (DDE)

The newest GUI's provide for dynamic linking between documents or files running under different applications. When cutting and pasting is done, a dynamic link is established between these parts of the two documents. As a result, when anything is changed in the linked area of one of the documents, then the other document or file is automatically changed.

To repeat the example above, a user might want to incorporate a graph and tabular data from a spreadsheet in a word processing document. With this capability, all or part of the spreadsheet can be cut and pasted and entered into the word processing document at any place the user desires. From this point forward, changing any of the data in the spreadsheet or in the word processing document in the linked area will cause an equivalent change to occur in the other document.

Clearly, this is a very useful capability. It makes the preparation of reports and analysis a great deal easier. It also strongly supports the re-use of data which is now resident in one file under one application by making it available for manipulation or re-use in another application.

To have this capability, there are two requirements. Firstly, the operating system must support these capabilities. Secondly, the application systems, that is the spreadsheet package and the word processing package, need to be special versions which can take advantage of the capabilities of the operating system and link the documents for these purposes.

The use of GUI operating systems requires a lot more memory, considerably more hard disk storage space, and if one of the older and slower processing chips is present in the microcomputer being used, the response times from the users' perspective may be unacceptably slow.

Also, with DDE, it is important to take extra caution on the management of files. For example, if only one file is copied and then sent by E-mail or by other means to a fellow employee, he or she will not have access to all the linked files. If you update a linked file which you did not forward, your other document will be updated but the document in the possession of your fellow employee will remain unchanged.

It is also possible to accidentally back up only some of the files that are linked together and not others. This could result in an inability to reproduce an important composite document drawn from many files.

Thus, it is a good idea whenever two or more documents are linked, to put them all together as a set of files in a separate subdirectory. Procedures should be established to forward, copy, or back up the entire subdirectories instead of individual files.

NON PROCESSING CONTROLS

The non processing controls necessary to support office automation have already been discussed in previous chapters under local area networks and end user computing. A proper application of these control concepts will help ensure that the confidentiality and accuracy of data and files is reasonably secure and the proper backup and disaster recovery arrangements have been put into place.

As previously noted, employees can become highly dependent on the continuing availability of their microcomputer workstations in order to conduct business. Thus, the ability to quickly replace or repair microcomputers which break down needs to be continually assessed in the light of continuing reliance on the availability of this hardware.

If enough microcomputers are used for enough time, it is inevitable that a microcomputer will break down and/or will have a hard disk crash. Thus, it is a very good idea to have emergency arrangements with a local retail store to

177

borrow microcomputers while those of the organization are being repaired. Also, it is good to have a repair and maintenance contract in place which provides both for preventative maintenance of the hardware.

Some organizations have gone to the extent of training one or more employees to look after minor microcomputer hardware failure. These employees are trained in how to isolate bad areas on hard disks so the rest of the disk can continue to be used, as well as the replacement of boards or floppy and hard disk drives. Spares are kept on the premises to provide for speedy maintenance.

Users need to be supported as well in the use of the applications and receive training on them. Many occasions will arise when a user will have difficulty getting a report to print on the LAN, successfully reformatting a file or because they have used the application in such a way that it "locks" and refuses to proceed. There should be one or more individuals available in the organization who have extra in-depth knowledge and training on the major office automation products in use so that they can provide support and assistance when such problems occur.

THE NATURE OF MAJOR OFFICE AUTOMATION PRODUCTS

The major features and capabilities of the more widely used office automation enabling technologies are described below, together the most important features which should be considered in selecting a product.

It should be noted that this discussion is not meant to be exhaustive or indepth. Rather, the goal is to provide the reader with an overall appreciation of the nature of office automation technologies which are available at the time this book was published.

Features Applicable to any Office Automation Product

No matter what office automation enabling technology is under consideration, the following should always be considered:

- Is there a good and sufficient business reason for acquiring the office automation capability? Will the increase in the quality of customer service, presentation materials, management information etc., be sufficient to warrant the cost? While some people will argue that office automation technology can lower overall costs, in the experience of the writer, this is not always the case. If the argument for an office automation technology is based principally on cost savings, it should be reviewed with a jaundiced eye. Users should agree in advance to reduce their budgets for any anticipated cost savings once the new technology has been installed and is working.

- What will be the impact of the new office automation technology on the structure of the organization and its need for support personnel both from a hardware and application point of view?
- Is the current size of computer hardware and operating systems sufficient to support this new office automation technology or will upgrades to hardware and operating systems be required?

In respect of any particular office application package or supplier, the following questions are usually appropriate.

- How long has this particular product been in use? Are the people using it happy with its capabilities or does it contain bugs or problems which have not yet been rectified? There is always a risk in being one of the first users of a new office automation technology or indeed a new package or offering by a supplier.
- Does the supplier offer network versions (e.g., multi-user) of its package? Does the supplier offer, or will they offer in the near future, GUI versions of their packages so that the advanced features of such operating systems can be taken advantage of?
- What is the quality of the user manual? Is it extensive and thorough and is it easy to read and understand? Does the supplier provide tutorials on diskette which are interrelated with the user manual and can be used by personnel to gain a working knowledge of the software?
- While support is usually somewhat limited for office automation products on LANs, is there at least a hotline number which one can call if problems arise? How many hours per week is the hotline support available and what is the cost of using it?
- Will the supplier make a site license available or even better a license for use of the product throughout the organization, representing a considerable cost saving over buying many individual versions of the software?
- Does the software license provide sufficient latitude so that additional copies of the software may be made and stored for backup purposes?

If an organization is considering extensive use of office automation technologies in areas which are key to the conduct of its business, it would be good to spend the money on a professional consultant to advise both in the selection of an office automation product as well as to train the staff and assist in the implementation of the product. For example, an organization may decide to maintain its sales catalogues and price lists using desktop publishing technology. If sales catalogues and price lists change frequently, then the organization is dependent on being able to effectively and efficiently use this software in the conduct of its business.

There is an absolute wealth of material on office automation products in a wide selection of well recognized and respected microcomputer magazines. These magazines often have feature issues on a particular office automation technology, including a comparison of the price, features and support for various packages. Back issues of these magazines can always be obtained either from the supplier or from the local public library.

Against the background of these general comments, a discussion follows on various office automation enabling technologies.

WORD PROCESSING

Word processing has been around for a number of years, and its use is well known. Many word processing packages are being expanded to include a host of other capabilities. Some packages now support limited calculations, such as totalling and cross adding and other basic functionalities of a spreadsheet. They may also enable columns and rows of figures to be converted into fairly simple graphs and charts. In addition, the newer packages will support a wide variety of preformatted style sheets and will enable users to incorporate logos and symbols into documents which they produce.

Put another way, many word processing packages are now presenting themselves as being the equivalent of more simple and basic desktop publishing support tools.

The ability of a word processor to import and export files for electronic mail packages should be assessed. This requires that both the electronic mail and the word processing package be reviewed. Indeed, it is preferable if users only have to learn one word processing package rather than having to learn an additional word processor imbedded in an electronic mail system.

Many organizations have sought to control costs by making word processing packages available to middle management and supervisors and encouraging them to do their own document preparation. The argument then continues that secretarial support costs can be considerably reduced. In some organizations, this is undoubtedly true. However, one has to also carefully consider the use of executive time in performing typing tasks and the ability and indeed willingness of users to acquire basic or advanced typing skills.

Also, the word processing functions which might be performed by the knowledge worker or middle management employee should not necessarily be all encompassing. For example, many organizations would encourage middle management to prepare documents of two or three pages in length in the sense of entering in the words. However, the actual formatting and printing of the document may best be left to a secretary who has special training in these functions. The sharing of these functions between word capture and document layout and preparation can easily be co-ordinated where local area networks exist and the file can be electronically passed to a secretary.

ELECTRONIC MAIL

Electronic mail is useful for correspondence within an office as well as to outside parties. Using a local area network or minicomputer, an electronic mail package can allow anyone in the organization to create a document and then forward it on to one or more individuals within the office. In addition, most electronic mail packages allow other documents such as a spreadsheet package template to be attached to the electronic mail document. The recipient can store the spreadsheet, document, or other attached file in his own microcomputer or LAN and then view and edit it using the appropriate application package.

The use of electronic mail may grow when there is an ability to send and receive electronic mail to others outside the organization. This can be accomplished by joining one of many electronic mail services that have secure "mail boxes". In this way, messages can be sent to people in other organizations who have joined the same service. Furthermore, employees at home or away from the office can access their electronic mail or send messages to others without the need for the organization to install, support, and control their own dial-up telephone lines. If the organization wishes to use an electronic mail service, then the electronic mail package supplied by that outside organization, or that at least one that is compatible with that service system, should also be used internally.

Electronic mail today is so widespread that to question its usefulness seems unusual. However, the use of electronic mail should indeed be questioned, as there are alternatives and an organization can end up with a proliferation of expensive and overlapping alternatives.

For example, if there is a desire to send information to others outside the organization, fax can be used. This may be sufficient for many organizations. Furthermore, software can be purchased today which, with the installation of a special board in a microcomputer, can turn any microcomputer into a fax machine. With this software, the microcomputer can take any document that has been stored, and convert its output format into a fax format and transmit it. Similarly, the software can receive fax messages, store them and then display them on the screen.

Many organizations have installed both electronic mail and electronic voice management systems. The electronic voice messaging systems allow employees to leave telephone messages for each other. They can also receive and store messages from anyone who dials in from outside. The owner of the electronic mailbox, by dialling a special telephone number and entering his or her password can retrieve and listen to his messages from any touch tone telephone. Most people are familiar with these systems if only from having come into contact with them when calling others.

Organizations should question whether they really need an electronic mail system as well as an electronic voice messaging system for internal use. After all, voice mail can be accessed from anywhere there is a touch tone phone. It is thus easier for employees away from the office to contact their voice mail than to take a portable microcomputer along and find a telephone plug with which they can connect. Also, voice messaging systems today support group definition functions, whereby a voice message can be given once and then sent to a list of predetermined individuals. The key point here is to consider whether an organization requires both systems for internal purposes.

DESKTOP PUBLISHING

Desktop publishing software provides the ability to lay out documents and brochures in complex ways and supports a host of printing fonts and styles. The major purpose of desktop publishing is to allow an organization to produce its own pamphlets, brochures, sales catalogues, presentation overheads and slides and other documents for external consumption and thus avoid the expense of using outside publishing houses.

Unlike word processing, spreadsheets, and electronic mail, desktop publishing supports a variety of talents that many of us do not possess. While all of us prior to the age of microcomputers were used to writing documents, creating financial models, or receiving and sending mail, very few of us had any knowledge of graphical arts. Thus, the mere acquisition of a desktop publishing package will not in itself provide the typical user with the ability to produce good looking brochures, catalogues, and proposals. It is not only the knowledge of the software which needs to be acquired, but the graphical arts knowledge as well.

Thus many organizations train an employee skilled in graphical arts in the use of the desktop publishing software. For efficiency, it is highly useful that the desktop publishing software be able to capture and make use of documents which had been created on a word processing package. In this way, the typical user can concentrate on the contents or message which he or she wishes to have incorporated in some document. This can then be loaded electronically by the desktop publishing employee into the software, and the final product created.

For the average user, the more limited capabilities and layout styles available in most word processing and spreadsheet packages are sufficient for the production of internal reports and graphs.

PROJECT MANAGEMENT SOFTWARE

Project management software exists to help individuals create, analyze, and maintain fairly complex projects. Most of these software packages allow interdependencies of tasks to be defined, as well as tracking the availability of employees working on each sub project. They support critical path or PERT analysis as well as the production of GANTT charts. Thus, it is usually possible to produce graphs and flowcharts displaying tasks chronologically with their interdependencies noted. The software usually also supports the entering of actual accomplishments to date and adjusts future anticipated completion dates of dependent tasks accordingly.

Once again, it is desirable to adopt one package for the organization. In this way, people will be able to understand the output from other's project management activities as well as being able to share the actual project management plans in electronic form.

To make good use of this software, it is necessary not only to learn the software but to have an appreciation of project management techniques and the concepts of critical path, task interdependencies, GANTT charts, etc. Thus, in encouraging the widespread use of such software, an organization needs to consider training in both these respects.

IMAGE PROCESSING

Image processing refers to the capability of scanning any document and then storing its image in machine-readable form in a file. The documents are indexed with headers and footers by the person doing the scanning so that, for example, incoming mail can be referred to the right person and a copy of the document placed in the correct "correspondence file". In more elaborate image processing systems, the recipient of a document is then able to add or append a note to the document and after performing his or her task, forward the document plus the notes added onto the next person.

Image processing is based on already existing and robust technologies. For example, the technology in the document reader used to scan documents into machine-readable files is based on fax technology. The indexing and filing of documents into logical files by recipient and subject area is based on data base technology.

The overall purpose behind image processing is to create electronic files so that correspondence and documents may speedily be passed from one individual to another, documents can move from individual to individual to support the processing of a transaction, and so that document images may be speedily and efficiently retrieved.

For example, a corporation might scan in sales orders received through the mail. Through indexing, the sales orders are forwarded to the sales order department as well as a copy of the sales order document being filed under the particular customer. As the sales order is approved, it can be transferred to the shipping department for shipment as well as forwarded to the invoicing department for billing. The system might track all sales orders received but still in the order department, all orders approved but not yet shipped, etc. Thus, as well as efficiently forwarding and filing documents, some image processing systems can assist in measuring workflow and spotting bottlenecks.

While the technology to support image processing is fairly simple and well understood, the problem today is in the amount of disk storage space required to store an image. Typically, at the time of writing, it can take up to 50k to store a one page image. This means that only 20 pages can be stored in one megabyte on a hard disk.

To get around this particular difficulty, CD ROM disks which have a huge storage capability can be used. Today, with the low cost of CD writers and readers, the use of image processing by smaller organizations is becoming more feasible. However, image processing systems have not come into use in smaller organizations, except in rare circumstances where there is a special and unique need which this technology can support.

Today, image processing systems are on sale or under development which support OCR or optical character recognition. In these systems, it is possible for the image processing system to interpret type written, or possibly in the near future, block printed documents. In this way, the creation of the electronic image will at the same time include data capture activities. For example, in the previous example the sales order itself could be interpreted and the results stored in the sales order processing system. It should be pointed out that OCR technologies at this moment are new and somewhat complex. Approaches and procedures have to be put into place to deal with the documents or sections thereof which the image processing system is unable to interpret.

Perhaps the major message for smaller organizations in relation to image processing is to recognize this as a developing area which deserves monitoring. As image processing grows and becomes more integrated with fax technologies, image processing systems may be a good alternative for smaller organizations to electronic data interchange which is now being demanded by many major organizations from all their suppliers.

CHAPTER 11

A Word About Computer Viruses

THE NATURE OF A COMPUTER VIRUS

Computer viruses are computer programs which are able to replicate themselves from program to program and thus can spread rapidly throughout computer systems. They usually contain only a very small amount of code and are capable of hiding themselves in places which are very hard to find. For example, a computer virus can be hidden in an existing computer program in such a way that even the total number of bytes which the program consists of as reported by a disk operating system is unchanged. Computer viruses are often hidden in the file allocation tables on hard or floppy diskettes or on the master boot sector of a hard disk.

To date, almost all instances of viruses have occurred on microcomputers and LANs. However, they may in the future appear on minicomputers and mainframes, despite the better defenses these larger computers have.

Computer viruses are aptly named because they spread quickly. Fundamentally, a computer virus works its way into the operating system and then causes a copy of itself to be replicated into other programs as they are brought into memory. Whenever one of these infected programs is used, this causes other programs to become infected.

Thus, a computer virus which exists in a network server can spread to all of the workstations on the network, or even worse, can spread from one local area network to another if both LANs are part of a wide area network.

Generally speaking, viruses are usually so constructed that they remain latent until they become widely spread. This means that viruses usually seek out the opportunity to replicate themselves in a large number of programs before any activity is undertaken which might bring to the user's attention that a virus is present and is spreading.

Once the virus has been sufficiently spread, then it "activates its payload" or starts to interfere with the operation of the computer programs and files in the manner intended by its creator. Some viruses spread very rapidly and cause damage in a very short amount of time.

Because a virus is a computer program, it can do a great deal of damage. It can erase or distort files, destroy or eradicate programs, scramble the content of allocation tables so your operating system is no longer able to find files and programs, or interfere with the proper operations of your software. In other words, it destroys your ability for some period of time to use your hardware and software. In the absence of proper backup, your data can be gone forever.

Because the writer of the virus is not familiar with the layout of the data in your files, it would be unlikely, if not impossible, for a computer virus to change the value of somebody's gross wage or write off an amount you have recorded as an accounts receivable. But there is widespread opportunity for tremendous malicious damage in destroying files so they are no longer usable or altering programs so they no longer function.

Some viruses work by simply putting in processing loops which tie up the hardware's processing capacity or fill the channels connecting devices to the LAN so they are choked with garbage and cannot perform their functions. Others create more serious damage by erasing or altering files or programs so they may no longer be used.

The author's worse virus fear has not yet appeared, but it is only a matter of time. Indeed, for reasons of security I am afraid to describe what it would be in this book, but it would be simple and effective to create and would cause even more widespread damage than those currently in existence.

The Extent of the Threat

The threat of a computer virus is very real. Major accounting firms, financial institutions, and governmental agencies have suffered from viruses. The frequency of virus infection is on the rise and the damage viruses are doing is more pernicious and painful. A recent survey in the United States disclosed that 40% of the companies surveyed had suffered a virus infection in the last six months.

At the time of writing, viruses have almost been exclusively restricted to microcomputers and the local area networks and wide area networks which use microcomputers as network servers.

This is because operating systems in the microcomputer environment do not have the boundaries between themselves and applications systems which exists in most minicomputers and almost all mainframes. For the virus to replicate, it has to get itself from an application program up into the operating system or its utilities so it is present there to infect another program as it comes into memory. These boundaries are very well defended in most mainframes and strongly defended in most minicomputers. However, in the microcomputer world these boundaries are very fuzzy and in fact operating systems have little or no defense to prevent application systems from seeding viruses into the operating code. This statement is true regardless of the type of operating system software being used on a microcomputer.

There have been instances of viruses reported on mainframes and on minicomputers where these systems have been operated in such a fashion so as not maintain the integrity protection which the operating system has to prevent its own alteration. In addition, two microcomputers who communicate with each other via a minicomputer or a mainframe can infect each other. That is, a program passed by one microcomputer to another using a mainframe or minicomputer as a telecommunications device can pass the infection from microcomputer operating system to microcomputer operating system, even though the transmitting mini or mainframe computer itself may remain uninfected.

What Some Viruses Have Done

To date in North America, the payload of most viruses has been somewhat benign. Often, the virus simply creates a message on your screen saying that it is present and presents some silly joke or graphic written by the virus creator. Other North American viruses are not so kind. Some of them create additional meaningless processing loops so that the processing power of your microcomputer or LAN is used up in performing meaningless tasks and is unavailable to do business. Other viruses scramble the allocation tables on your hard or floppy diskettes so your operating system cannot find the files or programs it needs to perform a task.

In North America, we have been fortunate compared to our cousins in Europe. In Europe, there are many more computer viruses which are more cleverly written and hidden and which are far more damaging. One European virus erases the contents of the hard disk. Another virus infects programs so that when a call is made to save a file, the file is not saved even though the application system reports that a save has been performed. One particularly nasty virus fills up all the memory and buffers in the CPU of a microcomputer so completely that is almost impossible to get in to eradicate the virus. It is sort of like trying to push yourself into a room that is already full of balloons to remove them, but the balloons are pushing so much against the doors and windows you can't get in. One manufacturer of anti-virus software reports that their research files contain over 1000 different types of viruses they have encountered, an increase from about 100 different types two to three years ago.

How Virus Infection Occurs

To date, the vast majority of computer viruses have been caught when an executable code (e.g., a computer program) is put on a microcomputer and that executable code already contains the virus. The virus is able then to travel from the application program into the operating system and start replicating itself. It doesn't take a great deal of time for this to occur; it can be measured in fractions of a second as soon as the program is loaded into memory. The virus can spread from the microcomputer into the LAN and from there to all other attached microcomputers. It can then spread from LAN to LAN if the two LANs are connected in any way.

Some of the newer viruses hide in the file allocation part of a floppy diskette. In this case, merely putting the diskette into your disk drive and then causing the operating system to point at or read that particular diskette will cause the infection to occur, even if the program on that diskette is left unloaded or unused, or even if the diskette contains only data.

There is a lot of theoretical debate as to whether a computer virus could be hidden in a data file. At the date of writing, this has not occurred and the best information the author can get is this is highly unlikely. However, the templates in many spreadsheet packages or the documents in wordprocessing programs to a certain extent get incorporated within the wordprocessing or spreadsheet package executable code. Thus, no one can say it is absolutely impossible for a virus to be spread in this manner. At the date of writing, viruses have been built into macros of spreadsheet programs by anti-virus researchers, but have not appeared as yet in the real world.

The writers of computer viruses are a group of hackers who are dedicated to writing them as an intellectual hobby or challenge. Particularly in Europe, they have banded together into user groups and share information as to the latest techniques which work best. Because viruses often cross international boundaries and there are legal differences in many jurisdictions, it is very hard to find out who the virus writer is, let alone successfully prosecute these individuals.

*The increase in incidence of virus infection in microcomputer and LANs is
such that every organization should plan on the grounds that sooner or later
they will get a virus infection.*

Thus, the rest of this chapter is devoted to firstly reducing the incidence of virus
infection, but of greater importance, to spelling out what should be done to be
able to recover from such an unfortunate incident.

How to Reduce the Incidence of Infection

Like a virus that gives us colds, the flu or makes us ill, the best way to avoid a
virus is not to come in contact with it.

Thus, every organization should have very strict rules which are to be followed
whenever programs or diskettes are received from third parties. Furthermore,
policies should carefully control the use of bulletin boards, including the
downloading of free software which they often make available.

Fundamentally, employees should be strongly discouraged if not prohibited
from running programs on their microcomputers or on the local area network
that have not been obtained for valid business purposes from a well known
supplier. This step by itself is the most important one that you can implement.

Many organizations scan all diskettes and all programs received for viruses
before the diskettes or the programs can be used.

The scan makes use of virus detection software which has been written to detect
computer viruses. It is important to point out that virus detection software is not
infallible. Firstly, they can only detect viruses which were known at the time the
particular detection package was created. There is a good probability that new
viruses will escape the detection pattern. Secondly, most detection packages do
not scan all code in programs as to do so would take too much time. Thus, the
makers of detection software tend to search for places in programs or parts of
diskettes where viruses are much more likely to be found.

Where virus detection software is used, arrangements should be made with the
supplier to obtain updated versions of the detection software say every two to
three months. In this way, the organization will be using the most up-to-date
detection software which has a better chance of deleting a virus.

Virus detection software is not that expensive. Often, copies can be acquired for
about $100. Furthermore, if there is a desire to install this software on all
workstations on the network (a recommended procedure as discussed below),
the cost can well drop to $40 to $60 per workstation.

To summarize, effective and cost efficient steps that can be taken to seriously reduce the incidence of computer virus infection include:

- Prohibiting all employees from directly using diskettes or computer programs they have acquired from third parties. This prohibition is especially important for computer games or what is known as "freeware" or "shareware", being apparently useful programs available from bulletin boards or on the street for which the creator does not demand any purchase price, or asks only for a token voluntary payment.
- All new programs or diskettes before they are used should go through an appointed systems administrator who will subject the diskettes and programs to a virus detection scan.
- Virus detection software should be kept up-to-date, with new versions obtained whenever they are issued by the supplier.

Reducing The Pain When A Virus Infection Occurs

The first statement obviously is that any organization must have backup files for all of its computer programs and data which are kept up-to-date and maintained on a regular basis. This is just good discipline against accidental destruction of data or programs. Should you be hit by a virus, these procedures will be a lifeline.

The analogy between computer viruses and viruses that affect human bodies continues. A virus does far less damage and is much easier to deal with when it is detected early.

As mentioned earlier, viruses seek to replicate themselves in all of the computer programs on the workstation or network. Thus, if a virus can be caught early, then there is less infection to eradicate. Furthermore, viruses usually want a period of time to spread themselves widely before they "activate their payload". That is, the writer of the virus wants to ensure that the virus is completely spread before it shows itself by doing damage. If you can catch the virus at this early stage, then obviously less damage has been done.

As previously discussed, one way of detecting viruses early is to have virus detection software installed on the network server and on all workstations. This detection software should be installed in such a manner that it runs every time the system is turned on. Employees may be tempted to interfere with the execution of this detection software, as it causes them to wait for a few moments while the software does its job. Instructions should be issued to employees to not interfere with the operation of this program. Sometimes microcomputer workstations and network servers are left running for a long time without being shut down. In this eventuality, the systems administrator should be responsible for ensuring the virus detection program gets run daily.

The purpose of these procedures is to check the memory and programs on workstations and LANs daily for the presence of a virus and should a virus get through the preventive procedures described earlier, hopefully it will be caught early before much damage is done.

As mentioned earlier, virus detection programs have their limitations and viruses can go undetected. Thus, some organizations wanting a higher level of security against viruses have gone to a fingerprinting technique.

Fingerprinting involves a special software program that does a complex bit map of every program on the network or in a workstation. Any disturbance or change to a computer program is then easily identified by doing the complex calculations on the bits in the program once again and comparing the results with the original value. The fingerprint software executes every time a program is called into memory to work.

Often, this technique is more effective than virus detection software to determine whether a virus has gotten into a computer system. However, there is a lot of overhead and administration associated with its use.

Firstly, the fingerprint software executes every time a program is loaded into memory. This takes time and causes users to wait. Secondly, maintenance is required as every time a program is changed, a new original fingerprint value has to be computed and then saved. This can be especially difficult with some of the new programs such as windows which tends to reconfigure itself to respond to users needs as it is being executed. In this case, a simple reconfiguration, for example, of the desktop changes the actual format of the windows program and would require its re-fingerprinting.

Thus, at the time of writing this book, fingerprinting is a technique which is best saved for only those organizations who have a high security requirement.

One manufacturer of anti-virus software has created an interesting and less burdensome variation on the fingerprinting technique.

This software stores a copy of sensitive parts of an application program when it is first called into memory. When the user of the program completes his or her work, the anti-virus software again looks at the application program in memory and compares it with the program which was originally loaded. If the program "has caught a virus" while in memory, it will have been altered and this alteration would then be caught and reported to the user by the anti-virus software. This is a good approach as it provides a defence (or at least a warning) against all types of viruses.

The organization is not solely dependent upon virus detection or fingerprinting software to notice the presence of a virus. Some alert users may report an inexplicable drop in systems response or efficiency or the programs may seem particularly slow or are not responding in the normal manner. These kinds of complaints should be investigated from the point of view that they may be due to a virus. Of course, they may be due to a host of other reasons as well, but it is a good idea to have employees report such concerns to your systems administrator for his or her consideration.

Of course, you may find out about the presence of a computer virus in the worst possible way, when it delivers its payload. In this unfortunate eventuality, at best your users will see annoying and funny messages or graphics on their screen and at worst you will find that the entire contents of your hard disk and network server have been erased.

At this stage then, steps need to be taken.

How to Recover From a Virus

The best advice is that an organization who knows it is suffering from a virus should seek professional help from individuals trained to deal with these problems. If a virus is not completely eradicated, it will only appear again in a short time.

Some viruses can be quite simply and quickly eradicated with little or no cost or disruption to your operation. At the other end of the scale, it may be necessary to completely erase the entire contents of all workstations and network servers right down to the degree of cleanliness that they would have had when first removed from the box from the manufacturer. In this latter case, the restoration of programs and files can be indeed very time consuming, as all of the directories and subdirectories need to be rebuilt and in a network environment all of the file and program attributes, password and user ids etc. need to be reconstructed.

The other perplexing problem is that while you have backup files, some of your backup files may already have the virus in them. For example, if you backup your programs and files daily, the virus may have entered your system on Monday and only have been detected on Thursday. Thus, your backups for Tuesday and Wednesday contain the virus as well. In this eventuality, the expert has to go into the backup and examine each executable file and eradicate the virus from the programs, file allocation tables, and other places where it may have been seeded.

Summary

Viruses are a real and growing threat in the microcomputer environment. All organizations should take measures to reduce the likelihood of infection. As infection is likely to occur eventually, there should be a plan developed in advance to deal with this problem.

While virus prevention and early detection can and should be everyone's responsibility, the eradication of a virus really requires the help and involvement of a specialist.

Control Considerations for the Owner/Manager

INTRODUCTION

This summary is written for the owner/manager chief financial officer, or other member of senior management having overall responsibilities for information technology. It outlines the activities required to acquire, implement, and then use small computer systems. The summary will also be useful to management of branches or departments in larger organizations who use small computer systems, who can read the text below thinking of themselves as fulfilling an owner/manager role.

Clearly, the owner/manager should be deeply involved in any computer acquisitions, although some outside help will usually be required. There are certain decisions about computer systems that only the owner/manager can make. Matters of a more technical nature, however, will require the involvement of someone, perhaps an independent EDP consultant, having more detailed knowledge of EDP (electronic data processing) and related internal control concepts. In a large organization, departmental management would turn to the information systems department for assistance.

Of course, there is no inflexible line between overall management decisions and the more technical aspects. Owner/managers interested in increasing their knowledge of EDP systems and their control should read some or all of Chapters 1 to 11.

ACQUISITION DECISIONS

Overall Decisions and Strategic Plans are Required

While the primary focus of this book is on financial systems, information processing decisions need to be made on an overall basis to meet the total needs of the organization. These overall needs include financial systems, office automation support software, and end user or personal computing.

Information technology now affects virtually every service provided by an organization as well as most of its internal activities. Thus, every organization needs a strategic information systems plan or SISP. The basic purpose of an SISP is to ensure that information technology required by an organization will be available and will be obtained in a coordinated and cohesive manner and in a logical sequence respecting priorities and needs.

A SISP can not be properly prepared unless the organization has a strategic plan. Only then can a SISP be drawn up that supports the critical success factors and major goals of the organization.

When an organization has a proper SISP (which need not necessarily be longer than 5-10 pages), then decisions on the acquisition of individual pieces of hardware or specific applications can be made in concert with this overall plan.

In drawing up overall plans, and indeed in making decisions on individual systems, it is important to bear in mind that local area networks or LANs are now a viable alternative for virtually all information processing needs for the small organization or department. Furthermore, the multiple ways in which microcomputers can be used should be considered to get the most value from computer expenditures. For example, microcomputers can be used on a stand alone basis for personal computing requirements. Attached to minicomputers or local area networks, they can access a wide variety of accounting and office automation applications and perform a wide variety of functions.

Often a new system is needed when the current system (either manual or computerized) shows one or more of the following symptoms:

- Information is costly to obtain.
- The system no longer supports changing business requirements.
- Information needed by management is not produced by the current system.
- Information is difficult to obtain.
- Information is inaccurate or incomplete.
- Information is not available on a timely basis.

Computerized systems do not necessarily save money. They should be considered not just from the point of view of reducing costs, but also from the point of view of improving efficiency because they can provide more and better information more quickly and reliably.

Getting Help in Getting Started

As noted earlier, there are certain decisions only the owner/manager can make. What information is required to profitably manage the company? How often and how quickly is that information needed? Who should have access to it? How much business growth should the new system be able to accommodate?

This information and related control requirements then have to be expressed as technical system requirements. How many terminals will be required to handle input activity at peak times? How fast should the printer be to generate the required reports? What size of disk drives are required to store all the information needed? Which computer hardware and software configurations will have the upwards compatibility necessary to provide for future growth? What kinds of controls are required to make sure that all and only authorized data is entered into the computer system and that it is safely and accurately stored? What safeguards should be put into place to reconstruct records if stored data (or even the computer) is accidentally destroyed?

The owner/manager decides why a computer system is needed and what it is to be used for and then persons with EDP skills determine the best way to fulfil those needs and estimate the cost.

There are four basic ways to obtain access to the required EDP expertise:

- Hire employees with the required EDP knowledge and skills.
- Train existing employees in basic or advanced computer skills.
- Hire EDP consultants to assist in making acquisition decisions and for support and periodic assistance once the system is in operation.
- Rely on (and possibly pay additional fees to) a software supplier for assistance (but recognize this advice may not be free from bias).

Making Decisions for Individual Computer Applications

As stated earlier, LANs as well as minicomputers are both viable alternatives as a base upon which the overall information systems needs of the organization can be built. Indeed, most of the discussion that follows applies equally to these two alternatives.

However, there are major differences between minicomputers and local area networks as regards the nature and availability of help which can be obtained from third parties. This, of course, impacts on what the organization must be able to do for itself.

In a minicomputer environment, often an outside supplier is willing, or indeed eager, to act as a sole source for the organization in meeting its hardware, operating systems and application systems requirements. If needed, the application packages which these suppliers sell can be tailored or altered to the specific requirement of the organization. In addition, an outside supplier is often willing to assist in providing or locating training courses for employees. Should problems arise, the outside supplier would provide on-site support and assistance for an additional fee.

The market for local area network support services is quite different. The hardware, the operating systems, and the applications used in local area networks are effectively sold on a retail basis. Retail stores selling any or all of the above are just that, retailers. While some help or assistance may be available, they are generally not in the business of providing an integrated service to help an organization select all of its hardware, operating systems and applications from a business perspective. These stores usually do not provide training courses and indeed may not necessarily be aware of what training courses are available for the organization's employees. Also, support in the organization's office to deal with problems or difficulties may not be available.

Thus, as a generality, purchasers of local are networks have to be far more self-sufficient than those who are seeking an integrated solution from a software supplier involving mini-computers and complex and expensive application software.

This discussion is not meant to deter organizations from looking toward local area networks as a solution. As a generality, the hardware and the software is far less expensive for local area networks. Local area networks can be a better vehicle to serve the entire processing needs of the organization, when one considers additional requirements for personal computing as well as office automation. However, when local area networks are acquired, it does mean the organization must take appropriate steps to have EDP skills in-house to be appropriately self-reliant. Thus, employees should be hired or trained to be competent "network managers", familiar with the hardware, network operating systems, and other factors needed to successfully implement and then support the use of local area networks. Local area networks are complex and powerful. The employees managing them should have appropriate EDP experience and training as well as be knowledgeable in the particular hardware and operating systems being acquired.

With these differences in mind, the following discussions apply equally to the minicomputers and local area network environment.

If the owner/manager wants to have custom computer programs written in-house for his minicomputer or LAN, people with proven EDP experience in the kind of systems to be developed should be hired. An EDP consultant can help assess prospective employees and can also be a short-term resource to help with the extra tasks during program development and implementation. (As explained later, however, it is usually best to buy rather than write programs.)

Before owner/managers can fully understand their role in choosing a computer system, they need to become familiar with the three basic parts of it:

1. The computer hardware, including peripherals such as printers, screens, keyboards, disk drives, etc.
2. The operating system software and related utilities which allow the various components of the computer hardware to work together and to interact.
3. The application software which is written to perform specific tasks such as payroll or accounts receivable.

In most cases, the application software should be chosen first and then the hardware and operating systems which will support the applications can be selected.

How to Choose an Appropriate System

The key elements to be considered in choosing application software, hardware, and operating systems are discussed below.

Application software

Whenever possible, software packages should be purchased from recognized and responsible vendors, rather than creating computer programs in-house. This is especially true if the owner/manager is a first-time computer user.

There is a wide variety of software packages, ranging in cost from a few hundred dollars for microcomputers and LANs up to tens of thousands of dollars for the most sophisticated packages for large minicomputers. Packages are not only available for different business applications such as inventory, accounts receivable, payroll and general ledger, but also for law firms. medical practices, travel agents, insurance agents, etc. through the many customized industry packages available. Usually, a package will provide most of what is required at a fraction of the cost of developing programs within the business.

Most packages provide options as to how data can be processed and the content and format of output reports. Often, they can be integrated with general ledger packages so that details are automatically posted. For larger, more sophisticated packages, the software supplier can be asked to make special modifications. The cost of even modest changes can, however, add up to be many times the cost of the original package.

Owner/managers might decide to purchase packages for most of their needs and custom develop only that one application where available packages do not really meet needs adequately. If programs are to be developed in-house, personnel with EDP expertise may have to be hired not only to initially develop, but also to continually modify and amend the programs as business circumstances, legal regulations, and the information needs of the company change. With a package, such services are usually provided by the supplier for an annual maintenance fee. Because most small computer systems use packages, the following discussion is limited to that option. The book itself discusses other options.

The first step in deciding on appropriate software is to carefully define system requirements. Failure to adequately define needs can result in systems that cost too much, do not provide all the information required, or cannot be properly controlled.

Requirements should be carefully defined, even when the perceived solution is the purchase of relatively inexpensive microcomputer software to run on a LAN. While the cash outlay might be small, the success of the system in producing relevant, accurate, and timely information is of fundamental importance to the business.

A preliminary survey to define requirements should identify:

- The procedures in the current system and the needs of management to be met by the proposed system.
- Problems or weaknesses in the current system that require correction.
- Additional useful information not currently being produced.
- Business expansion implications.

This approach will identify and document the requirements of the new system, including desired management information. Detailed definition of output and exception reports required, and management trails (defined later).

If the likely answer is to acquire a sophisticated minicomputer package, then systems requirements can be documented in a formal "request for proposal" (RFP) and suppliers can be asked to respond in writing on how their packages meet the needs stated and what the cost will be, including ongoing annual maintenance fees. Usually, the assistance of an external advisor possessing appropriate EDP technical skills is needed to prepare such RFP's and to evaluate supplier's responses. If the solution is relatively inexpensive, for example an off-the-shelf microcomputer package for a LAN, these are sold on a retail basis. Demonstration packages and manuals can be borrowed to determine whether the package meets the needs specified, or articles in microcomputer magazines can be read.

Application systems consist of much more than the programs themselves. They also include:

- Manual procedures used to obtain the information to be recorded in the computer.
- Data entry procedures.
- Procedures to operate the programs.
- Manual procedures to review and balance information output.
- Proper and effective use of information produced.
- Alternative procedures for use when the computer system is inoperative.

Documentation explaining all these procedures is important, but because it is not always automatically provided by software suppliers, the owner/manager should enquire into its availability. Also, employees need to be properly trained on how to use these systems.

Selecting computer hardware

The application software packages chosen will usually run on only a limited number of computers.

Speed and capacity will also limit choices. The hardware selected must be able to provide for all present applications as well as allow for both new applications and increased business volume.

In assessing these factors, the volume and frequency of transactions should be identified, as well as the number of related records to be stored on disk and the number of hours a day or number of shifts during which the system will operate. From this data, the required speed and capacity of hardware and peripherals can be estimated. Because of the detailed and complex technical tasks involved, this is often best done by someone with considerable EDP expertise.

Although application software is usually chosen first, a review of the hardware it will run on may cause software decisions to be re-examined. For example, a particular application package may fit a company's needs exactly, but it runs on only one type of computer that does not appear to have the additional capacity to allow for future growth. Or, the owner/manager may find an ideal payroll package for the first computer application, but the appropriate computer for that particular package may not have good packages for general ledger, sales, inventory or other applications that might be required at a later date.

Operating systems

The purpose of this discussion is to give a brief explanation of the nature and purpose of operating systems, including network operating systems which perform similar functions for local area networks. EDP expertise is required to select them.

Operating systems coordinate the various devices that make up a computer system. They transfer information from the keyboard to the central processing unit and to and from the disk drives. They send information to the printer and to screens. In addition, some operating systems will support a greater variety of peripheral equipment such as high-speed laser printers, tape drives, concurrent use of multiple terminals, etc.

In addition to the basic functions, operating systems can perform other routines. These additional functions, usually referred to as "utility programs" or "application support software programs", can be part of the operating system or may need to be purchased separately.

Utilities perform many tasks that would otherwise have to be programmed for each individual application. Utilities copy files, assist in backing up files daily or weekly, sort files in to order, manage databases, and support the receiving or sending of information through telecommunications networks. Of greatest interest, from a internal control point of view, they can provide security against unauthorized use or changes to computer files by restricting access to programs and files through passwords.

Where such functions are not built into the operating system (or cannot be purchased separately), the application packages would have to be expanded to include the capabilities required. Thus, a review of operating systems capabilities by an EDP expert could identify additional requirements for your application packages.

While utilities are necessary and make the functioning of computer systems much more efficient, they are also a considerable control risk. Utilities can be used to copy files of sensitive company data. Also, utilities usually contain routines to allow the operator to directly change the value of data stored in computer files. While this is necessary from time to time when a computer malfunction arises, it also represents an opportunity for operators to make unauthorized alterations to such items as pay rates, value of credit notes, amounts of inventory on hand, or other sensitive data (sometimes these alterations can occur without leaving any trail).

The necessary internal controls to offset these risks are discussed later on.

Making the Actual Purchase

The costs of acquiring the new computer system (including all hardware, program and maintenance fees) should be calculated, as well as the projected monthly operating costs. Any costs in excess of what the existing system costs should be considered in light of the additional benefits that might be obtained. As with any other purchase, it should be made only if the cost-benefit relationships make sense.

As previously mentioned, the hardware, operating systems, and applications for local area networks are generally sold on a retail basis. As always, it pays to shop around. Also, the ability and willingness of the retail store chain to provide assistance and help in assuring the compatibility between various parts of the hardware and software and during installation should be considered. It will also be useful to discuss with the retail chain the nature of on-site support they may be able to offer should problems and difficulties arise.

Where the more expensive minicomputers and related packages are being bought as an integrated whole from outside software houses, then it is possible to proceed in a more traditional way in obtaining quotations and bids and entering into formal contracts.

Once suppliers have been selected, a clear concise contract is needed. The contract should cover all aspects of the transaction and should be reviewed by the company's lawyer. The contract should provide for a clear understanding by both parties of their respective responsibilities, commitments, and representations, and should usually address such matters as the computer hardware, expected performance criteria, payment and financing arrangements, title or ownership to the operating software and application software, preparation and approval of detailed system specifications prior to commencement of programming (if any modifications are being requested), annual renewal and maintenance fees, and payment arrangements. The right to return the equipment and receive a refund if performance falls short of representations should also be spelled out. It should be recognized that vendors' standard contracts are usually written with the vendor's particular interests very much in mind.

The Issue of Internal Controls

The CICA Handbook (paragraph 5205.0-5) summarizes management's internal control objectives as follows:

"Management's objective for internal control is to ensure, as far as practical, the orderly and efficient conduct of the enterprise's business, including:

(a) discharge of statutory responsibilities, for example maintaining accountability to owners;
(b) profitability and minimization of costs;
(c) prevention and detection of fraud and error:
(d) safeguarding of assets;
(e) reliability of accounting records;
(f) timely preparation of reliable financial information".

Internal controls include all the procedures, activities, and methods within the company that ensure only authorized data is recorded, and it is recorded completely and accurately. Internal controls built into the operating and application software are an important part of such procedures.

The quality of application software and its features are important elements in an overall system of internal control. For example, application software should be able to edit transaction data as it is being recorded. (Edits are a series of programmed routines that assist in checking the completeness and accuracy of the data being recorded.) It should produce appropriate transaction lists or control reports so that the owner/manager or staff can verify the completeness, accuracy, and authorization of the data recorded in the computer system. Also, it should be able to list changes made to any of the data stored in computer files, including semi-permanent data such as customer names and addresses, credit limits, salary rates, and sales tax rates.

Security software (including password procedures) is important to the enforcement of an adequate division of duties within the company. As explained later, an adequate division of duties is essential for creating an effective internal control system, and proper password structures are important in creating and maintaining those divisions.

As for computer hardware, most of it is highly reliable and has the necessary checks within its circuitry to ensure that mathematical results are accurate. The owner/manager should consider, however, how to quickly obtain access to replacement hardware should the computer equipment malfunction and/or need repair.

Testing the Computer System

Packages should be fully tested before use, whenever possible by the people who will be using the new system. Testing should be comprehensive and include all phases of the system from data collection, data input and processing to production of daily, monthly, and yearly output reports. Backup and recovery restart procedures should also be tested.

Parallel testing can be effective. It involves the concurrent processing of transactions by both the software being tested and the current system being replaced. The results from both systems are compared and reconciled to ensure that the new system is functioning properly.

Test packs — creating a separate set of test files and input data — can also be used. The input data is processed against the test files using the application package. and the results are compared to manually precalculated results that show what the results of processing should be.

Packages not in widespread use should be more thoroughly tested than well established ones. Unamended packages generally need less testing than packages where you have requested the software supplier to make amendments.

On rare occasions, owners of small computer systems will choose to write their computer application software in-house, using their own EDP personnel. It is a challenging task to control the software development process and to ensure that the resulting computer programs process data accurately and completely. The most important activities to be undertaken in this environment are described in Chapter 1 under the heading "Application Software Development Implementation and Documentation".

Conversion to the New System

It is necessary to have correct opening files for the new system. Data, once recorded, can be printed and compared to source documents. Also, data entered to create the new files can be edited by the new system and manually predetermined totals for data can be balanced to output reports.

All data initially stored in the new system should be verified. For example, in an accounts receivable and sales system, in addition to checking the dollar balance for each customer, it is important to check such items as names, addresses, credit limits, sales tax status, and rates.

In other words, the records, output, and owner/manager controls discussed later in this Appendix should be appropriately applied to the initial data entered into the new system.

NON-PROCESSING CONTROLS

Non-processing controls are organizational controls that provide an appropriate segregation of duties and controls to ensure that application systems and operating systems are properly maintained and properly used. They also include controls necessary to provide security over information stored in the computer and to ensure that backup and recovery procedures are in place in case some or all of the data or programs stored in the computer are lost or destroyed.

All these controls are preventive in nature. They are designed to reduce the occurrence of errors in the first place, rather than detecting them once they have happened. Detective controls are also an important element of internal control and are discussed later under the heading "Records, Output and Owner/Manager Controls".

Organizational Controls

Because personnel resources are limited, it has always been difficult for small business to divide responsibilities among employees so that errors (accidental or otherwise) will be prevented.

The introduction of a computer system increases these concerns as:

- Computer systems tend to further concentrate duties that were segregated in manual systems.
- Certain authorization procedures (e.g., authorization of customer shipments based on credit limits) may be performed in part by computer programs.
- There may be a requirement for technical EDP expertise that existing employees do not have.
- Additional training may be necessary to provide employees with new skills.

Unless counter measures are taken, organizational problems may compromise controls in the company.

Basically, there are two modes of operating EDP systems, each of which may require a different response in the organizational structure.

1. Businesses that purchase packages usually may not employ full-time EDP specialists. Instead, EDP activities, such as copying of files, printing of reports, etc., are performed by one person who has received sufficient training.
2. In the "limited in-house EDP staff support" mode, the small business has one or more employees with EDP skills who may initially write and subsequently maintain application programs. In any event, these EDP employees operate the computer equipment, print out reports, and copy files.

Regardless of how the EDP function is organized, for the vast majority of small computer systems transactions are entered through data entry terminals in the source and user departments. Those departments also balance input and output. Thus, an accounting clerk who previously created sales invoices in a manual system may now use a terminal to record sales or create invoices.

Employees who enter transactions through terminals are recording these transactions. Such employees should not have any responsibility for initiating and authorizing transactions or have access (directly or indirectly) to related assets (e.g., bank accounts, inventory or credit notes that reduce accounts receivable).

The work of those recording transactions should be checked through the use of batch controls or transaction lists. With batch controls, all transactions are added up prior to recording and that total is then compared with a control total produced by the computer system. Transaction lists are a printout of all transactions recorded, with the details on the listing being subsequently agreed to the original source documents. Because the purpose is to check the work of the data entry clerk recording the transactions, those functions should be performed by someone else.

In ideal circumstances, initiating transactions, authorizing transactions, recording and performing batch control or transaction lists procedures should be carried out by different people. If this is not possible, Chapter 2, under the heading "Organization Controls", provides a number of examples of how duties can be divided to achieve some level of control.

Certain data entry functions may be performed in operating areas. For example, order-taking or shipping personnel may enter data directly into the computer system. If it is possible to have the same segregation of duties as in a manual environment, the impact on controls is minimal. The shipping supervisor who enters shipment data on a terminal is essentially performing the same job as filling out a shipping document. The data entered on the shipping department terminal must be subject to the same or equivalent control as a shipping document would receive in a manual system.

The requirements for organizational control in an automated small business are therefore comparable to the requirements in a manual environment. However, the means to make sure that a division of duties is respected is very different. Records are no longer locked away in filing cabinets or physically controlled. Any terminal can access any computer record unless restrictions are put in place. A large part of the solution is to use passwords to limit operating and accounting personnel to the functions properly assigned to them.

Where a company has a small EDP staff, it is important to properly segregate duties between them and the rest of the employees. The EDP department or employees performing such functions should have no responsibility for initiating transactions, recording transactions, or custody of or access to assets. If the EDP department has more than one employee, duties should be divided as much as practicable. For example, those designing systems or writing programs should not operate the computer.

Owner/managers may find it difficult to review and supervise EDP employees. Furthermore, an in-house EDP specialist may be a programmer/analyst who does not have the administrative and management skills necessary to provide assistance for strategic planning and resource allocation purposes. Sometimes the best solution is to obtain the services of an EDP consultant who can, from time to time, review the work being performed by the EDP staff and assist with strategic planning activities.

EDP employees tend to change employment frequently. If all EDP technical functions are performed by one person, and that person leaves, much knowledge of the computer systems might leave as well. Once again, the ongoing services of an EDP consultant can provide some backup knowledge. Another line of defence, especially where custom programs have been developed in-house, is to ensure that all programs are completely and fully documented.

Employees who are responsible for entering data, running the programs to produce output, and copying files should be adequately trained and have adequate documentation to instruct them in these duties. These concepts are equally important to administering passwords and see that all files are backed up.

Many internal controls performed by people in a manual system are now "automated controls" performed by software. Such controls include edit routines, computations such as sales taxes, extensions, and footings on sales invoices, and password procedures to help enforce the required segregation of duties. The application software may effectively authorize transactions, for example, by comparison of balances outstanding and the value of sales orders with credit limits prior to shipment. Thus, program changes to applications must be controlled. Obviously, changing software could affect how internal control is exercised in the organization.

RECORDS CONTROLS, OUTPUT CONTROLS, AND OWNER/MANAGER CONTROLS

All of these control areas, which can be described as "Processing Controls", are the most important element of any system of internal control.

Processing controls are controls over the actual processing of transactions through the system. They should be designed to provide reasonable assurance that accounting records are complete, accurate, and, authorized. In addition, adequate management trails should be produced; that is, the system should supply sufficient detail, both to properly control and use computer reports and to meet legislative requirements (i.e., those of the Income Tax Act).

Before discussing all of these controls, it is necessary to define a few terms. Also, an example is given which will be referred to when discussing processing control concepts.

Computer data basically takes two forms: transaction (or accounting) data and semi-permanent data.

1. *Transaction Data*

   Transaction data relates to individual transactions flowing from day-to-day activities with third parties or employees. Thus, shipping reports, purchase invoices, time cards, cheques issued, and deposits made all contain transaction data. Each transaction data item relates to an individual economic event, such as the shipment of particular goods or the time worked by a specific employee.

2. *Semi-permanent data*

   Semi-permanent data is information that is not changed as the result of day-to- day business events. It is stored in machine-readable form to be used over and over again. It is more cost effective to store and re-use this information than to enter it each time a particular transaction occurs.

   For example, in relation to customers, the following semi-permanent data might be entered in to the computer system:

   - Customer number
   - Customer name
   - Mailing address
   - Ship to address
   - Credit limit
   - Payment terms
   - Sales tax status.

Therefore, to prepare a sales invoice for a particular customer, it is necessary only to give the customer's number and to enter details of the goods or services rendered. The programs can refer to the stored semi-permanent data to get the customer's name and address and to check the credit limit to see if the rendering of the service or shipment of goods will exceed the pre-authorized credit limit.

Semi-permanent data is stored for many kinds of business transactions, including:

- Customer information (as illustrated above)
- Product information and costs for the inventory records
- Vendor information for accounts payable systems
- Payroll information for personnel and payroll systems
- Product descriptions and sales prices for sales systems
- Inventory costs for inventory cost systems.

Semi-permanent data may be recorded in separate computer files, may be built into look-up tables stored on disk, or can be contained within the application software.

Computer systems can be structured to capture data off-line or on-line and can process data in batch or real-time mode.

1. *Off-line*

    In off-line data capture, data is captured in a separate device not attached to the central computer hardware. For example, to record sales orders, a special machine may be used that is not attached and cannot communicate to the central processing unit, except by the physical transfer of the medium on which the machine has recorded data (i.e., floppy disk, tape cassette, etc.).

2. *On-line*

    On-line usually means that the device used to capture data, for example, a data entry terminal, is connected to the computer hardware. This means that the data can be edited by computer programs stored in the computer as it is being entered and many types of errors can be corrected "on-line".

3. *Batch systems*

    In batch systems, transactions are accumulated in a separate file. Then, periodically, the stored data is processed against other files. For example, shipping reports would be written into a separate shipping report file as they are recorded. Computer programs are run periodically to produce the sales invoices, post them to the accounts receivable records, and to reflect the shipments as reductions in inventory.

4. *Real-time*

In real-time processing, all related computer files are updated immediately as the data is captured. Thus, as each shipping report is recorded during the business day, sales, accounts receivable, and inventory records are updated. In a real-time mode, though, printed output (i.e., sales invoices, etc.) is generally prepared at the end of the day.

Because the majority of small business systems run in an on-line, batch update mode, this mode will be discussed here. Other modes of operation are covered in the main text.

A Typical Computer Application

A company has purchased a system to computerize its accounts receivable records and the recording of related shipments, sales invoices, credit notes and cash receipts. The cash receipts portion is described below.

Mr. Small, the owner/manager, opens the mail, reviews cheques from customers, and separates the remittance advices from the cheques themselves. He adds up the cheques on an adding machine tape for eventual agreement with the bank deposit and gives the cheques to Mr. Baker (the chief accountant) for deposit. The remittance advices go to Mrs. Jones, the receptionist.

Mrs. Jones uses a listing showing each customer's name and account number to enter an account number on each remittance advice. She also splits the remittance advices into batches of 10 and runs an adding machine tape to show the total for each batch. The remittance advices and batch totals are given to Mrs. Cooper, whose duties include recording cash receipts.

Mrs. Cooper sits down at a data entry terminal, turns it on, enters her valid user ID and password, and sees a screen that appears as follows:

```
                1.   BILLING
                2.   CASH RECEIPTS
                3.   PAYROLL
                4.   ACCOUNTS PAYABLE
                5.   DISBURSEMENTS
                6.   JOURNAL ENTRIES


                     YOUR CHOICE   [        ]
```

The cash receipts recording function is accessed by entering a 2, but Mrs. Cooper accidentally enters a 3 (payroll). The system responds with a message that the password is not authorized for the payroll function requested. Realizing her mistake, Mrs. Cooper returns to the main menu, selects 2 for cash receipts processing, re-enters her password, and the system now responds with the following screen:

```
                     CASH RECEIPTS
                      PROCESSING


    CUSTOMER NUMBER     [        ]    _____
```

The computer system is asking Mrs. Cooper to enter the account number for the first payment. Mrs. Cooper enters 4673. Referring to the semi-permanent data, the computer system finds this customer number and responds with the customer name. It is Mrs. Cooper's responsibility to compare that customer name on the screen with the remittance advice. If it is not the same, the receptionist probably coded the customer number incorrectly. If Mrs. Cooper does not notice the error, the wrong customer will be credited.

If the names correspond, Mrs. Cooper enters the amount of the cash receipt. The cash receipt is for $693.00 and Mrs. Cooper enters $693. The system responds by telling Mrs. Cooper there is an input error as she has failed to enter a decimal point. Mrs. Cooper enters the amount by adding the decimal point and two zeros. The system responds by reporting that the customer is entitled to a $5.35 cash discount (based on program logic allowing cash discounts of 1% where the date of payment is within 20 days of the date of shipment). The customer, however, is claiming a cash discount of $7.00. Mrs. Cooper now must choose to allow the computer-produced amount to stand or override the system to record the cash discount the customer has claimed. She decides to do the latter and enters an override of $7.00.

The next nine remittances are entered in a similar manner. After 10 remittances have been recorded, the system prompts Mrs. Cooper to enter a batch control total and she enters the amount predetermined by the receptionist. The program compares the total of the ten remittances it has recorded so far with the total entered by Mrs. Cooper and reports a difference of $90. Mrs. Cooper selects an option in the system to display the name and amounts of all remittances entered so far. By comparison with the remittance advices, she notes that the cash remittance from Thomas Limited is incorrectly recorded as $890, instead of $980. She selects a menu option which allows her to correct this and the computer system accepts the batch. Mrs. Cooper then proceeds to record all other remittance batches.

Mrs. Rosen is responsible for daily batch processing. Accordingly, at the end of the business day, using an appropriate menu selection and her password, she has the computer system process the cash receipts recorded by Mrs. Cooper (and other transactions recorded by other employees). Among other reports, the computer system produces the following transaction listing for cash receipts:

```
              Cash Receipts Transaction        October 2, 19XX
                       Listing

   Customer      Customer      Cash       Discount     Standard     Total
   Number        Name        Received      Given       Discount     Credit

    4673       J. JONES        693.00       7.00         5.35        700.00

    4269       D. THOMAS LTD.  980.00        -            -          980.00
```

```
   TOTALS                   $17,492.60   $1,426.20    $1,312.80   $18,918.80
                            ==========   =========    =========   ==========
```

Note the listing of cash receipts shows each cash receipt processed. This will provide a backup for transactions should it be necessary to re-enter them if the updated accounts receivable file were destroyed or lost. The report also shows cash discounts as calculated by the computer system and a separate column of actual cash discounts allowed. Mr-Small can review the instances where Mrs. Cooper has over-ridden the system and allowed a cash discount greater than the computer system suggests.

This report goes to Mr. Baker, chief accountant, who compares the total cash receipts on the listing with the total on the bank deposit receipted by the bank. In turn, Mr. Small will agree the total of the bank deposit with the adding machine list he made first thing in the morning to make sure that all cash was deposited.

The chief accountant then enters the total cash receipts, discounts allowed, and total of accounts receivable credits in a batch control log and initials the log to show he has checked these totals. The control log appears as follows:

```
┌─────────────────────────────────────────────────────────────────┐
● ┆                          CONTROL LOG                            ┆ ●
●                                                                     ●
● ┆                        CASH RECEIPTS                            ┆ ●
●                                                                     ●
● ┆                        OCTOBER, 19XX                            ┆ ●
●                                                                     ●
●                                                          Total      ●
● ┆                   Cash          Discounts           Credits     ┆ ●
●                                                                     ●
●      October 1       $20,246.30      $2,006.40        $25,252.70    ●
●                                                                     ●
●      October 2        17,492.60       1,426.20         18,918.80    ●
●                                                                     ●
●                                                                     ●
●                                                                     ●
──────────────────────────────────────────────────────────────────
● ┆     FOR MONTH        $40,738.90      $3,432.60        $44,171.50 ┆ ●
                        ==========      =========        ==========
● ┆                                                                 ┆ ●
└─────────────────────────────────────────────────────────────────┘
```

An important use will be made of this control log either weekly or monthly. Note that the control log shows the total value of credits to accounts receivable from cash receipts. Other control logs would show the total changes to accounts receivable resulting from the processing of sales transactions, credit notes, or journal vouchers.

Control logs can be used to determine that only authorized transactions have been processed against receivable records, thus helping identify whether utility programs or other methods have been used to make unauthorized changes to receivables without leaving a trail.

The control logs are used as follows:

- Take the balance of accounts receivable on the most recent prior accounts receivable trial balance.
- Add the total of debits to accounts receivable arising from sales since the last trial balance.
- Subtract the total of credits to accounts receivable arising from cash receipts, credit notes or adjustments, since the last trial balance.

The resulting total should equal the total of accounts receivable on the current computer-produced trial balance. If it does not, perhaps unauthorized transactions have been made to accounts receivable or perhaps the staff has processed transactions against out-of-date or incorrect versions of the accounts receivable files. In any event, the difference should be investigated and any errors corrected.

217

Total value of accounts receivable

October 1, 19XX per trial balance and general ledger		$ 88,600.27
Add value of sales invoices processed during October, per invoice control log		61,426.20
		$ 150,026.47

Less

cash receipts for October, per manually maintained control log	44,171.50	
credit notes for October, per manually maintained control log	1,746.21	
adjustment per journal entry No. 21	3.46	
		45,921.17
Predicted balance October 31, 19XX		$ 104,105.30
Total per computer-produced accounts receivable trial balance		$ 104,105.30
Differences requiring investigation		$ NIL

Using the above typical application, several categories of internal control will now be identified and discussed in general terms.

Asset protection controls

Asset protection controls serve to protect assets against theft or loss. In the above example. cash receipts assets are protected by restricting access to cheques received in the mail to the owner and chief accountant. Clerical staff were given only the remittance advices.

Asset comparison controls

These controls compare assets on hand as shown in the books with a source that is independent from the accounting records. In the example, the transaction listing of cash receipts was compared to the bank deposit receipted by the bank, thus ensuring that entries in the books agreed with some external source. Other examples of asset comparison controls would be physical inventory counts and bank reconciliations.

Collectively, asset protection and asset comparison controls can be thought of as owner/manager controls because such controls normally require an involvement of the owner/manager or the chief financial officer. All small businesses should have owner/manager controls, regardless of whether they are using computerized or manual systems.

Balance controls

Balance controls provide an independent check over the completeness and integrity of accounting records. In the illustration, the balancing of totals from the accounts receivable trial balance to an independently determined control total (derived from control logs) is a good example of balance controls.

Balance controls recognize that there are ways to change data in computer files other than using application software and authorized procedures. Therefore, balance controls seek to prove that important computer files have been affected by only authorized transactions processed in an approved manner. If utility programs had been used to accidentally or fraudulently alter the company's accounts receivable records in the example, this would probably have been detected by the balance controls.

Records controls

Records controls — all controls over the recording of data (input controls), over computations performed by the system (computation controls), and over the output produced (output controls) — are the controls most affected by the introduction of computer processing.

In the example, input controls were applied to cash receipts by providing batch control totals (computed by the receptionist and balanced by Mrs. Cooper in detail and by the chief accountant in total) and having edit routines in the programs to check the accuracy of Mrs. Cooper's work.

Computation controls existed in that the computer program was calculating discounts actually earned by customers. In addition, the correct processing of the cash receipts in the daily update routine depends on the correctness of the computer programs that ensure cash receipts are credited to the customer entered, that new unpaid balances for each customer are correctly computed, that totals on output reports are correct, etc. These controls actually consist of correct logic in the application software.

Output controls determine the accuracy and completeness of output before it is accepted. In the example, the cash receipts transaction listing was shown to be correct by agreeing it in total to the bank deposit slip. In addition, differences between cash discounts calculated by the system and other amounts that may have been recorded by Mrs. Cooper were subject to review and approval.

Menus

Menus are an excellent way of structuring computer applications so that employees can readily "set up the computer" to perform a particular task, when those employers do not have any special knowledge of computers or how they work. Also, by tying particular menus and the functions which they contain to particular passwords, a good division of duties can be created. Employees will quickly learn that their passwords will enable them to activate and use only certain menus.

Passwords

Passwords are an important control as they serve to enforce a division of duties. In the example, Mrs. Cooper had to use the correct password to record cash receipts; her password would not allow her to perform other functions. The company that Mrs. Cooper works for also has a data entry terminal in the shipping department, used to record shipments to customers. The shipper's password would permit the entry of only shipping data.

Similarly, Mrs. Rosen, who runs the daily update routines, has a password that only permits her to produce these output reports and does not allow her to enter transactions.

Management trails

Adequate management trails supply sufficient detailed information to enable the reconstruction of records and help ensure that control can be exercised by the owner/manager. Management trails are also important should a third party question a balance with them or should some regulatory authority (such as Revenue Canada) want to audit the records. Certain legislation requires management trails to be left until permission is received to throw the records out.

In the example, the cash receipts listing provides a good management trail. It lists details of all cash receipts recorded every day and could be used to re-enter cash receipts transactions should the current accounts receivable file be accidentally destroyed. The highlighting of differences between cash discounts actually due to customers and those Mrs. Cooper has decided to allow enables management to review any extra discounts granted for customer relations purposes.

The various aspects of all of these control areas are now discussed in more detail.

Input Controls

Input controls relate to information requiring a record to be made in the company's accounts. Thus, input has to do with such things as recording shipments, receiving reports, purchase invoices, cash receipts, changes in customer's credit limits, and changes in the prices of products.

Entering a transaction normally starts when the data entry clerk receives a source document. The clerk enters the data using a terminal. The transactions then update previously stored data. It should be noted that the entry of a transaction will often trigger further business activity as well as having an impact on other transactions. For example, entering a sales order can lead to the shipment of goods or entering a raise in wage rates will increase future pay cheques.

In some instances, no physical source document will exist. For example, sales orders may be accepted over the telephone from customers, with a sales order clerk entering the data directly into a terminal. In such cases, it would be prudent to print out all orders, or at least larger orders, for subsequent approval before any shipment takes place.

Input controls are also needed for semi-permanent data. For example, credit limits, sales prices, and salary rates change from time to time. Incorrect sales prices or salary rates can result in selling goods at a lesser price than intended or paying employees more than they have earned. Because some semi-permanent data is used over and over and can affect numerous business transactions, an error in that data can actually create a greater loss than would occur from the incorrect recording of a single transaction.

All the procedures discussed below, from the creation of source documents to the recording and balancing of the information and producing the output report, should be applied to both semi-permanent and transaction data.

Approval of source documents

All source documents should be approved by the owner/manager or someone authorized to do so for that particular type or value of transaction. Application software can assist the approval process by:

- Providing computer-produced exception reports of significant transactions (i.e., over a certain value) for owner/manager review.
- Using programmed authorization routines, such as checking a sales order to see whether the customer's authorized credit limit would be exceeded if a sales order were accepted.

Edit routines

Edit routines check input for errors to the extent possible through programmed logic. In the earlier example, some input errors by Mrs. Cooper were caught by these programmed routines.

The sufficiency and correct operation of edit routines are tested at the time an application system is acquired or amended. Edit routines cannot catch all errors. For example, they cannot catch unauthorized transactions or incorrect transactions that have plausible values. Therefore, batch control totals or equivalent procedures are also required.

Batch controls

Batch control totals are an effective control over the completeness and accuracy of the work of terminal operators.

In the earlier example, Mrs. Cooper entered a cash payment as $890.00 when it really was $980.00. If Mrs. Cooper had not corrected the error, the total cash receipts report would not have agreed with the bank deposit. In this case, the bank deposit prepared for another purpose also served as an independent batch control total. In many instances, such as controlling total quantities recorded for shipments, batch totals are created purely for control purposes.

A data entry clerk does not need a source document to enter information into a computer system. It would be quite possible for Mrs. Cooper to either accidentally or on purpose record cash receipts even if she did not have a remittance advice. Thus, the balancing of recorded transactions with some independently predetermined control total is an effective and required technique to detect this kind of error.

Batch control totals can check the accuracy of only the particular information for which the total is created. It cannot check other aspects of the transactions being recorded. For example, batch control totals would not catch an error if Mrs. Cooper had credited Mr. A's payment to Mr. B's account.

For better control, transaction lists can be used. They show all the details of the transactions recorded. Another employee then checks all the details to the original source documents.

A control log should be kept to document that transaction lists or batch control totals have, in fact, been compared and balanced. In addition, the totals in the control logs will be important in performing balance controls discussed later.

Rejected transactions

Edit routines often lead to the rejection of incorrect data. Any rejected transactions should be controlled to ensure they are promptly and accurately resubmitted for processing. If it is not possible to correct the error and re-record the transaction at the time, unprocessed rejects result. This should be detected when differences are identified between predetermined batch control totals and the value of transactions accepted by the system or when source documents are compared to transaction lists. Unless the transactions are subsequently corrected and re-entered, the accounting records will be incomplete.

The proper use of a control log can manage the error correction activity. Details of differences between batch control totals and the totals of transactions processed are documented in the control log, together with details of the rejected transactions making up the difference and the dates when the rejected items were properly recorded.

Batch control totals, transactions listings, and control logs should also be used to control the recording of semi-permanent data. Examples of batch controls and transaction lists to control semi-permanent data are found in Chapter 4.

Division of duties

Data entry clerks should not have access to assets. Access to assets includes the authority to approve credit notes, sign cheques, ship inventory, etc. as well as physical access. It is a basic tenet of good internal control that custody of assets and the accounting function should always be separated.

To summarize, it is important to segregate the following functions as much as possible:

- Initiation and authorization of transactions.
- Recording of transactions.
- Custody of assets.
- Balancing of batch control totals (or transaction lists).

Password procedures

In a computerized environment, it is difficult to enforce a division of duties without password controls (some technical books refer to this as logical access controls). In the absence of passwords, any computer terminal could be used for any purpose, allowing a knowledgeable employee to record any kind of transaction, change computer files, or even change computer programs.

As data entry terminals or microcomputers serving in this capacity are frequently dispersed throughout an organization. it is extremely important to implement password procedures. The maximum ability of a system to provide password control was fixed when the application software and related operating systems were selected. It is now important to make use of those capabilities.

To gain access through a password protection system, users should have to enter both a password and their own, unique user identification. The password and user identification are compared by the computer system with passwords on a password file. If there is a match, the user is assumed to be the authorized user and is allowed to continue to perform any function permitted by that password. If there is no match, the user cannot continue.

Of course, one password could provide access to the entire system. Such powerful passwords should generally be restricted to the owner/manager. Typically, passwords allow access to only a specific function (e.g., cash receipts) or can be based on the function to be performed (deletes).

Passwords are not only important to ensure that employees are restricted to functions they are authorized to perform, but are indeed important to ensure that the entire computer system is protected against unauthorized access by outsiders. This is particularly important when the computer system (including LANs) has dial-up lines which allow company employees or management to access computer files from outside the office. Chapter 8 on local area networks has an exhaustive discussion as to the additional controls and password protection procedures which may be needed when dial-up lines exist.

The foregoing discussion of password procedures has been simplified in order to illustrate the concepts. In practice, the creation and maintenance of logical access security so that passwords are present and effective is a very complex and technical area. It is necessary to protect access to the computer records initially at the operating system level and then, once access is gained to the entire system, to focus the user and channel him or her only to those particular functions within a given application that they are authorized to use. Thus, often passwords have to be designed or at least correlated at both the operating system and application system level. This is another example of why employees running computer systems within a smaller business or department must receive adequate technical training and support and have an appropriate background of skills and knowledge of the EDP environment.

Output Controls

In a computerized environment, output may include negotiable instruments (e.g., cheques), accounting reports (e.g., general ledger trial balances), control reports (e.g., transaction listings), and other documents such as invoices, customer statements, and payroll registers.

It is important to remember that all computer output is the result of transaction data (including changes to semi-permanent data) and the application of logic in computer programs.

As previously illustrated in this Appendix, errors can and do occur in either of these processes. Therefore it is very important to check computer output. Do not believe that "computers cannot make mistakes". People entering transactions into computers, creating or changing computer programs, or operating utility programs can and do make mistakes.

The output control procedures suggested below are neither time consuming nor complex and are particularly appropriate for the small business environment. Output controls are not infallible, however, and do not necessarily detect every error. For example, transactions not written up initially on source documents and incorrect information entered on source documents will probably not be detected by output controls. For these reasons, both input and output controls are needed.

No output should be accepted as valid until it has been subjected to one or more of the following:

- Balance controls (by far the best choice).
- Review by the owner/manager or another senior employee designated to do so.
- In some instances, a periodic test check of calculations.

Most owner/managers are familiar with how, in a manual environment, subsidiary ledgers are controlled by use of the general ledger control account. Such a control account contains a summary of all entries in the subsidiary ledger and, as such, should always be equal to the sum of the accounts in the subsidiary records. If the control account is posted from a source different than that used for the subsidiary ledger, it provides an effective check on the subsidiary ledger.

Usually, no such distinction exists in a computer environment. Normally, the computer programs both keep the detailed records (subsidiary ledgers) and create totals for entering into the general ledger control account, always in reference to the same source documents entered by the same person.

Control can be re-established by building up totals in manually maintained control logs to predetermine the overall control total that should be contained in a computer file such as accounts receivable, accounts payable, bank accounts, or total payroll costs.

Such a balance control in the cash receipts was cited in the example given earlier. In that case, all cash receipts as recorded in the control log were totalled. Similar control totals for sales, credit notes and adjustments were then used to predetermine the total value of accounts receivables before the accounts receivable trial balance was produced by the computer system. The cash receipts total would also be used to help predetermine the bank balance.

Normally, balance control procedures would be established over those files which act as subsidiary ledgers, such as accounts receivable, accounts payable, inventory, fixed asset, and other files that are accumulations of one transaction type (such as total sales, month, and year to date).

It is also important to maintain balance controls over semi-permanent data. As previously explained, errors in semi-permanent data can be very costly because the processing of all transactions that refer to the semi-permanent data will be in error. Balance controls are maintained over semi-permanent data in a similar manner to the process described above.

For example, sales prices may be maintained on the computer system. One could take the total dollar value of all sales prices at the beginning of a period, add the dollar value of prices of all new products, deduct the sales prices of all products deleted since the last balancing procedure and adjust for changes in any sales process. (All of these figures would come from control logs.) This predetermines the total dollar value of sales prices in the computer files, which could be agreed to a printout of the total of sales prices in the computer file as at the end of a period. Such totals for control purposes are often referred to as "hash" totals.

It is often a good idea to periodically print out all semi-permanent data and check it thoroughly (or at least review it for reasonableness). The depth and frequency of such efforts will depend on the following:

- The frequency of additions, deletions and changes
- The dollar value of accounting transactions that would make use of a semi-permanent data
- The number of semi-permanent data items.

Some semi-permanent data is changed annually, for example, when all employees are given pay increases at a particular time of the year. Thus, strong controls would be instituted at that particular time while less formal controls might be required throughout the year when changes are minimal.

Because balance controls are so important, they should be performed by someone who does not have custody of assets or is not involved in day-to-day data entry functions.

Wherever possible, output reports should be verified before they are used. For example, an analysis of sales by customer, product, or region can be agreed to independent "sales year-to-date" totals.

It also makes good sense to review output before it is used or distributed. Thus, sales invoices should be briefly reviewed before they are mailed. Payroll cheques and payroll registers should not be accepted without review simply because they have been printed by computer. The owner/manager should use knowledge of the business, the employees and their pay rates to make sure that payroll register and payroll cheques seem reasonable.

It is still advisable to manually re-perform and verify the accuracy of important computations from time to time. The frequency of such checking will vary with:

- The sensitivity of the calculation
- The complexity of the calculation
- The chance that a required change may not have been made
- The frequency of program changes
- When changes occur (new changes are more likely to contain undetected errors as errors usually come to light with the passage of time).

Management Trails and Computer Operations Controls

Management trails

These controls help ensure that an adequate management trail exists and that the system is properly run each day.

A management trail allows one to subsequently determine that each transaction has been processed and is included in the summary totals in the general ledger and other accounting records. It also allows a summary total to be taken from the general ledger (for example, total sales or total repair expense for a month) and, at a later date, identify the individual transactions that comprise that total.

Without management trails, it may not be possible to trace any differences that come to light back to the source and to then correct them. Moreover, it will be impossible to determine what employee processed which transactions making it difficult to hold employees responsible for inadvertent or purposeful errors. Furthermore, a good management trail is an essential element in the backup of the system.

Good management trails usually have most of the following features:

- The appearance of each transaction entered on a control report, indicating who entered the data. Note: This rule should apply to both transaction and semi-permanent data.
- Unique numbers or codes identifying each transaction to facilitate tracing to and from computer output.
- Daily or periodic printouts of transaction totals or transaction lists.
- Printout of sufficient information to enable a manual check of the accuracy of computer computations.
- Clearly defined retention policies for source documents, printouts, and master accounting and semi-permanent data in machine-readable form.

A good management trail also provides sufficient information for management decision purposes. Output is used in making vital decisions in a company. Therefore, output should be produced in sufficient detail to assist in making management decisions. For example, it probably would not be useful for a computer system to report only total sales each month; instead, total sales by product line, salesperson, major customer, etc., would be more useful.

Finally, there are many legislative requirements for the production and maintenance of detailed data. Business records are necessary in order to meet the requirements of the applicable corporations acts, the income and sales tax acts, the consumer protection acts, etc. Legislative requirements should be addressed when application packages are acquired or developed. In addition, it is essential to establish retention policies covering all data in machine-readable form and printouts of the management trail, which together will ensure adherence to those legislative requirements. This can be a complex area and usually some consulting advice is required.

Controls over system use

All transactions must be processed using the correct data files. For example, suppose that on Wednesday morning, the computer operator starts up the system using accounts receivable and sales data files from Monday rather than Tuesday night. The operator then proceeds to enter Wednesday's sales and other transactions. All transactions processed on Tuesday will not be in the system.

Programmed routines can help ensure use of the correct data file. For example, many packages require the operator to enter today's date when the system is turned on in the morning. The system compares that date with the date of creation recorded on the file being used. Should there be a difference of more than one day, a warning message is sent to the operator, which unfortunately is sometimes ignored. Other technical means are available which may be even more effective.

Where removable disks or tape cartridges are used, each disk or tape should be labelled stating its creation date on the outside of its container. In this way, the operator can check the date to ensure that apparently the correct data file is being loaded into the computer.

Also, the balance controls discussed previously can be of great use in detecting the use of incorrect files.

Finally, it is essential to ensure that control reports such as batch control totals or transaction lists are printed and copies of files needed for backup are created. Written instructions are helpful. They should list in detail the control and management trail reports for each application to be produced daily, weekly, and monthly. It can be useful to photocopy the instructions and have the operator sign off and file the photocopies daily to show that all required output and copies were produced.

Some small computer systems provide software controls to encourage good discipline. For example, a sales/receivable system may "refuse" to print sales invoices unless the transactions listing for shipments has been produced; or it may "refuse" to update the accounts receivable balances for cash receipts until the cash receipts file has been copied for backup purposes.

Unfortunately, data files can be damaged quite easily and while not a common occurrence, it happens sufficiently frequently that recovery plans to recoup the lost data must be in place. Tapes or disks can be lost, accidentally erased, or scratched by read/write heads if there is any dust on the surfaces.

Recovery begins with the backup copy and then transactions since that backup was made are re-entered; it is important to copy the backup file before proceeding with the above reconstruction.

Asset Protection and Comparison Controls

Although asset protection and comparison controls are among the most important controls in a small business environment, they are the ones least affected by computerization. Therefore, most owner/managers are familiar with these controls.

Books and records by themselves do not provide any protection over a company's assets. No matter how complete, accurate, and authorized records may be, it would still be possible, in the absence of other controls, for assets to be stolen, lost, or misplaced. It would also be possible for the company to become committed to transactions that are not economically advantageous and that contravene the policies established by the owner/manager.

Asset protection controls are separate and distinct from other controls. Nevertheless, they are applied on a day-today basis, often at the same time as the other controls. They are discussed in more detail later on in this Appendix.

The final and most important group of controls consists of comparison controls. Their purpose is to determine whether any assets have been lost or stolen or to determine whether there are any errors in the accounting records and correct them. They include procedures such as taking a physical inventory and comparing the results to book records, and bank reconciliations which compare cash in the bank with amounts recorded in the company's books and records. These controls function on a periodic basis only.

Comparison controls can be thought of as the keystone or final method of proof in any system of internal control. On the one hand, records controls exist to ensure complete, accurate, and authorized books and records. On the other hand, asset protection controls help ensure that a company's assets are not lost, misplaced, or stolen. In theory, a comparison of assets on hand with the books and records should never disclose any differences. In practice, however, differences almost always exist, as all systems of internal control have inherent limitations and are designed with cost effectiveness relationships in mind. Frequently, the owner/manager thinks it is better to incur a modest loss than to spend more than the amount of the potential loss to prevent it.

Where a comparison discloses significant differences, they should be carefully investigated to determine whether they are primarily due to errors in the books or whether assets have been lost, misplaced, or stolen. If errors caused the differences, they should be corrected and steps taken to strengthen the internal accounting controls to prevent an unacceptable level of inaccuracies or incompleteness in the records. If they are the result of assets being lost or stolen, steps should be taken to determine how that occurred and then to strengthen the internal controls to reduce the probability that it could happen again. More frequent comparisons in the future would also be advisable until differences settle down to an acceptable level.

Controls over books and records, controls to protect assets, and controls to make comparisons are all interrelated. Books and records help safeguard assets by providing a source against which assets on hand can be compared (this was the major purpose of accounting for many centuries). Asset protection controls depend, for the most part, on the availability of documentary evidence supplied by the accounting process (for example, goods should be released for shipment only when a properly approved shipping order has been presented, and cheques should be signed only after supporting vouchers have been reviewed). Finally, comparison controls serve to compare assets on hand with those recorded in the books and records.

Asset protection and comparison controls can often effectively serve as compensating controls for absent or weak controls in other areas. Unacceptably large losses could, however, be incurred if such controls were applied too infrequently or if preventative controls were so weak that large losses could be incurred over a short time.

Basic nature of asset protection controls

Assets need to be protected against a range of risks such as fraud by company employees or third parties, accidental loss or misplacement, and loss by fire. While the precise nature of the controls used will vary from asset to asset, the techniques employed will be one or more of the following:

1. Ensuring proper division of duties between those having custody of or access to assets and those who keep books and records.
2. Having custodians (often the owner/manager) release assets only after they have carefully reviewed appropriate documentation.
3. Providing, where appropriate, joint access to assets by two employees.
4. Implementing appropriate physical safeguards to protect assets against unauthorized access.
5. Reviewing the adequacy of insurance coverage on a regular basis is also a good idea.

Each of these techniques is discussed below.

1. *Division of duties*

   The effectiveness of using books and records to verify that all the company's assets are accounted for, is for the most part, impaired if physical custody over assets and the ability to make entries in the books and records are in the hands of one employee. This is the primary reason why accountants have always stressed the necessity of dividing custody of assets from recordkeeping activities.

   It is important to realize that custody does not mean just physical control; any person who has the authority to reduce or release an asset has effective custody over that particular asset. For example, employees who are able to sign cheques have effective custody over the company's bank accounts. Those who are able to approve credit notes or journal entries to reduce accounts receivable have effective custody of the accounts receivable.

   Even when a company has only a small number of employees, it is usually possible to divide duties involving custody of assets and the authority to record entries or otherwise affect books and records. This division of duties should come before any other division of duties suggested in this text.

   Chapter 7 gives several examples of how custody of assets might be segregated from recordkeeping for major business functions.

2. *Review of appropriate documentation*

   For effective protection, those having custody of assets should obtain and review appropriate documentary evidence before releasing any asset. Without this safeguard, asset protection controls serve little or no purpose. For example, a shipper should make sure that he or she has a valid shipping order, initialled as required by company procedures, before shipping any items to a customer. Owner/managers or others signing cheques should obtain and review underlying supporting documents such as purchase invoices, purchase orders, and receiving reports before signing cheques.

3. *Joint custody over-assets*

   Where assets, either because of their nature or value (for example, small but valuable inventory items), are vulnerable to theft or physical loss, joint custody is appropriate even though a later physical inventory might disclose a shortage.

   Similarly, unless the owner/manager is also the one signing the cheques, banking resolutions should require the signature of two employees before the cheque is honored by the bank. The bank would be instructed not to cash cheques made payable to the company but to require their deposit instead. A withdrawal of the funds would, of course, be possible only with the joint signatures.

4. *Physical safeguards*

Physical safeguards are the oldest internal controls used by companies and include safety deposit boxes, locks, fences, guards, etc. In designing a system of physical safeguards, the following factors should be taken into account:

- Physical assets such as inventories need safeguarding. The books and records (including computer programs and data) also constitute an asset and need protection. For example, if accounts receivable records are lost or destroyed, the company could suffer a significant monetary loss. Physical safeguards exist to keep people outside the company from getting access to the company's assets. They also exist to fix responsibility to a particular company employee. For example, an employee responsible for the custody of valuable inventories cannot be held responsible for any shortages if the inventory was stored in a place where other employees could easily obtain access to it.
- Blank forms should be physically safeguarded. Blank cheques, credit notes, and journal vouchers should also be carefully controlled as they could be used to obtain unauthorized release of assets.

5. *Insurance coverage*

Insurance is part of an effective overall system of internal control. Insurance should not only cover employee theft (through bonding), but also cover loss by outside theft, fire, etc. Insurance should be considered for physical assets such as inventories and fixed assets, as well as for potential losses of other assets if the books and records were destroyed.

Insurance should not be considered as a replacement for an adequate system of internal control. Unless the system of internal control can detect that a loss has, in fact, taken place and provides sufficient documentary evidence to support a claim, insurance recoveries may not be possible.

Basic nature of comparison controls

Comparison controls comprise the final detective control to determine whether there are any errors or omissions in the books of account and/or whether any assets have been stolen, lost, or misplaced.

Comparison controls should not be limited to inventories and fixed assets, but should encompass almost all assets owned by a company. For example, a bank reconciliation constitutes a comparison of cash in the bank (according to the bank's records) with that shown in the company's books. Reconciling items require investigation and can disclose errors or omissions in the company's books or items recorded incorrectly by the bank. Similarly, if a company sends out an accounts receivable statement and the customer complains, the probability is raised that there is a difference between the real asset (what the customer is willing to pay) and the books and records.

While the precise nature of comparison controls will vary from asset to asset and company to company. the following techniques are often useful in applying such controls:

- Frequent comparisons should be made, taking into consideration the relevant strengths of other controls. so that losses, errors, or theft of assets would be disclosed before they become unacceptably large.
- Differences should be investigated by or under the supervision of employees who are not responsible for the custody of assets or the maintenance of books and records on a day-to-day basis.
- Differences should be adequately investigated to determine their cause, and errors or omissions should be corrected in the books of accounts. In addition, appropriate steps should be taken to prevent further unacceptable errors in the books and records or a further loss of assets.
- Physical counts should be taken periodically under the close supervision of the owner/manager or supervisory personnel. If people who keep inventory or fixed asset records, or who normally have custody of the assets, participate in the count process, they should be only one of the two employees who make up each count team. Differences between physical count results and book records should be investigated by supervisory personnel and the owner/manager should review and approve any adjustments to the books of account to reflect physical count results.

Many factors need to be considered in determining how frequently assets on hand need to be compared with the books and records. Factors the owner/manager should assess include:

- The comparative strengths of other aspects of the overall system of internal control, especially input and output controls and asset protection controls.
- The nature of the asset in question and whether it is relatively vulnerable to loss or pilferage.
- The amount of loss the owner/manager is willing to sustain (potential for loss increases in proportion to the time between count comparisons).
- Prior experience.

Certain differences can always be expected from the comparison process. If the differences which arise are normal, all that will be necessary after the review is to adjust the books and records to correct any errors or omissions.

In considering whether differences warrant further investigation, individual differences, and not just the net value of differences, should be considered. For example, the overall difference in physical inventory results might be quite small. That small net difference could, however, include large differences where counted quantities exceed book amounts offset by other large differences where book records show greater quantities than the physical count. Such differences should be investigated as the former might be due to errors in the books and records and the latter due to inventory loss or theft.

CONCLUSION

Many of today's owner/managers recognize that they must take the lead if the benefits of computerization are to be realized and the risks which come with computerization are to be avoided.

Only the owner/manager can ultimately determine the information needs of the business and ensure that the experienced personnel and other necessary resources and support material are put in place, including the policies and procedures needed to ensure that information is relevant, complete, accurate, and timely.

Computerized systems, the data they process, and the reports they produce need to be properly controlled just as manual accounting systems are controlled. As has always been the case, this control requires active owner/manager participation.

List of Control Considerations

This list of control considerations should be of use to owner/managers and Chartered Accountants advising them in helping to ensure that all control areas covered in the publication are considered when acquiring, implementing, and using small computer systems. As explained in the introduction to the book, it should also be useful to management of departments in larger organizations in respect of any departmental systems. The list does not purport to be exhaustive or complete.

The list has been designed so that "no" answers generally indicate an area where further attention is required to obtain good controls. While "yes" answers are positive, care should be exercised in interpreting them as a detailed consideration of the factors underlying the general premises could reveal that further action is required.

Unless indicated otherwise, questions are applicable to all types of computer systems and hardware configurations, including local area networks.

ACQUISITION DECISIONS (Chapters 1, 8, 9, 10)

Is there an overall strategic information systems plan (SISP) for the organization and does it cover all needs including financial systems, end user and personal computing and office automation requirements?

Has the possibility of meeting all the above requirements on one set of hardware been carefully considered?

Does the intended approach to new systems make the best possible use of microcomputers including personal computing, office automation, and their use as terminals on local area networks for financial systems?

Has a precise statement of the business problems which the new system (or systems) is intended to solve been prepared?

Are the necessary personnel resources available that are needed to initially acquire and then implement and operate EDP systems? Have one or more of the following sources been considered?

- using existing personnel
- providing additional training for existing personnel
- hiring new staff with appropriate EDP skills
- relying on software houses or vendors
- obtaining assistance from EDP advisors or consultants

How will the data processing activity be organized? Will there be a separate EDP department or will existing departments be responsible for computer operations? Are in house skills sufficient and appropriate for those EDP activities the company will perform for itself?

For any local area networks, do personnel exist with adequate overall EDP knowledge and specific training to act as network administrators?

Has a preliminary survey been performed and does it clearly document the requirements of a new system or systems?

Has a cost benefit analysis been performed for the new systems and have both the costs and the benefits been realistically estimated?

After considering the preliminary survey results, is the owner/manager. satisfied that the business should proceed with the system?

Will the new system require the acquisition of new or additional hardware and operating systems'? If so, have the services of an outside EDP advisor been obtained to help determine hardware and operating system needs?

If it appears that needs can be met through the purchase of relatively inexpensive software packages, have arrangements been made to obtain copies of these packages for evaluation?

If more expensive and sophisticated packages are needed, has a formal request for proposal been prepared? Does it cover all essential features and considerations?

In developing the criteria to evaluate proposal responses, have plans been made to appropriately involve both the owner/manager and an outside EDP consultant and are both parties aware of their respective responsibilities?

Before any consideration is given to the development of custom software either inside the company or through an outside software supplier, is the owner/manager satisfied that the additional costs are warranted in terms of needed features that packages will not provide?

Have appropriate contractual arrangements been negotiated between the business and the software supplier?

APPLICATION SOFTWARE DEVELOPMENT, IMPLEMENTATION AND DOCUMENTATION (Chapter 1)

For Microcomputer Packages Bought Off The Shelf To Execute On Local Area Networks

Has the package been adequately tested?

Does the software contain the necessary procedures to provide for proper internal controls when the system is implemented? Consider:

- exception reports
- edit routines
- control totals or transaction lists
- terminal access controls (passwords)
- management trails

Is the user documentation adequate?

Has the conversion of existing information for the new system been adequately controlled?

Has the completeness and accuracy of data conversion been verified?

Will the addition of the new application(s) cause overall systems performance to degrade unacceptably? Has the need for new hardware to ameliorate this situation been considered?

For the Purchase of Complex Packages, Development of Custom Systems by Third Parties or by Company Personnel

Have arrangements been made for appropriate user participation in detail design specifications?

Does the software contain the necessary procedures to provide for proper internal controls when the system is implemented? Consider:

- exception reports
- edit routines
- control totals or transaction lists
- terminal access controls (passwords)
- management trails

Has the software been adequately tested?

Is system, programming, and user documentation adequate?

Has the conversion of existing information into the new system been adequately controlled?

Will the addition of the new application(s) cause overall systems performance to unacceptably degrade? Has the need for new hardware to ameliorate this situation been considered?

Additional Considerations for Custom Application Systems or Where Complex Packages will be Significantly Amended

Have the services of an outside EDP consultant been engaged to help monitor and control the development process?

Do the arrangements with the suppliers include a recognition of the supplier's responsibilities to supply a total package, including necessary operating systems and utilities?

Have the application programs been subjected to rigorous testing?

OPERATING SOFTWARE DEVELOPMENT AND IMPLEMENTATION (Chapters 1 and 8)

Where applications are being developed by company employees, have the services of an outside EDP advisor been engaged to help control and monitor the acquisition and installation of operating systems?

Have any weaknesses in the operating system and related utilities been thoroughly determined so that they may be offset when designing records controls and owner/manager controls?

ORGANIZATIONAL CONTROLS (Chapter 2)

Has a proper segregation of duties been achieved within the EDP department (where one exists)?

Where a separate EDP department exists, does its responsibilities exclude:

- custody of assets?
- initiation and authorization of transactions?
- recording of transactions?

Within the source or user departments, are the following activities segregated from each other wherever possible:

- initiation of transactions?
- authorization of transactions?
- recording of transactions?
- balancing batch controls (or similar control activities)?

If all the above duties cannot be segregated, has the best possible segregation been achieved along the lines outlined in Chapter 2?

Wherever possible, are automated controls used to help ensure the completeness, accuracy and authorization of data?

OPERATING SOFTWARE MAINTENANCE (Chapter 2)

Are changes to the operating system, other than those recommended by the third party supplier, prohibited or at least restricted to unusual circumstances where a clear need can be demonstrated?

When modifications are made to the operating systems, are such changes controlled to the degree possible? Has the need for assistance in this regard from an external advisor been considered?

Are changes to operating systems, including those made available by third parties, tested before the revised operating system is used on live records?

APPLICATION SYSTEMS MAINTENANCE AND DOCUMENTATION (Chapter 2)

Where packages have been purchased off the shelf on a retail basis:

- is information on new versions of the package regularly reviewed to see if the organization could benefit from new functions?
- if an improved version of the software is acquired, is it appropriately reviewed and tested before being put into use?

Where packages have been acquired from an outside vendor under a contract which provides for possible amendments or enhancements, is there a user group of representatives from companies using the package in which the company can participate?

Are changes to the software by employees limited to those that can be made through maintenance screens or otherwise through the use of routines incorporated in the package and described in the systems manuals?

Are requests to outside suppliers for modifications to packages by them held to a minimum to reflect only those circumstances where the value of the change to the business warrants the cost?

Are all such changes properly reviewed and tested, both by the software vendor and by the organization's employees, before they are accepted?

Where changes are made to application programs that were written by company personnel, are all such changes:

- properly authorized?
- tested by someone other than the person affecting the change?
- properly documented?

Are ALL program changes appropriately tested before the amended application is used to process the company's transactions or records?

Are program change logs used to help control and then document ALL changes to application programs?

PREVENTION OF RECORD AND EQUIPMENT LOSS (Chapter 2)

Are there written procedures for computer operators to follow which require the regular copying of files to create backup copies?

Are all copies of transactions since the last backup was performed stored in an orderly way to facilitate their re-entry should this be required?

If the computer system generates a file of all transactions recorded, is this transaction log copied onto tape or disk which is then stored as outlined above?

Has a disaster plan been prepared?

Does the disaster plan distinguish between essential systems which would have to be recreated quickly and non-essential applications which could be regenerated later?

Have copies of all of the following been stored off premises?

- operating systems (including application support software)
- application programs
- systems, program, and user documentation
- sufficient copies of input and output forms for emergency use

Are there procedures requiring that recent copies of data files are sent to off-premises storage frequently? Does the frequency of such procedures reflect the risk to the company that transaction data since the last transfer might be permanently lost?

Have arrangements been made for the use of alternative hardware in the event of a disaster and have the hardware and related peripherals been carefully reviewed or tested to ensure they will execute the company's operating systems and application software?

Have steps been taken to ensure that the disaster plan will be kept up-to-date by:

- changing all manuals, forms, and software in off-premises storage whenever the live systems and programs are changed?
- redetermining the compatibility of alternative hardware whenever systems are changed or periodically in any event?
- sending recent copies of master files to off-premises storage on a regular and predetermined basis?

Have insurance arrangements to offset losses due to business interruption and to defray the cost of data reconstruction been considered?

INPUT CONTROLS (Chapter 4)

NOTE: The following procedures should be applied to all input transactions, including those which record or change semi-permanent data.

Are input transactions authorized by operating area personnel?

Are standardized input forms used and are they pre-numbered with the numerical sequence being accounted for?

Are input forms checked for completeness and accuracy before they are submitted for data entry?

Are source documents cancelled by data entry clerks to prevent duplicate data entry?

Is the maximum possible use made of semi-permanent data to reduce the amount of data which has to be entered to record transactions'?

Where transactions are rejected by the software because they fail to pass edit routines or for other reasons, are there procedures in place to ensure that the input document is corrected and then re-entered into the system on a timely basis?

Where transactions require correction, are they returned to the originating department for correction?

Are transaction totals (batch controls) or transaction lists used to control the correct and complete entry of ALL transactions?

Are transaction totals or transaction lists balanced or verified by someone other than the data entry clerk?

Has the maximum possible division of duties over data entry and related activities been achieved? (see questions above on Chapter 2 organizational controls)

In any event, as a minimum, are the following activities performed by different individuals

- initiating and recording transactions on the terminal?
- authorizing transactions and transaction control (e.g., balancing) procedures?
- having custody of assets?

Are terminals physically located in such a way as to minimize the chance that they could be accessed by unauthorized personnel?

Have the use of keys or badges with magnetically encoded strips to control access to terminals and computer equipment been considered?

Have passwords been properly used to restrict employees from performing incompatible functions by only allowing them to perform their individually authorized activities?

Is the password system itself properly designed and maintained, for example:

- passwords are kept confidential
- passwords are changed from time to time and always when an employee has a change in responsibilities
- passwords for employees leaving the company are deleted
- passwords do not appear on screens or output
- the password file itself is protected by a password and wherever possible is encrypted
- the ability to add, delete, or change passwords is restricted to the owner/manager or systems administrator.

Does the owner/manager periodically scan the password file and review reports of terminal activities and invalid access attempts?

MANAGEMENT TRAILS AND COMPUTER OPERATIONS CONTROLS (Chapter 5)

Management Trails

Is the management trail adequate to:

- provide the information needed for control purposes?
- provide all the information needed by management to run the business?

- satisfy legislative requirements, including record retention for Revenue Canada?

Is the application designed in such a way that data can be summarized or reported in different ways to meet the changing information needs of management?

Does every transaction entered appear on a control report, showing the person who entered the data?

Are detailed reports available which facilitate the checking of computations?

Are there retention policies in place covering data in machine-readable form as well as print-outs of the management trail which are sufficient to cover legislative requirements?

Computer Operations Controls

Are systems controls (designed to help ensure that the correct files are being processed) used to the maximum possible extent?

Do controls exist within the application systems to ensure that correct start-of-day, end-of-day, and transaction control routines are executed by the computer operator?

Where the above controls are not built into the application software, are there checklists of procedures to be followed by the operator to ensure that all the necessary control reporting, backing-up of files, and other operations procedures are performed?

OUTPUT CONTROLS (Chapter 6)

Have output controls been designed to help offset any weaknesses that may exist in controls over the use of operating systems and utilities?

Is all computer output subjected to one or more of the following controls before being used?

- The file from which the output is drawn has been subjected to file balance controls.
- The output has been reviewed by the owner/manager or senior personnel. In some circumstances, a periodic check of calculations has been made.

Is all important stored data, either of a semi-permanent or accounting nature, subjected to balance control procedures on a regular basis? Are balance control procedures carried out by an employee who has no responsibilities for data entry or custody of assets?

For semi-permanent data not controlled by balance controls, is the data printed out for review by an appropriate employee on a regular basis?

Is all output reviewed by the owner/manager or an employee with a sufficient knowledge of the business that he or she could spot obvious errors?

Are important computations made by computer program checked for accuracy from time to time by manually performing the calculations and agreeing the results to computer output?

Are cheques produced on computer agreed to source documents before they are signed?

ASSET PROTECTION AND COMPARISON CONTROLS
(Chapter 7)

Asset Protection

NOTE: Protection procedures should be applied to all of a company's assets including cash in banks, cash receipts, and accounts receivable and not just to physical assets such as inventories and fixed assets.

Is there a proper division of duties between those who have custody of assets and those who keep books and records?

Do those having custody of assets (frequently the owner/manager) only release them after carefully reviewing appropriate, approved documentation?

Where appropriate, is custody to assets on a joint basis requiring two employees to gain access?

Are there good physical safeguards?

Is the adequacy of insurance coverage (including fidelity insurance) reviewed on a regular basis?

Comparison Controls

NOTE: As with asset protection controls, comparison controls should apply to all assets.

Are comparisons between book records and actual assets made with sufficient frequency so that losses, errors, or theft would be disclosed before they become unacceptably large?

Are differences investigated by employees who are not responsible for the custody of assets or the accounting records? (If this is not possible, then as a minimum the investigation should be supervised by an employee who does not perform these functions).

Are differences investigated to determine their cause and is corrective action taken to prevent further occurrence?

COMPUTER VIRUSES (Chapter 11)

NOTE: At the time of writing, virus concerns were restricted to microcomputers and LANs.

Are all diskettes received from third parties scanned for viruses by the network administrator before they are used?

Is only the network administrator allowed to add new programs to any microcomputer or the LAN?

Is some form of virus detection software in use?

Have arrangements (including professional help) to recover from a virus infection been determined and documented?

Glossary

acceptance test

A test of a system or program in as close to operating conditions as possible in order to determine whether the system or program is ready for implementation. Sometimes referred to as user acceptance or user testing.

application software

Software written to perform certain tasks, such as payroll or accounts receivable.

application support software

A general term for a variety of programmed routines, often supplied by the equipment manufacturer, to perform standard recurring functions. The main categories of application support software are source language compilers/interpreters, general utility programs, on-line support software, and file organization and data management utilities.

application system

An information system designed to perform a specific task, e.g., accounts receivable.

assembly language

A programming language which is machine-oriented but uses symbols rather than binary code to ease the programmer's job.

asset comparison controls

Controls to compare assets on hand as shown in the books with a source that is independent from the accounting records.

audit asset protection controls

Controls to protect assets against theft or loss.

audit trail

Synonym for management trail.

backup

Relating to information systems resources that are available for use in the event of service interruptions, or destruction of original equipment, programs or files.

backup copy

A duplicate of data or software that can be used if the original is damaged or destroyed.

balance controls

Controls to provide an independent check over the completeness and integrity of computerized accounting records.

batch control

A procedure whereby all transactions are added up prior to recording and that total is then compared with a control total produced by the computer system.

batch system

A system whereby similar items are collected into groups (batches) for processing by a computer.

CPU

Acronym for central processing unit.

CRT

Acronym for cathode ray tube. A screen similar to a television screen that is used to display information in a computer system.

cell

An area, one column wide by one row high, on a spreadsheet.

central processing unit

The component of a computer system where the arithmetic, logic and data transfer control is carried out.

check digit

A digit, formed by performing a calculation on the digits of a number according to a specified formula and then appended to that number, which is used to provide protection against transposition, transcription, and random errors.

code

The ordered list in a program language of the successive computer instructions representing computer operations for solving a problem.

compile

To translate program instructions written in near natural language code into machine language instructions.

compiler

A program that translates program instructions written in near natural language code into machine language instructions.

computation controls

Controls over computations performed by the computer system consisting of correct logic in the application software.

configuration

A grouping of one or more computers and peripheral equipment which are programmed to operate as a system.

console

The component of the computer which is used by the operator to control the actions of the computer.

control log

A written record used to document the balancing of batch controls and control the resubmission of erroneous or rejected transactions for processing, or: a computer generated print out of actions and operating system instructions initiated by a computer operator.

control report

A report generated by a computer program whose purpose is to aid in balancing or checking input or stored data.

control report indicator

An indicator maintained in machine-readable form by a person to indicate whether or not a control report has been printed.

control total

A sum of numbers which is computed prior to the start of a process being checked. This total is then compared to the equivalent total recomputed by the process and any difference between them indicates an error.

conversion audit

An examination of change-over procedures and new accounting procedures and files which takes place when there has been a significant change in the accounting system (e.g., a change from a manual to a computerized system or a change of computer systems).

Corporate Systems

Application systems supporting functions or containing data of overall importance to the organization taken as a whole, such as financial systems and systems supporting service to customers.

custom software

Programs written specially for a particular user.

database

A collection of related data stored together in computerized form that is shared and used by different users for different purposes.

database management system

Generalized software programs used to handle physical storage and manipulation of databases.

data centre

A data processing installation that provides service to several users.

data duplication

A process whereby programs and data exist on two separate disk drives so that the second disk drive can be used as back-up should damage occur to the first or primary disk drive.

data element

Any of the units of data that are grouped together to form a record.

data entry

The process of entering data into an information system for processing purposes.

data file

A collection of similar and related data records dealt with as a unit.

decision table

A tabulation of all the conditions that may exist and the corresponding possible courses of action, selections, or alternatives which can be possible.

detective controls

Internal controls designed to detect, or maximize the chance of detection of, errors and other irregularities.

disk

A storage device in which data is recorded on a number of concentric circular tracks on magnetic disks.

disk drive

A device that reads and writes data stored on a disk.

disk pack

A set of magnetic disks designed to be placed in a processing device for reading and writing. Their design permits them to be interchanged with other disk packs.

diskette

Flexible magnetic storage medium (i.e., a floppy disk).

display

(noun) The visual representation of data on a console screen.

distributed processing

Processing in a complex computer information network in which data relevant only to individual locations is processed locally, while information required elsewhere is transmitted either to the central computer or to another local computer for further processing.

documentation

The collection of records, reports, workpapers, and other documents that describe the information system and the procedures for performing data processing tasks.

dynamic data exchange

A special capability of operating systems and application programs running underneath them to interconnect parts of different files so that a change made to the part of one interconnected file will automatically update the other file.

EDP

Acronym for electronic data processing. Data processing by computer.

edit

An input control technique used to detect input data which is inaccurate, incomplete, or unreasonable. This function can be performed manually or by computer either before or during regular processing.

encrypt

To encode information according to predetermined rules so that it cannot be understood without knowledge of those rules.

error message

A message produced by the program to describe or designate an error encountered during execution of the computer program.

exception report

A report from an information system, produced upon request or in response to certain specified conditions, which highlights exceptions from the normal or anticipated situation.

execution

The carrying out of the operations specified in the instructions of a program.

fallback

Relating to the use of special computer or manual functions when a disruption in operations has occurred.

field

An area established in a computer record to provide for the storage or collection of a unit of information for processing (e.g., a customer name or inventory quantity); or a set of one or more characters recorded in such area.

file server

See network server

fingerprinting

The tagging of a computer program with a unique identifier that can be used to detect whether a virus infection has occurred.

flowchart

A graphic presentation of the movement in operational sequence of goods, documents or work flow.

general and environmental controls

Controls which apply to all applications systems within an organization and thus are not unique to any individual application such as payroll, inventory, or accounts payable.

gigabyte

One billion bytes of computer storage, or the equivalent of 1,000 megabytes.

graphical user interfaces

The feature of an operating system which presents to the user a menu with Icons which appears like a desk top surface and enables the users to choose particular functions or programs for execution. Often, operating systems which provide this feature also support dynamic data exchange.

hard copy

A printed copy of computer output.

hard disk

A storage disk made of a rigid base coated with magnetic material that can store many millions of bytes of data.

hardware

The physical equipment or devices in an information system, consisting of mechanical, magnetic, electrical, and electronic devices such as central processing unit, tape drives, disk files, etc.

hash total

A control used to establish accuracy of processing whereby a total of data is made by adding values which would not normally be added together (e.g., the sum of a list of part numbers) and subsequently compared to a computer generated total of the same values.

header

A file record that contains information identifying the file or record.

high level language

A programming language that is not dependent on the machine language of a computer, requiring a compiler to translate it to machine language and designed to allow the use of words similar to those used in the English language.

in-house

Within the entity.

input

(noun) Information introduced into a data processing system.

input controls

Controls over the recording of data.

input/output

A general term for the techniques, devices, and media used to communicate with data processing equipment.

integrated system

An information system in which data entered for one application is made available for a number of applications without having to re-enter the data for each application.

interface

(noun) A shared boundary in which two systems, devices, or programs interact.

internal control

The plan of organization and all coordinate systems established by the management of the enterprise to assist in achieving management's objectives of ensuring, as far as practicable, the orderly and efficient conduct of its business, including the timely preparation of reliable information.

interpreter

A program that translates the instructions of a program written in a high level language to machine language one statement at a time, causes the instruction to be carried out for that statement, and then repeats the process until all the instructions in the program have been carried out.

job schedule

A list of the jobs and the sequence in which they are to be processed.

K

Two to the tenth power 2^{10} or 1,024, when referring to computer capacity. It is derived from the prefix "kilo" which represents 1,000 in decimal notation.

load

To transfer a program or data into the computer memory from a storage device.

local area network (LAN)

A series of microcomputers interconnected by a network operating system allowing users to share files and programs which are usually resident on a network server.

log/log book

A chronological record of the activity of a computer system, including work performed and malfunctions.

logical access

The access provided to an individual user under logical security whereby his or her password permits access to specific programs, files, and capabilities, or: the processes and related software whereby access to programs or data is restricted to authorized individuals, each of whom is restricted to his or her authorized capabilities.

logical security

A specialized computer program which through passwords and by other means can restrict general access to programs and files stored on computer, as well as restricting accesses of individual users to particular programs, files and functions.

lookup table

A tabulation of information such that an intersection of labelled rows and columns serves to locate specific information.

machine code

The system of combinations of binary digits that a computer is designed to recognize as instructions and data.

macro

A single instruction that represents a set of several instructions.

management trail

The predetermined route by which the processing of data can be traced either forward or backward through the application system.

master file

A file containing semi-permanent information, as well as transaction data, or its result.

menu

A listing of available items displayed on the screen of a terminal to enable the terminal operator to select the system, program, or transaction option to be performed.

microcomputer

A general term referring to a small computer with a microprocessor.

minicomputer

A general term referring to a small computer that is generally physically larger, has more data storage, and is more expensive than a microcomputer.

multi-processing

The simultaneous execution of more than one computer program.

multiuser systems

Application systems that allow two or more users to operate contemporaneously using the same programs and data files.

network operating system

Operating system that acts as the centre of a local area network by providing telecommunications, multi-user, and logical security functions, thus allowing two or more users on different terminals or work stations attached to the LAN to share programs and files in a controlled manner.

network server

A larger microcomputer, part of a local area network, where the major part of the network operating system together with programs and data to be shared by users resides. Sometimes referred to as a file server.

non-processing controls

Organizational controls that provide an appropriate segregation of duties and controls to ensure that application systems and operating systems are properly maintained and used.

off-line

Pertaining to equipment, devices, or operations that are part of a computer system but which are not directly controlled by the central processing unit.

office automation

The reference to hardware and software used in a manner to allow employees within an office to share functions and files such as word processing, electronic mail, etc., in electronic format.

on-line

Pertaining to equipment or devices under the control of the central processing unit.

on-line system

An information system which maintains files of information in a form which is immediately accessible for either the acceptance of input transactions or the reporting of information through a device which is connected to the computer system.

operating software

A general term for operating system software and application support software.

operating system software

A programmed set of routines provided by the equipment manufacturer to control all operations of the computer hardware.

operating system

A set of programs designed to provide a facility for controlling the allocation and use of computer resources.

output

(noun) Information produced by a data processing system.

output controls

Controls over the output produced by the system which determine the accuracy and completeness of output before it is accepted.

package

A generic term referring to any group of detailed computer programs necessary to achieve a general objective; e.g., "accounts receivable package", which is sold by a software supplier to a broad base of organizations.

parallel run

Concurrent data processing using the new system and the system to be replaced.

parallel testing

Concurrent data processing using a new system and the system to be replaced, with subsequent comparison of the output from both systems.

password

The unique set of digits or characters by which a user is identified when logging on to a computer for any purpose.

payload

The particular function in a virus program which actually causes damage to the contents of computer memory, programs or files.

peripheral

A component of the computer system other than the central processing unit.

physical inventory

An inventory determined by actual observation count, weight,or measurement.

preliminary survey

An initial investigation to gather and organize pertinent information about the business, its activities and its information system, and identify future business and information requirements.

preventive controls

Internal controls designed to prevent, or minimize the chance of occurrence of errors and other irregularities.

print-out

(noun) Computer output in printed form.

processing control

Controls over the processing of transactions through the computer system.

program

(noun) The complete sequence of machine instructions and routines necessary to solve a problem on a computer.

program library

A collection of computer programs and routines.

program logic

The way a computer program is designed to solve a problem and the processing steps and decisions involved in solving the problem.

programmed controls

Automated control procedures contained within the computer programs.

programmer

A person who prepares programs for a computer.

programmer/analyst

A person who defines problems, analyzes and develops solutions for those problems, and prepares the computer programs to solve them.

RAM

Acronym for random access memory. Storage that allows information to be read from, or written in, a location direct rather than by reference to other information in storage.

real-time processing

On-line processing in which an item is processed quickly enough to produce output which can be used in directing or controlling a process as it is occurring.

record

(noun) A collection of fields of information established in the program relating to one item of activity; for example, an inventory record would consist of separate fields for a product code, product descriptions, product location. quantity on hand, etc.

record count

A control used to establish accuracy of processing, whereby a count is made of the number of records in a file or in the number of records processed by a program.

record layout

The arrangement or organization of fields in a record.

records control

Controls over the recording of data, the computations performed by the system and the output produced.

recovery

The process of resuming processing without irreparable loss of the data in the system after an error in a program or a malfunction in equipment has occurred.

request for proposal

A document specifying the attributes of a computer or computer programs required which is sent to potential suppliers who, in turn, use it as a basis for hardware or software proposed by them and price quotations for their proposals.

response time

The amount of time that elapses between entering an inquiry at a terminal and the receipt of a response at the terminal.

restart procedures

The instructions to allow processing to resume after an error in a program or a malfunction in equipment has occurred.

routine

A subdivision of a computer program consisting of two or more instructions that are functionally related.

security software

A generic term for the security features available with various types of logical access control software.

semi-permanent data

Information that is not changed as the result of day-today business events. It is stored in machine-readable form to be used over and over again.

server duplexing

A process whereby an operating system or network operating system keeps in real time two complete copies of programs and data on separate physical machines. Under this arrangement, one physical machine can then be used as back-up should damage occur to the primary machine.

service bureau

Refers to a company or organization which is in the business of providing computer and related facilities for the performance of data processing to different users.

software

Instructions to a computer, prepared in the appropriate computer language.

software package

See package.

source code

The original program code written by the programmer.

source document

An original record or evidence of a transaction.

source language

The high level language in which a program is written.

spreadsheet

A rectangular grid containing cells arranged in columns and rows on which data or formulae is entered.

stored data

Any information previously recorded on disk, diskette, or tape which will be referred to at a later stage. This might include program and accounting information.

strategic information systems planning (SISP)

A process whereby the entire information systems needs of an organization are assessed and documented and a plan developed to meet the needs.

subsidiary ledger

A ledger in which individual accounts of the same type are kept (e.g., customers' accounts), the aggregate of those accounts being maintained in a control account in the general ledger.

system design

The specification of the interrelationship among all the parts of a system in handling an application.

system documentation

See documentation.

systems programmer

A programmer who is responsible for the installation and maintenance of the operating system and operating system software.

tape

A tape made of nylon or plastic, coated or impregnated with magnetic material, on which alphabetic or numeric characters can be represented in code form by means of polarized spots.

tape cassette

A cartridge containing a reel of magnetic tape and a take-up reel.

tape drive

A device that reads and writes data stored on a magnetic tape.

terminal

A device used to perform input/output operations in a computer system.

test pack

A set of test files and input data which is created to test a computer system.

trailer record

A file record that follows a group of records and contains summary information on the group of records.

transaction data

Information relating to individual transactions flowing from day-to-day activities with third parties or employees.

transaction list

A print-out of all transactions recorded, with the details on the listing being subsequently agreed to the original source documents.

transaction log

A record of the transactions initiated and transmitted to the main computer system. The log may be a by-product of a remote terminal input process, or may be prepared manually with control totals for verifying that all the information sent was correctly received by the system.

utilities/utility programs

Programs used for standard routines such as sorting, adding, printing, copying, and tracing.

virus

A computer program designed to render useless computer memory or files and programs. Viruses spread from one computer program to other computer programs or damage data files by gaining entry to the operating systems and replicating themselves.

virus detection software

Specialized application software designed to determine whether or not computer memory, programs, or files contain computer viruses.

wide area network

A network resulting from connecting together two or more of any combination of local area networks, minicomputers and mainframes so that users on one of these nodes may have access to, or be able to communicate with, other nodes in the system. Wide area networks or WANS are usually geographically dispersed.

Index

A

Accounting data
    input controls on, 75, 76-78
    output controls on, 115-16

Acquisition
    contractual negotiations, 20-21
    criteria
        application software, 7-8
        EDP activity, 12-13
        hardware, 9-10
        operating software, 10-11
    defining requirements, 15
    interrelationship of decisions, 4
    LAN
        application software packages based on, 21-22
        reasons to acquire, 138-39
        vs. minicomputer, 139-46
    new computer system (reasons), 3-4
    office automation, 174-75
    preliminary survey, 15-18
    process, 12-36
    proposal
        evaluation of, 19-20
        request for, 15-18

Application software. *See also* Custom software; Software acquisition of
        custom-designed, 14
        LAN-based packages, 21-22
        minicomputer packages, 23-25
        specialized industry systems, 14
        standard application packages, 13-14
    changes to, 50-54

B

Batch controls
    illustrations, 42-46
    input control, 92-94

C

Comparison controls, 121-23, 127-33. *See also* Asset protection controls
    division of duties, 128
    example, 129-33
    frequency of, 127
    investigating differences, 129

Compilers, 33

Computer operations controls, 108-11
    system controls, 108-9
    within application software, 109-11

Computer viruses, 187-95. *See also* Loss prevention
    extent of threat, 188-89
    history, 189-90
    how infection occurs, 190-91
    nature of, 187-88
    recovering from, 194-95
    reducing incidence of, 191-92
    reducing pain of, 192-94

Confidentiality (end user computing), 166-67

Control features
    as acquisition criteria, 11
    effect when application software chosen first, 8
    effect when hardware chosen first, 10
    effect when operating software chosen first, 11

Control record, 110

Controls. *See* Asset protection controls; Comparison controls; Computer operations controls; Input controls; Interrelationship of controls; Organizational controls; Output controls

Conversion to computer-based system, 25-26

Cost (minicomputer vs. LAN), 140

G

H

I

L

M

N

O

P

Passwords
    assigning of, 101
    changes of employee status, 101-2
    characteristics, 100-2
    files, 102
    LAN, 148-52
    use of, 101

Personal computing. *See* End user computing

Prevention. *See* Loss prevention

Processing speed (end user computing), 159

Program controls (end user computing), 162

Program documentation. *See* Documentation

R

RAM (end user computing), 159

Records controls, 64-65. *See also* Input controls

Request for proposal document (RFP), 17-18, 20

S

Security. *See also* Passwords
    LAN, 148-52
    minicomputers vs. LAN, 145

Segregation of duties
    asset protection controls, 124-25
    comparison controls, 128
    electronic data processing (EDP), 40-46
    input controls, 102-5
    LAN, 148-52